H. G. Wells
under Revision

H. G. Wells under Revision

*Proceedings of
the International H. G. Wells Symposium
London, July 1986*

Edited by

Patrick Parrinder and Christopher Rolfe

Selinsgrove: Susquehanna University Press
London and Toronto: Associated University Presses

Associated University Presses
440 Forsgate Drive
Cranbury, NJ 08512

Associated University Presses
25 Sicilian Avenue
London WC1A 2QH, England

Associated University Presses
P.O. Box 488, Port Credit
Mississauga, Ontario
Canada L5G 4M2

The paper used in this publication meets the requirements
of the American National Standard for Permanence of Paper
for Printed Library Materials Z39.48-1984.

Library of Congress Cataloging-in-Publication Data

International H.G. Wells Symposium (1986 : London, England)
    H.G. Wells under revision : proceedings of the International
H.G. Wells Symposium, London, July 1986 / edited by Patrick Parrinder and
    Christopher Rolfe.
        p.   cm.
    Bibliograhpy: p.
    Includes index.
    ISBN 0-945636-05-9 (alk. paper)
    1. Wells, H. G. (Herbert George), 1866–1946—Criticism and
interpretation—Congresses.   I. Parrinder, Patrick.   II. Rolfe,
Christopher, 1938– .   III. Title.
PR5777.I58   1986
823'.912—dc20   88-43425
                                                                      CIP

PRINTED IN THE UNITED STATES OF AMERICA

Contents

Acknowledgments

We would like to express our thanks to all the contributors to this volume, and to the other speakers (both from the platform and the floor) who helped to make the 1986 International Wells Symposium such a memorable occasion. The symposium would have been impossible without the dedicated work of organization, planning, and day-to-day supervision carried out by a number of members of the H. G. Wells Society. In particular, we would like to record our gratitude to our fellow members of the steering committee, Sonia Burgess, Michael Draper, and David Jarrett; and to Jeanne Pingree, the former archivist of Imperial College. For secretarial help in the preparation of the manuscript, we are indebted to Lilian Argrave and Jenny Bevan of the Department of English, University of Reading, and to Margaret Ward of the School of Literary and Media Studies, Polytechnic of North London.

Quotations from *In the Days of the Comet, Men Like Gods, The Wealth of Mr Waddy,* and *Tono-Bungay* appear by permission of A. P. Watt Ltd. on behalf of the Literary Executors of the Estate of H. G. Wells. Quotations from H. G. Wells's *Experiment in Autobiography* are reproduced by permission of Faber and Faber Ltd. and Little, Brown and Company.

General Introduction

1

"H. G. Wells under Revision" may sound—as one participant in the 1986 International Wells Symposium remarked—a faintly menacing title. It alludes, however, to Wells's own lecture, "Democracy under Revision," given at the Sorbonne in 1927 and subsequently reprinted in his collection of "Guesses and Forecasts of the Years Ahead," *The Way the World Is Going.* In that lecture, Wells said that the phase of what he called "Democracy as release" was coming to an end, to be superseded by the "phase of Democratic Synthesis." Similarly, the present volume comes at the end of a twenty-five year period of expansion in the scholarly study of Wells, accompanied by a steady growth in his literary and intellectual reputation. For many years after his death in 1946, that reputation was at a very low ebb. When it began to recover in the early 1960s, two quite different and even antagonistic traditions of Wellsian appreciation grew up. The first emphasized his achievement as a literary artist, concentrating on his early work and accusing him of having sold his artistic birthright in midcareer for what G. K. Chesterton memorably called a pot of message. The second tradition in Wellsian studies was primarily concerned with the message and its continuing relevance: Wells's great gifts as a writer were simply seen as a means to a propagandistic end. Behind this split loomed, of course, the shadow of Wells's famous quarrel with Henry James over the nature and purpose of literary art.

H. G. Wells under Revision aims at a synthesis of the two traditions of Wellsian studies. The 1986 symposium in London was the first major international conference on Wells since the 1960s and the first to provide a forum for contributors from a number of separate disciplines. Naturally, our attempts at interdisciplinary coverage fell short of Wells's own magisterial achievement as a successor to the eighteenth-century Encyclopedists. Nevertheless, the present volume includes papers by literary critics, historians, sociologists, and educationalists, as well as by an anthropologist and a leading novelist. (If some of our contributors would find these labels unduly limiting, that is perhaps an indication of the extent to which they are imbued with the Wellsian spirit.) A still wider range of specializations was represented at the symposium itself, which took place within the severely scientific ambience of Imperial College, not much more than a stone's throw from the building that once housed the Normal School of Science, of which T. H. Huxley was dean and H. G. Wells a lively but somewhat unruly young student.

Here, in front of an audience that ranged from science fiction writer and spaceflight consultant Arthur C. Clarke to a former British foreign secretary, the opposing views of Wells as artist and as prophet (forcefully stated in this book by Brian W. Aldiss and by W. Warren Wagar respectively) were passionately debated. But, at the same time, the exploration of an unusually wide proportion of Wells's oeuvre from numerous perspectives took the argument far beyond the stark oppositions of the Wells-James quarrel, revealing the interconnections and consistencies between the different branches of Wells's work in several new lights, and leaving all the participants with an enhanced respect for his many-sided and complex achievement. Although it cannot serve as a complete record of the 1986 symposium, *H. G. Wells under Revision* will, we believe, serve as a definitive refutation of those prejudiced and over-simplified views of Wells that continue to find expression in general literary surveys, encyclopedias, and histories of ideas, and that from time to time still infect scholarly discussion.

The remainder of this introduction outlines in more detail the recent development of Wellsian scholarship and the way in which that development is reflected in the various papers in this volume. In conclusion, we shall touch on one crucial area of discussion at the 1986 symposium: the immediate future of Wellsian studies. First, however, it is worth remarking that—although there is sometimes a degree of discrepancy and incongruity attaching to conferences on famous writers and thinkers—there is nothing odd about a symposium devoted to H. G. Wells. Not only was Wells a highly gregarious man, a publicity seeker, and a public figure; but the idea of a great conference or symposium at which the world's problems could be thrashed out and solved held a strong and continuing imaginative appeal for him. Whether one thinks of the absurd literary colloquium by the sea in *Boon*, or of the Brissago conference that initiated the new world order in *The World Set Free*, it is clear that Wells was inclined to measure the human race's ability to survive and to build a better future in terms of its capacity to hold successful symposia. We cannot say whether H. G. would have approved of "Wells under Revision," but it is hard not to imagine him throwing himself into its proceedings with gusto.

2

When H. G. Wells died in 1946, he was an old man who had perhaps outlived his time, but he remained an awesome intellectual presence. "No writer of our time, at any rate no English writer, has so deeply influenced his contemporaries as Wells," wrote George Orwell in a hitherto unreprinted obituary. "He was so big a figure, he has played so great a part in forming our picture of the world, that in agreeing or disagreeing with his ideas we are apt to forget his purely literary achievement."[1] John Middleton Murry, in another obituary, described him as the "last prophet of bourgeois Europe."[2] But in the years after 1946, both Wells's ideas and his literary achievements *were* forgotten, or, where not forgotten, taken for granted. Just as the first half of the twentieth century had shown scant respect for many of the intellectual giants of the Victorian age, so the second half of the century looked with a sceptical and often a jaundiced eye on the leading reputations of the first. Indeed, it was Orwell, in his much better-known essay on "Wells, Hitler, and The World State" (1941), who registered what was beginning to happen to Wells's own standing. It was, the younger man then wrote, "just the singleness of mind, the one-sided imagination that made [Wells] seem like an inspired prophet in the Edwardian age [that] make him a shallow, inadequate thinker now."[3]

Here, much aided by the wide influence of Orwell's *Collected Essays* in the late 1940s and 1950s, was a strategy for the posthumous pigeon-holing of Wells. First say that he was in his prime back in the Edwardian age, or even earlier, and then accuse him of mental laziness and imaginative self-repetition. Nearly all the best literary criticism of Wells until the mid-1970s followed this strategy. Its most influential exponents were the late Gordon N. Ray, who was responsible for the establishment of the magnificent H. G. Wells archive at the University of Illinois at Urbana in the 1950s and for the first publication of materials from that archive, and Bernard Bergonzi. Bergonzi's incisive and elegant account of *The Early H. G. Wells* (1961) portrayed its subject as a fin-de-siècle writer and literary symbolist whose best work, the scientific romances, was all published before 1900 and whose later decline was the inevitable fate of a good man fallen among Fabians. Bergonzi's emphasis on the scientific romances was endorsed by a widely read account of science fiction which came out in the same year, Kingsley Amis's *New Maps of Hell*. In the succeeding two decades, a high proportion of the literary criticism devoted to Wells appeared in the new field of science fiction studies, in which the author of *The Time Machine* and *The War of the Worlds* was recognised as a founding father. At the same time, it was Wells's science fiction books which continued to sell, often in cheap and lurid paperbacks. Commentators who observed—often with ill-concealed delight— that Wells's once-enormous hold on the popular imagination had faded seemed never to notice the undiminished appeal of these books, which were now shelved in places where only the science fiction enthusiast could find them.

Wells's literary-critical rehabilitation, it may fairly be said, came about through his science fiction (though there were important articles on his social comedies and *Tono-Bungay*). But, in the same year that *The Early H. G. Wells* appeared, Yale University Press brought out W. Warren Wagar's very different study of *H. G. Wells and the World State*. For Wagar, an intellectual historian, Wells's interest was not primarily that of a storyteller or transient imaginative genius; rather, he was concerned with the writer who "bridged the gap between the man in the library and laboratory and the man in the street," the "journalist, teacher, preacher, and prophet on the grandest possible scale."[4] Wagar's enthusiasm for Wells the prophet proved to be less contagious, in the short run, than Bergonzi's portrayal of an insecure, imaginatively obsessed fin-de-siècle symbolist. Nevertheless, the endorsement of Wells's ideas was for many years the distinguishing feature of the H. G. Wells Society, founded in 1960 by J. R. Hammond (who himself has become known for his illuminating and forceful literary criticism of Wells). And Wells's centenary year, 1966, brought forth some well-publicised commentaries on Wells's thought from such luminaries as A. J. P. Taylor, C. P. Snow, and Lord Ritchie-Calder.

The last twenty-five years have seen a steady accumulation of books and articles on Wells's science fiction and of general studies of Wells as a novelist. There have been a few notable studies of his thought (such as Roslynn D. Haynes's *H. G. Wells: Discoverer of the Future* and John R. Reed's *The Natural History of H. G. Wells*) and a steady accumulation of bibliographical and scholarly aids: collections of Wells's early literary and scientific articles, of contemporary reviews of his work, and of his letters to James, Gissing, and Bennett; editions of early versions of books such as *The Time Machine* and *Kipps;* and an anthology of his unreprinted short stories. But it is not exactly this work which has captured the public imagination and turned Wells's life and writings into a well-tried source of material for TV drama, radio programs, and the Sunday literary supplements. A series of biographical revelations, stemming from the works of Gordon N. Ray, Lovat Dickson, Norman and Jeanne Mackenzie, and—above all—Wells's son Anthony West has done that, together with the well-kept secret of the third volume of *Experiment in Autobiography,* published in 1984 (as *H. G. Wells in Love)* when virtually all its dramatis personae were dead. It was not the fault of Wells's biographers if they found a sensationalist role thrust upon them, for the mixture of carefully maintained secrecy and sotto voce scandal surrounding Wells's name during the lifetimes of Rebecca West and Amber Reeves ensured that, once the full story could be published, it would be avidly and sometimes maliciously heard. But it can be said that the Wells "under revision" in 1986 was a Wells whose private life had been scrutinized as closely, and with as much publicity, as that of any twentieth-century writer. David C. Smith, whose *H. G. Wells: Desperately Mortal* was published shortly after the symposium, was perhaps the first major biographer since Geoffrey West in 1930 whose "revelations" chiefly concern Wells's public career rather than his private relationships. Nevertheless, analysis of the connections between Wells's experimental private life and his public imagination and ideas now has an important role to play in Wells studies, as both Smith's biography and several contributions to the present volume make clear.

3

The 1986 symposium began with Brian W. Aldiss's lecture, "Wells and the Leopard Lady," which also introduces the present volume. Perhaps inspired by an H. G. Wells Society schools competition that he had generously helped to judge (and for which the prizes were presented immediately before his lecture), Aldiss addresses the dichotomy between the artist and the prophet in Wells by way of a discussion of the role of the leopard and other great cats in Wells's fiction. This highly personal account by one of Wells's science fiction successors suggests that the broad argument between Wellsians is still that between W. Warren Wagar and Bernard Bergonzi, as set out in their books published in 1961. In this argument, Aldiss unhesitatingly sides with Bergonzi, maintaining that Wells is no longer the "great prophet whom earlier generations foresaw, but the brilliant if eccentric writer who—almost by his own decision—went off the gold standard."

It is fitting, then, that "Wells and the Leopard Lady" appears side-by-side with Wagar's bold reassessment of Wells as a prophet, which occupied a later session at the symposium. Nevertheless, each critic develops his case in ways that would have been unlikely or even unthinkable a generation ago. Aldiss's illustrations of Wells's excellence as a novelist are by no means all drawn from the early works generally acknowledged to be "on the gold standard." Wagar, in turn, is severely critical of the element of "messianic scientism" in Wells's thought. Both writers illustrate what they find most characteristic in Wells with references to such unsung novels as *The Shape of Things to Come* and *In the Days of the Comet*. Like almost every subsequent contributor to *H. G. Wells Under Revision,* Aldiss and Wagar can be seen as stressing the need to base critical judgments on a broad range of Wells's oeuvre, not just on those parts that can be most easily categorized and that best suit a particular critic's prejudices.

Middleton Murry once described Wells as belonging to the "rare type of men . . . who become national and international symbols."[5] Kirpal Singh's paper, subtitled "Towards an Asian Understanding of H. G. Wells," speaks directly on behalf of this wider readership. For Singh, the dichotomy of artist and prophet arising out of Bergonzi's and Wagar's books is the product of a limited, narrowly European perspective. Perhaps, Singh suggests, the Wells who set out to become both an imaginative writer and a social teacher and sage was not such an eccentric figure after all, when seen in a global context; it is in the West, with its demand for a strict separation of the responsibilities of artist and citizen, that a genius like Wells's is most in danger of being misunderstood.

The theme of Wellsian revisionism gathers strength in Part II, "Wells and the Novel," with a series of papers seeking to undo the (partially self-inflicted) damage done to Wells's literary reputation in the course of his arguments with other contemporary writers. After his quarrel with Henry James and the influential "modernist" attack on his work by Virginia Woolf in "Mr Bennett and Mrs Brown," Wells hastened to exclude himself from the "hierarchy of conscious and deliberate writers"[6] whom both James and Woolf championed. John Hammond, critic, bibliographer, and founder of the H. G. Wells Society, argues vigorously that Wells's novels are far more experimental in form and substance than is usually allowed. He was a more restless and less easily classifiable author than his

Edwardian counterparts Galsworthy and Bennett. His habitual narrative self-consciousness is just one of the structural and symbolic features of his novels which seem calculated to appeal to present-day readers.

In other papers in this section, Christie Davies reviews Wells's ability to transform his own painful experiences in the labor market into the hilarious exploits of his comic heroes, while Maria Teresa Chialant offers a new view of Wells's artistic relationship to Dickens (a relationship that has been rather little explored since E. M. Forster and Geoffrey West spoke of it sixty years ago).[7] Bonnie Kime Scott offers a thoughtful feminist critique of Wells's "social romances" such as *Ann Veronica, Marriage* and *The Wife of Sir Isaac Harman*. These novels, some of them now back in print for the first time in many years, had a stimulating and sometimes a decisive impact on the lives of an earlier generation of feminists. Whether Wells's "Patented Feminism" was as perishable as sometimes alleged, his outspoken engagement with the "Woman Question," as it was then known, remains both challenging and topical.

It is curious that hardly any of the contributors to the 1986 symposium offered papers dealing exclusively with Wells's science fiction; perhaps that vein has been very fully mined in the last twenty years, as is shown by the number of articles on Wells published by such journals as *Extrapolation* and *Science-Fiction Studies*. In *H. G. Wells Under Revision,* readers primarily interested in the science fiction will find it discussed in interdisciplinary ways and under a variety of headings. John Huntington, for example, analyzes *The War of the Worlds* in the course of his essay on Wells as an "amorous utopian," and K. V. Bailey compares the apocalyptic imagery of the scientific romances with the writings of C. S. Lewis. The most frequent references to the science fiction came, as might be expected, in the section devoted to "Wells and Science." Wells in the 1890s was simultaneously writing scientific romances and scientific journalism (see the important anthology by Philmus and Hughes).[8] It could be said that he never ceased to combine the two modes.

Leon Stover is author of a book-length study of the 1936 Wells/Alexander Korda movie *Things to Come*.[9] During the 1986 symposium, the fiftieth anniversary of *Things to Come* was marked by a special showing at the National Film Theatre in London. Stover introduced the film with a twenty-minute slide show, and then fielded questions from a capacity audience. (The first question, as it happened, was asked by H. G. Wells Society vice president Arthur C. Clarke, author of *2001: A Space Odyssey,* which may be seen as a lineal descendant of *Things to Come.*) A few hours earlier, at Imperial College, Stover had delivered one of the most challenging papers of the symposium, in which he questioned the universally accepted view of Wells as a faithful disciple of his biology professor T. H. Huxley. "Does it follow," Stover asks in "Applied Natural History: Wells vs. Huxley," "just because he worshipped Huxley as man and teacher, that he stuck to the man's teachings?" Stover's trenchantly argued case is that Wells effectively turned Huxley's "Evolution and Ethics" thesis inside out.

John R. Reed's intricate analysis of the concepts of natural and human law in *The Island of Doctor Moreau* touches on several of the questions raised in Stover's essay, while W. M. S. Russell's paper on "Wells and Ecology" defends Wells as an ecological thinker against the rather disparaging assessment of T. H. Huxley's grandson Julian. Russell looks appreciatively at the ecological wisdom embodied in two of Wells's more neglected science fiction tales, *The Food of the Gods* and *Men Like Gods*. Finally in this section, Romolo Runcini in "H. G. Wells and Futurity" relates Wells's faith in scientific planning to the narrative structures of his early science fiction, especially *The Time Machine*. Both as a novelist and a scientific thinker Wells was responding, in Runcini's view, to the specific changes in modern industrialised society that occurred at the beginning of the twentieth century. Once again this essay is devoted to suggesting the unity of Wells's work, whether as artist or as scientific prophet.

Part IV of *H. G. Wells Under Revision* is entitled "Educationalist, Utopian and Visionary." The interdisciplinary character of the 1986 symposium is strongly evident in this section, and nowhere more so than in the first essay, where John Huntington ranges from the early Wells of *The War of the Worlds* to the posthumously published memoir *H. G. Wells in Love* in his concern to unravel some of the unconscious strands that complicated Wells's philosophy and determined the structure of his utopian fictions. "Problems of an Amorous Utopian" is followed by Martha Vogeler's study of "Wells and Positivism," which (like Stover's earlier essay) constitutes a powerful revisionary statement of Wells's place in the history of ideas. Vogeler's essay, like Krishan Kumar's, has as its starting point the long neglected paper on the "So-called Science of Sociology," which Wells read to a meeting of the Sociological Society in 1906. In this paper, with its recommendation of utopian thought as a central concern in the social sciences, Kumar finds a persuasive argument for a sort of sociology very different from any that has been known up to now. Cliona Murphy, by contrast, looks at one of the gaps in Wells's work, his failure to depart very far from the conventional views of his time with regard to the education of women. K. V. Bailey, in a remarkable evocation of Wells's visionary qualities, traces connections and contrasts between his work and that of another influential educator and literary fantasist, C. S. Lewis. Bailey's essay points toward the sublime and apocalyptic elements of the Wellsian imagination. Robert Crossley's concern, however, is much more down-to-earth. "Wells's Common Readers" offers a unique insight into the blend of excitement, intellectual stimulation, and sheer human warmth that Wells was able to communicate to his most enthusiastic followers.

What these readers felt may be reconstructed from the fan mail Wells received, much of which survives in the University of Illinois Wells Collection. Typical of the writers is one from Surrey who said that he or she had read *Joan and Peter* and was left "tingling with desire to be a worker in the new world." Crossley's insistence is that we should consider such responses alongside the influential and often condescending comments of a Henry James, an F. R. Leavis, or a Virginia Woolf. Wells has sometimes been mocked for presenting himself as a "conscious common man,"[10] but after reading this essay, it is impossible to doubt that he possessed the common touch as perhaps no other modern writer has done. Clearly Wells's books can never again arouse the tide of emotion that greeted *Mr Britling Sees It Through* when it came out in the middle of the First World War. Nor are his vistas of the future as immediately compelling as they were in the days when his latest prophecy was part of the staple diet of every newspaper reader. But that Wells can still appeal to a very wide range of readers, as well as exciting a loyal and erudite following, was evident throughout a symposium at which Robert Crossley's essay was unquestionably one of the high points.

Inevitably, not all the papers that were read during four crowded days at Imperial College could be included here. One or two contributions, such as Lady Birk's delicious after-dinner speech (so delicious, it must be said, that it put the House of Lords catering to shame), and David C. Smith's rousing final address on "Wells Today and Tomorrow," were too much geared to a particular occasion to benefit from the transition into cold print. But there is one omission—from the symposium, not from *H. G. Wells Under Revision*—that we have happily been able to rectify. Julius Kagarlitsky, the Soviet critic, editor, and translator of Wells's works, had been encouraged by the Union of Soviet Writers to believe that he could travel to London in 1986, but was prevented from attending the

symposium at the last moment. At a special session chaired by
Arthur C. Clarke, the participants met to consider the political and
cultural issues raised for Wellsians by Kagarlitsky's absence, and to
draft a letter of protest. Happily, a long series of representations to
the Soviet authorities bore fruit ten months later, when Kagarlitsky
was at last able to accept the H. G. Wells Society's invitation to
come to London and deliver his paper. The discussion that followed, ranging over the history of Russian responses to Wells from
1920 to the present, was an unforgettable experience. We are happy
to include Professor Kagarlitsky's brief statement on "Wells the
'Culturologist' " as an epilogue to this volume.

4

Finally, a collection of papers such as this—delivered to an
audience that included not only the contributors themselves but the
authors of several other recent books on Wells—provides an opportunity to indicate some of the work that is needed to complete the
present revisionary phase of Wellsian scholarship. There is no lack
of urgent tasks requiring energetic and meticulous scholarship (not
to mention enlightened patrons and publishers). The state of Wellsian bibliography is quite unsatisfactory. It is to be hoped that
David C. Smith's hand list of the unreprinted journalism—totaling
well over a thousand items—will be published soon, for it will be
the first time this task has ever been attempted. The annotated lists
of Wells's books available in the H. G. Wells Society's *Comprehensive Bibliography,* and in J. R. Hammond's Garland bibliography,[11]
are of great use to scholars but do not supply the sort of detail
required by collectors and bibliophiles. The texts of those of Wells's
books that are currently available have, with one or two exceptions,
never been properly edited or even edited at all. Very few of the
surviving manuscripts have yet been studied. The Atlantic Edition
of Wells's works published during his lifetime is frequently taken as
the standard text, even though the circumstances surrounding the
production of this edition have never been studied at all—despite
the voluminous materials concerning this edition in the Wells Collection at Urbana. In addition, at least half of Wells's works have
not been reprinted since his death in any edition, and despite the
availability of his most popular fiction, it is almost impossible
(without haunting the library shelves and secondhand shops) to
gain any acquaintance with his nonfiction.[12] Only two general an-
thologies of the nonfiction have ever appeared, the first in 1924, and

the second, edited by W. Warren Wagar, in 1966, at the time of Wells's centenary.

The other major gap in Wells publishing is the lack of any general edition or selection of his letters. Only the correspondence with Gissing, Bennett, and James has so far been published in book form. The collection of letters to and from Wells at Urbana is, as readers of David C. Smith's recent biography will know, one of the richest early twentieth-century literary and historical archives in existence. Moreover—as may be ascertained from several earlier biographies as well as from *Experiment in Autobiography*—Wells was often at his sprightliest in his more intimate letters, and a magnificent collection could be made of his correspondence with his family and friends, illustrated of course by his endlessly fertile "picshuas"—themselves worthy of a separate volume.

Whatever new directions in Wellsian interpretation may be forecast, the primary need is for further work on the various categories of his texts. In the past, the Wells Estate and its agents, A. P. Watt Ltd., have exercised strict control over the publication of Wells's works, but the time is fast approaching when all the original copyrights will have lapsed. Already some of Wells's early science fiction is no longer covered by copyright in the United States. Thanks to the work of the last twenty-five years, we know far more about the range of Wells's formal and informal activities than was possible a generation ago; but it is very likely that new interpretations of Wells will be inspired by further discoveries. We have spoken earlier in this introduction of the enormous stimulus that was given to Wells studies in 1961 by the publication of such very different views of Wells by Bernard Bergonzi and W. Warren Wagar. It is surely significant that Bergonzi, in an appendix to *The Early H. G. Wells,* reprinted "The Chronic Argonauts" (the earliest version of *The Time Machine),* while Wagar, in *his* appendix, gave one of the earliest brief accounts of the riches of the Wells Archive. The first exhaustive study of the surviving drafts of *The Time Machine* has recently appeared,[13] but we still lack a full scholarly edition.[14] Biographers (notably the Mackenzies and Smith) and textual scholars have now published a fair amount of material from the Wells Archive, but many of its riches remain undescribed and—who knows?—undiscovered. In addition, the textual scholarship that is needed on Wells is by no means exclusively literary and historical in the traditional sense. A BBC radio program on Wells made during the 1986 international symposium featured interviews with some of the contributors to the present volume interspersed with recorded snatches from Wells's own broadcasts; at the same time, the largest and most public event of the symposium was the showing of *Things to Come* at the National Film Theatre. The Wells who is finding a new following today is not only the novelist and social thinker, but the communicator who was in advance of most of his contemporaries in adapting his vision and message to the demands of the visual and electronic media. The next phase in Wellsian studies will surely show an increased curiosity about the H. G. Wells known to radio listeners and cinemagoers, as well as about the author of that astonishing array of books and articles. A generation ago he was almost forgotten; today, not only has he bounced back to claim our attention, but he cannot any more than in his lifetime be confined to the printed page.

Notes

1. George Orwell, "The True Pattern of H. G. Wells," *Manchester Evening News,* 14 August 1946.

2. John Middleton Murry, "H. G. Wells," in *H. G. Wells: The Critical Heritage,* ed. Patrick Parrinder (London: Routledge & Kegan Paul, 1972), 327.

3. George Orwell, "Wells, Hitler and the World State," in *The Collected Essays, Journalism and Letters of George Orwell,* ed. Sonia Orwell and Ian Angus (London: Secker & Warburg, 1968), 2:143.

4. W. Warren Wagar, *H. G. Wells and the World State* (Freeport, N.Y.: Books for Libraries Press, 1971), 2.

5. Murry, "H. G. Wells," 326.

6. H. G. Wells, "Introduction" to Geoffrey West, *H. G. Wells: A Sketch for a Portrait* (London: Gerald Howe, 1930), 13.

7. E. M. Forster, *Aspects of the Novel* (Harmondsworth: Penguin Books, 1962), 24–25, 80; West, *H. G. Wells,* 297–99. See also A. H. Watkins, *Charles Dickens and H. G. Wells* (London: H. G. Wells Society Occasional Papers No. 2, 1970).

8. *H. G. Wells: Early Writings in Science and Science Fiction,* ed. Robert M. Philmus and David Y. Hughes (Berkeley and Los Angeles: University of California Press, 1975).

9. Leon Stover, *The Prophetic Soul: A Reading of H. G. Wells's "Things to Come"* (Jefferson, N.C., and London: McFarland & Co., 1987).

10. Wells, *Experiment in Autobiography* (London: Victor Gollancz and The Cresset Press, 1934), 2:418.

11. H. G. Wells Society, *H. G. Wells, A Comprehensive Bibliography,* 4th ed. (London: H. G. Wells Society, 1986); J. R. Hammond, *Herbert George Wells: An Annotated Bibliography of His Works* (New York and London: Garland, 1977).

12. Exceptions should be made for *Experiment in Autobiography* and *A Short History of the World,* both of which have been several times reprinted.

13. Bernard Loing, *H. G. Wells á l'Oeuvre (1894–1900)* (Paris: Didier Erudition, 1984).

14. Notwithstanding the appearance of a volume called *The Definitive Time Machine: A Critical Edition of H. G. Wells's Scientific Romance,* ed. Harry H. Geduld (Bloomington and Indianapolis: Indiana University Press, 1987.

H. G. Wells
under Revision

PART ONE
Artist or Prophet?

Introduction

In this section, Brian W. Aldiss, W. Warren Wagar, and Kirpal Singh offer conflicting overall views of what Aldiss names the "Himalaya of Wells Studies," the "long career punctuated so conspicuously by the ascent of literary heights and the decline into political shallows." W. Warren Wagar discerns a very different topography. For him it is the mixture of truth and falsity in Wells's attachment to socialism and science that constitutes the central challenge of his work. Wagar looks askance at Wells's assured position on the literary heights, since, as he points out, the whole notion of permanent canons of artistic excellence is currently under attack. The thesis and antithesis stated in these two essays reach a possible resolution in Kirpal Singh's paper with its reassertion of the "Asian" view that a writer is, first of all, a sage or seer with a duty to instruct his fellow citizens. The supposed split in Wells between artistic integrity and the prophet's calling can be seen to reflect a much larger duality in Western culture. Modern writers, Singh suggests, have customarily suffered a failure of nerve when faced with the responsibilities of mass communication. Wells saw his opportunity to become the prophet of the World State in which he believed, and should be honored for not drawing back.

Each of the three essays in this section has, of course, much more to offer than such a bald statement of the case can suggest. Brian Aldiss, the noted science fiction novelist and historian of science fiction, gives a marvelously suggestive (and highly personal) assessment of Wells's utopian imagination, starting from the curiously dream-like role played by "big cats"—tigers, panthers, leopards and "that enigmatic cat, the Sphinx"—in Wells's fiction. The latter's instinctive earthly paradise, Aldiss shows, is a garden in which the cat (rather than the dog) is friend to man, and the lion lies down with the lamb; yet in his utopias, where order and harmony have been brought out by political effort, we too often find that the cats have been "de-catted" or that personal pets have been outlawed. Seldom has the conflict between the instinctive, imaginative Wells and the political intellectual and world-reconstructor been more delightfully illustrated.

W. Warren Wagar is the author of *H. G. Wells and the World State* (1961), a book which for two decades occupied a lonely eminence as an exposition of Wells's political ideas. Here, in a forceful essay, he looks back on his earlier work, reflecting that Wells's expectation that power would pass into the hands of administrative and technical elites has come much nearer to fulfilment in the last twenty years. Yet this aspect of the Wellsian dream is the focus of Wagar's own misgivings. For him, Wells's vision of world order is at once broadly correct and flawed in one crucial respect. The English writer's Positivistic view of science, his "naive Victorian scientism and vulnerability to the steel-grey glamor of technocracy," are wholly discredited today. Wells's messianic faith in education and his willingness to allow the rule of experts to take over from democratic institutions can all be traced to his misplaced belief in the absolute value of knowledge. Though its author is a declared Wellsian, Wagar's essay is a searchingly critical account of the strengths and weaknesses of Wellsian thought. It is a powerful example of revisionist scholarship, being at once controversial and free of the polemical misrepresentations that have dogged earlier discussions of these issues, including those by such well-known essayists as George Orwell and Christopher Caudwell.

In "Wells and the Leopard Lady," Brian Aldiss cites Balzac as an author whose voluminous works reflected a spirit as unappeasable as Wells's. In his essay "Genius Misunderstood," Kirpal Singh (a science fiction critic who teaches at the National University of Singapore) illuminatingly invokes a very different parallel, that between Wells and his Nobel prize-winning contemporary Rabindranath Tagore. Tagore, like Wells, was at once artist, teacher and political thinker. Each writer gave voice to the demand for personal liberation in a way that expressed the aspirations of millions of his fellow citizens. Yet Tagore remained at one with his culture, while Wells's attempt to combine the roles of artist and prophet was largely misunderstood. Singh asks why Wells has had so few successors and why his was a success that (as Aldiss observes) no man of letters today could possibly emulate. Most critics would put this down to cultural changes—above all to the arrival of broadcasting and television—but Singh's "Asian perspective" suggests a very different answer: it is the message, not the medium, that is now lacking. "Characters may move us," he concludes, "but it is ideas that take hold of us." The three essays in this section present contrasting views of what it means to be taken hold of by Wellsian ideas and by Wellsian images.

Wells and the Leopard Lady

Brian W. Aldiss

"Really this is too much!" cried Mr. Burleigh with a note of genuine exasperation. "There must surely be police regulations to prevent this kind of thing."

"It's out of some travelling menagerie," said the gentleman with the eye-glass. "What ought we to do?"

"It looks tame," said Mr. Barnstaple, but without any impulse to put his theory to the test.

"It might easily frighten people very seriously," said Mr. Burleigh. And lifting up a bland voice he shouted: "Don't be alarmed, Stella! It's probably quite tame and harmless. Don't *irritate* it with that sunshade. It might fly at you. Stel-*la*!"

"It" was a big and beautifully-marked leopard which had come very softly out of the flowers and sat down like a great cat in the middle of the glass road at the side of the big car. It was blinking and moving its head from side to side rhythmically, with an expression of puzzled interest, as the lady, in accordance with the best traditions of such cases, opened and shut her parasol at it as rapidly as she could. The chauffeur had taken cover behind the car. Mr. Rupert Catskill stood staring, knee-deep in flowers, apparently only made aware of the creature's existence by the same scream that had attracted the attention of Mr. Burleigh and his companions.

The passage comes from the beginning of H. G. Well's's *Men Like Gods*,[1] where Mr. Barnstaple drives along what Wells calls "the Wonderful Road." Upon entering Utopia, Mr. Barnstaple and his party meet the leopard, which is benevolently inclined. By this symbol, Wells shows us the nature of an earthly paradise. The lion lying down with the lamb, etc. Dante on his journey to the inferno first meets a leopard as a sign.

Large cats, leopards, cheetahs, panthers, and other furry quadrupeds play a fairly active role in Wellsian imagery and are generally linked with Wells's perennial impulse to escape from the mundane world. While presenting these carnivores as tame and amiable, he also depicts himself, as he often says, as a carnivore.

This policy of reversal operates in many of his books, including one or two of the neglected ones.

The strangest reversal of all is the fact that—despite Wells's enormous success, which it would be impossible for any author nowadays to rival—there was a part of Wells, and a vital part, which no amount of success could ever appease, and which he was continually trying to suffocate under more work.

If modern opinion of Wells is to be revised, then it is first necessary to confront the Himalaya of Wells studies: that long career punctuated so conspicuously by the ascent of literary heights and the decline into political shallows. The Wells, in other words, with that marvelous sense of fun, the Great General of Dreamland, to use his own description, who became the hollow apostle of world order, who exchanged the cloak of imagination for the tin helmet of instruction—as the Chinese say. Wells was a dear and honest man; he would not mind, I hope, our looking into this puzzling question. For he has become, rather unexpectedly, not the great prophet whom earlier generations saw, but the brilliant if eccentric writer who—almost by his own decision—went off the gold standard.

Wells had a career problem. He rose from the unprivileged classes to a position of great privilege where he was free to travel around the world talking to Stalin and Franklin D. Roosevelt. This rise, this escape—one of Wells's numerous wonderful escapes—challenged his early identification with "the little man." *The Food of the Gods* is almost a parable of this dilemma. The novel starts on the side of the little men and ends up on the side of the big, the gods. Such reversals manifest themselves in numerous ways in Wells's life and thought.

One of Wells's most famous reversals occurs in *The War of the Worlds*. The author cleverly delays his description of an actual invading Martian until well into his story—in fact until chapter 2 of Book 2. Then the creatures are revealed as horrible enough to shock anyone. Not only do they exist by sucking the blood of living things—like those other monsters, the vampires, of which Bram Stoker had written only a year earlier—but they never sleep. And, mounting horror, they are "absolutely without sex".

These are, nevertheless, no alien creatures. Wells continues, remorselessly, "It is quite credible that the Martians may be descended from beings not unlike ourselves, by a gradual development of brain and hands . . . at the expense of the rest of the body."[2]

It is an evolutionary point Wells is making. Eighty years later, it may sound fairly conventional; that was not the case originally. Not only was Wells one of the first writers to use evolutionary themes directly in his work, but he was here using them against the grain of his generation's perception of the meaning of evolution. Whereas many interpreted evolution as a biological mechanism which had carried man to the top of the tree and would justify ruthless economic competition, Wells understood Darwin better; indeed, no English writer has shown a surer grasp of the scientific challenges of the modern age. *The War of the Worlds* demonstrates that the continuous process of evolution was as likely to work against mankind as for. If we continued as we were doing, there was no known way in which we could prevent ourselves becoming, in effect, Martians. The Eloi and Morlocks had already pointed that moral, with different emphasis.

Embedded in *The Time Machine,* Wells's first scientific romance, are many of the themes—not only the evolutionary one—which he would develop in the course of his next 120-odd books. The idea of utopia is there. The Eloi live in a kind of utopia. Present too is the dream of a perfect garden, which always haunted Wells. Perhaps when he visited his absconding mother, Sarah, at Uppark where she worked as housekeeper, he saw something like a perfect garden, a place without stress. Wells also traversed those bizarre underground passages through which the Uppark servants were forced to go, so as not to inflict themselves upon the upper classes. ("The evil was in the soil, he declared, *underground.* He laid great stress on the word 'underground',", says the narrator of haunted Dr. Finchatten in *The Croquet Player).*[3]

Here is the utopian descriptive passage from *The Time Machine:*

> After all, the sanitation and the agriculture of today are still in the rudimentary stage. The science of our time has attacked but a little department of the field of human disease, but, even so, it spreads its operations very steadily and persistently. Our agriculture and horticulture destroy a weed just here and there and cultivate perhaps a score or so of wholesome plants, leaving the greater number to fight out a balance as they can. We improve our favourite plants and animals—and how few they are—gradually by selective breeding; now a new and better peach, now a seedless grape, now a sweeter and larger flower, now a more convenient breed of cattle. We improve them gradually, because our ideals are vague and tentative, and our knowledge is very limited; because Nature, too, is shy and slow in our clumsy hands. Some day all this will be better organised, and still better. That is the drift of the current in spite of the eddies. The whole world will be intelligent, educated and co-operating; things will move faster and faster towards

the subjugation of Nature. In the end, wisely and carefully we shall readjust the balance of animal and vegetable life to suit our human needs.[4]

In summary, Wells says, "There were no hedges, no signs of proprietary rights, no evidences of agriculture; the whole earth had become a garden."[5] It's a clever comment, wedding the evolutionary with the social.

The gardens reappear. Meanwhile, there was all of mankind to be reformed.

The promising thing about mankind, as Wells perceived, is its mutability. Yet that mutability is also perceived as threatening.

If we had prognathous jaws only 2 million years ago, why not grossly overdeveloped crania two million years from now? The leopards and the big cats are another case. They were plain leopards two million years ago, not a spot different, and will presumably continue to be leopards 2 million years from now—unless we exterminate them next year. So that big cats in Wells's books are free not merely in the ordinary sense, in which big playful pussies always mean liberty, but in the way they appear to stand apart from that dreadful evolutionary machine which so inspired and alarmed Wells.

This link between big cats and freedom appears in one of Wells's best-known and most poignant short stories, "The Door in the Wall." You may recall that when Wallace the narrator was between five and six, that crucial age, he came upon the door somewhere in Kensington, that magical door through which he went, to pass into "immortal realities," and for the rest of his life was never again able to enter.

> "You see," he said, with the doubtful inflection of a man who pauses at incredible things, "there were two great panthers there. . . . Yes, spotted panthers. And I was not afraid. There was a long wide path with marble-edged flower borders on either side, and these two huge velvety beasts were playing there with a ball. One looked and came towards me, a little curious as it seemed. It came right up to me, rubbed its soft round ear very gently against the small hand I held out, and purred. It was, I tell you, an enchanted garden."[6]

Well, there are many enchanted gardens in fantasy writing, just as the symbol of the country house appears over and over in English fiction. None so poignant though as this one of Wells's. If you wonder why there is no big cat in that first garden, in *The Time Machine,* well, of course, there is: that enigmatic cat, the Sphinx.

Exactly how Wells felt is stated simply in *In the Days of the Comet*, when Leadford's mother is dying. "'Heaven,' she said to me one day. 'Heaven is a garden.'"[7]

The leopard in *Men Like Gods* also stands as a sort of sentinel to the magic which is to follow. It is about to allow itself to be stroked when it sneezes and bounds away, and the cattle don't stir a muscle as it runs past them. That's another reversal of the natural order.

Later we learn about this particular leopard. Like others of its kind, it was sworn off meat. "The larger carnivora, combed and cleaned, reduced to a milk dietary, emasculated in spirit, and altogether de-catted, were pets and ornaments in Utopia." In this Utopia, so we hear, "the dog had given up barking."[8] Wells was always dubious about dogs. They brought dirt into the house and disease with the dirt. Perhaps that dreadful late-Victorian London had given him special loathing of dogs and horses, whose mess was everywhere to be seen. They certainly aren't allowed in *A Modern Utopia*:

> It is only reluctantly that I allow myself to be drawn from my secret musings into a discussion of Utopian pets.
>
> I try to explain that a phase in the world's development is inevitable when a systematic world-wide attempt will be made to destroy for ever a great number of contagious and infectious diseases, and that this will involve, for a time at any rate, a stringent suppression of the free movement of familiar animals. Utopian houses, streets, and drains will be planned to make rats, mice, and such-like house-parasites impossible; the race of cats and dogs—providing, as it does, living fastnesses to which such diseases as plague, influenzas, catarrh and the like, can retreat to sally forth again—must pass for a time out of freedom, and the filth made by horses and the other brutes of the highway vanish from the face of the Earth.[9]

No wonder the horsey classes objected to Wells. All the same, there is a whiff of crankiness about his attitude to pets. Science would vote against him now, claiming that pets are good for psychic health, stroking them helps people get over heart attacks, and so on.

All utopians fear dirt. I've yet to read of a utopia where dogs were encouraged. Maybe in dog utopias there are no men.

The utopia in *Men Like Gods* is also likened to a garden. We read of the "weeding and cultivation of the kingdoms of nature by mankind."[10] Nowadays, as in so many other things, we would not trust ourselves with that same confidence to do a good job. The cultivation of Brazilian rain forest into timber is not an encouraging example.

In *The Shape of Things to Come,* we find more gardens, termed "enclosures and reservations",[11] in which specially interesting floras and faunas flourish. "Undreamt-of fruits and blossoms may be summoned out of non-existence." Here sex is directly linked to big cats. The Puritanical Tyranny, in suppressing sex, thought they had "imprisoned a tiger that would otherwise consume all." It was not so. Under the more relaxed dispensation following the Tyranny, people could now go naked and love as they liked—the old Wellsian aspiration. "Instead of a tiger appeared a harmless, quiet, unobtrusive, and not unpleasing pussy-cat, which declined to be in any way noticeable."[12] As early as *The Time Machine,* free love-making is a feature of utopia, without emotional attachment.

Sex and big cats. Also sex and childhood. Consider a passing remark in that large rambling volume, *The Shape of Things to Come,* which yokes such matters with a scheme for utopia.

> One must draw upon the naïve materials of one's own childhood to conceive, however remotely, the states of mind of those rare spirits who looked first towards human brotherhood. One must consider the life of some animal, one's dog, one's cheetah or one's pony, to realise the bounded, definite existence of a human being in the early civilizations.[13]

One's *cheetah,* indeed!

These strands of sexuality, utopia, and escape play a large role in Wells's work, both before and after that Himalaya in his career. Even "one's cheetah" turns up again. *The Research Magnificent* features the peculiar relationship between Mr. Benham and a beautiful woman called Amanda, whom he marries. Amanda, to him, is "the spotless leopard," while he, to her, is "Cheetah! big beast of my heart."[14] So they address each other. The terms are transposed from real life. In Wells's long involvement with Rebecca West, she was "Panther" to him, while he was "Jaguar" to her. They escaped into an animal world.

Not that there is a one-to-one relationship between the fictitious Amanda and Rebecca West. For after Mr. Benham and Amanda are married, he starts staying away from her, to her disgust, and Amanda shrinks into a Jane Wells role. Wells liked his freedom, and it is his voice we hear when Mr. Benham says evasively to Amanda, "We should meet upon our ways as the great carnivores do."[15] He then proceeds to trot round the world, overlooking the fact that jaguars occupy only narrow stretches of territory.

All this metaphorical use of cats—of which Wells was avowedly fond—and gardens and utopian innocence is immediately accessible to the imagination. The nature of a metaphor is not so much that it should be exact as that it should illuminate with a mysterious glow. That mysterious glow is certainly present in early Wells and accounts for much of his abiding popularity. But something got in the way of the glow, and that something manifested itself as politics.

If Wells needs reevaluation, I would say, in part, that Wells is interesting when he talks about people or social conditions or science or those possible worlds of his science fiction; but he was, or has become, outmoded when he goes on about politics, as after the mid-twenties he increasingly does. Remember the Open Conspiracy? The Life Aristocratic? The Puritanical Tyranny? The Voluntary Nobility? The World Brain? The New World Order? Such ideas are now lifeless, or, in some cases, flavoured by dystopian developments. We salute the endeavours and intellect of the man who conceived them; but it is as well to face the fact that Wells was too little a realist to make a true political seer, and there is nothing that turns to dust as promptly as yesterday's politics. A multinational corporation is the realization of a Wellsian dream—he loved big businessmen and moguls—but their autonomy is far from acceptable to most people.

Those reversals of which Wells was so fond in his fiction were carried into his life. He turned himself from creative writer into a sort of political journalist. Why did he do it? What drove him away from the literary to the ceaseless activity represented by *The Work, Wealth and Happiness of Mankind?*

Let's turn to that notorious big cat in *The Research Magnificent*, when Mr. Benham, taking a stroll in the Indian jungle, encounters a tiger.

They stand face-to-face, motionless for a while. Then Mr. Benham lifts his hand and says, "I am Man. The Thought of the world."[16]

The tiger disappears. Any right-thinking tiger would have eaten a man for saying something so pretentious. But the game little Wells individual has now become the bumptious Representative of Mankind, and such conceptions do not fit easily into works of literature with any claim to subtlety.

One more big cat in Wells's life and then no more on the subject. This cat leads us into what was next to come in the way of reversals. It is the Leopard Man who appears in *The Island of Doctor Moreau*. Rendered half human by Moreau's vivisection, the Leopard Man escapes, and Prendick tracks it across the island, to discover it at last "crouched together in the smallest possible compass," regarding Prendick over its shoulder. Then comes a passage we still find moving:

> If may seem a strange contradiction in me—I cannot explain the fact—but now, seeing the creature there in a perfectly animal attitude, with the light gleaming in its eyes, and its imperfectly human face distorted with terror, I realised again the fact of its humanity. In another moment other of its pursuers would see it, and it would be overpowered and captured, to experience once more the horrible tortures of the enclosure. Abruptly, I slipped out my revolver, aimed between his terror-struck eyes, and fired.[17]

The beast in the human, the human in the beast—is a powerful theme, one that seems in Wells's case to owe as much to inner emotion as to evolutionary understanding. At the end of *The Island of Doctor Moreau,* when Prendick gets back to civilization, he cannot lose his horror of the ordinary people round him, scrutinizing them for signs of the beast, convinced that they will presently begin to revert; an interesting passage derived from Swift's *Gulliver's Travels,* and possibly a precursor of the sad state of affairs at the end of *Animal Farm,* when the pigs can scarcely be distinguished from men or the men from pigs.

Wells has presented us with many striking images, of which this is not the least. Such coining of images is one of the true marks of imaginative genius, greater even than the creation of plot or character. But as Wells grew older, the ability to coin images grew fainter. From the image—enigmatic, disturbing, beautifying—he turned instead to elucidation, the image's opposite. It was another reversal. He set his considerable talents to educating and enlightening the world, stating, in his autobiography, "at bottom I am grimly and desperately educational."[18] That was the mid-1930s, when the urge to pontificate was taking over, when he became shut in a schoolroom of his own making, far from the sportive leopards of his youth.

So that remarkable short story, "The Door in the Wall," written when Wells was almost forty, is precognitive in showing what became of his fresh early vision. Wallace, the central character, spends his life searching for that door leading to the garden where the panthers and the beautiful lady were. In later middle age, Wallace comes across it again. In fact, he comes across it three times in a year, that door that goes into "a beauty beyond dreaming,"[19] but does not enter it. He's too busy with worldly affairs. He's a politician now, and has no time for such visions.

The reason Wells has never been properly accepted into the pantheon of English letters is mainly a squalid class one and has nothing to do with the fact that his original soaring imaginative genius eventually fell, like Icarus, back to earth.

Those of us who love Wells and his books have sought in the past to defend him by claiming that he was successful first as an artist and later as propagandist. This is approximately the view of Bernard Bergonzi in his book *The Early H.G. Wells*. Bergonzi says, "Wells ceased to be an artist in his longer scientific romances after the publication of *The First Men in the Moon* in 1901."[20] So persuasive is Bergonzi's book that many of us have gone along with the reasoning. Any considerable revision of Wells must take into account Bergonzi's arguments, just as any dismissal of Wells the Utopianist must take into account W. Warren Wagar's arguments that Wells's overall ideas are still viable.

All the same, the minor amendment I have to offer is based largely on what I see as Wells's second gambit to outwit the death of inspiration—second, that is, to the increasing doses of political speculation which fill his books. The second gambit is the policy of reversal, to which I have referred.

Even his role as educator is a role reversal. He had been the educated, the pupil. To education he owed his escape from drapers, ignominy, and boots. The great leap of his life was from student to teacher.

Teachers are forced into cycles of repetition to get the message to sink in. Wells's books work rather like that at times. The little men of earlier books—Hoopdriver, Kipps, Mr. Polly, Mr. Lewisham—are recycled as powerful figures, at times only semihuman: Ostrog, Mr. Parham, Rud Whitlow in *The Holy Terror,* Sargon the First, and the Grand Lunar.

With reversal went repetition. Other commentators have pointed out that the New Woman appears in more than one Wells novel. Ann Veronica has many sisters, not least Christina Alberta, and the charming Fanny Smith in *The Dream*. I don't find this cause for complaint. Nor can I complain that so many of the books chase that idea of human betterment; this is grandeur rather than narrowness. A justified complaint is that so many of those plans for the future reveal an almost willful lack of understanding of mankind's nature. It was Orwell who said that most of Wells's plans for the future had been realized in the Third Reich.

A fresh look at Wells's canon, however, reveals some unexpected pleasures. I have recently had the chance to defend in print *In the Days of the Comet,* [21] not as a science fiction novel, which it only marginally is, but as one of Wells's prime Condition of England novels—the phrase is Carlyle's. It is a reversal, demonstrating how *A Modern Utopia* might come about, and providing as abrasive a picture of Edwardian England as does *Tono-Bungay;* while in time it stands sandwiched between those two more extensive works.

This is a passage from *In the Days of the Comet,* a reminder of how brilliantly Wells could recreate life in the days before he decided instead to theorise about it. The humbly born Leadford is about to leave home forever, and to desert his mother, as Wells's mother later deserted him:

> After our midday dinner—it was a potato-pie, mostly potato with some scraps of cabbage and bacon—I put on my overcoat and got it (my watch) out of the house while my mother was in the scullery at the back.
> A scullery in the old world was, in the case of such houses as ours, a damp, unsavoury, mainly subterranean region behind the dark living-room kitchen, that was rendered more than typically dirty in our case by the fact that into it the coal-cellar, a yawning pit of black uncleanness, opened, and diffused small crunchable particles about the uneven brick floor. It was the region of the "washing-up", that greasy, damp function that followed every meal; its atmosphere had ever a cooling steaminess and the memory of boiled cabbage, and the sooty black stains where saucepan or kettle had been put down for a minute, scraps of potato-peel caught by the strainer of the escape-pipe and rags of a quite indescribable horribleness of acquisition, called "dish-clouts", rise in my memory at the name. The altar of this place was the "sink", a tank of stone, revolting to a refined touch, grease-filmed and unpleasant to see, and above this was a tap of cold water, so arranged that when the water descended it splashed and wetted whoever had turned it on. This tap was our water supply. And in such a place you must fancy a little old woman, rather incompetent and very gentle, a soul of unselfishness and sacrifice, in dirty clothes, all come from their original colours to a common dusty dark grey, in worn, ill-fitting boots, with hands distorted by ill use, and untidy greying hair—my mother. In the winter her hands would be "chapped", and she would have a cough. And while she washes up I go out, to sell my overcoat and watch in order that I may desert her.[22]

Everything comes beautifully together: the hatred of bad social conditions, poor hygiene, ugliness, disease, the mixed feelings for the old woman, the sense that one can only get out and go on. It's magnificent. There's added piquancy when we realize how soon *Comet* was written after the death of Wells's mother.

Later, in the mid-1920s, when, on the Bergonzi scale, Wells should be quite past it, we have a couple of novels which form reversals of an interesting kind. *Christina Alberta's Father* is about a man who believes himself to be the Sumerian Sargon the First, King of Kings. The Edwardian present of the novel becomes Sargon's future. In *The Dream*, Sarnac is a man of the future who relives a life in the Edwardian present. Both these novels are highly readable, and *The Dream* is excellent—overlooked, apparently, because Wells failed for once to find a noticeable title. The comedy and descriptions of low-life are in the best Kippsian manner. These novels date from 1924 and 1925, when Wells was under considerable mental stress. Indeed, *Christina Alberta's Father* strikes a new note. A theme of insanity is introduced for the first time, and the scenes in the mental institution are vivid.

Whereas Sarnac dreams himself back into an ordinary life, the low Mr. Preemby in *Christina Alberta's Father* imagines himself to be lord and protector of the whole world. It is a role Wells was clearly taking on himself.

There's much in Wells which reminds us of the productive French genius, Honoré de Balzac. Balzac wrote to a friend in 1820, saying, "Before long, I shall possess the secret of that mysterious power. I shall compel all men to obey me and all women to love me." He also said, "My only and immense desires, to be famous and to be loved."[23] He achieved both and killed himself by overwork. Fame and love together were not enough to quench that void within him which was the fruit of his mother's rejection and coldness to him. Wells is a similar case. His high and demanding productivity—*The Outline of History,* for instance, written in a year of "fanatical toil"—his deromanticized sexual activity, which continued into his seventies, point to an underlying anxiety and unhappiness.

Some commentators—among them the Mackenzies, I think—ascribe this to Wells's feelings of pique against the middle class, to whom he had been made to feel inferior. No doubt class enters into the matter, as it does into most English relationships. But something buried deeper fed on Wells, that unassuageable void which a derelicting mother can impose on her children. Sarah Wells, H. G.'s mother, did her best, but she left her husband and kicked Bertie, then almost fourteen, into the wide world, to fend for himself—or rather, into the narrow world behind the draper's counter—the same age at which another utopian, Aldous Huxley, lost his mother. The Mackenzies say that Wells bitterly resented this rejection, and we see that bitterness fermenting in his life.

His one escape from the draper's counter was through education. No wonder that in later days he saw life as a race between education and catastrophe. So it had been for him. But he had made another reversal, into a solipsistic universe, where what was true for him as a youth became true for the whole world in his age.

This turning away from the literary world to quasipolitical involvement still seems curious, and curiously unfruitful. Yet an explanation for it appears in the best book on creativity ever written, which explores the vagaries of the creative spirit. In his work, *The Dynamics of Creation,* Anthony Storr writes:

> The inability to stop working, to enjoy holidays, to allow time for relaxation or personal relationships, is often found among intensely ambitious men. In psychiatric practice, it is more often found among politicians and financiers than among artists. . . . Politicians often arrange life so that they are busily engaged all the time they are awake. . . . Political life is an ideal one for men who need to be ceaselessly occupied, who are driven to seek power by an inner insecurity, and who substitute extraverted activity for the self-knowledge which comes from cultivating personal relationships. . . . Creative production can be a particularly effective method of protecting the self from the threat of an underlying depression.[24]

We admire Wells. We also should spare him some sympathy. He who had so much drive was greatly driven. We have a right to our regrets when his wonderful early sense of fun dies.

Wells reverts to animal metaphors to describe his state of mind. He is "a creature trying to find its way out of a prison into which it has fallen".[25] Indeed, his life seems unsettled and unsatisfying, despite his encounters with the wonderful Moura Budbergs of this world, despite his escapes to the South of France, and the various households he maintained in England and France.

No wonder he dreamed of panthers and pleasant gardens. Big cats are symbols of a guiltless promiscuity. Wells worked hard at that activity, but there was no way in which the door in the wall would ever open again. Such doors have a time-lock on them.

Notes

1. H. G. Wells, *Men Like Gods* (London: Cassell & Co., 1923), 21–22.
2. Wells, *The War of the Worlds* (London: W. Heinemann, 1898), 211.
3. Wells, *The Croquet Player* (London: Chatto & Windus, 1936), 30.
4. Wells, *The Time Machine* (London: W. Heinemann, 1895), 50–51.
5. Ibid, 49.
6. Wells, *The Complete Short Stories of H.G. Wells* (London: Ernest Benn, 1927), 168–9.
7. Wells, *In the Days of the Comet* (London: Macmillan & Co., 1906), 276.
8. Wells, *Men Like Gods,* 87.
9. Wells, *A Modern Utopia* (London: Chapman & Hall, 1905), 230–31.

10. Wells, *Men Like Gods*, 87.
11. Wells, *The Shape of Things to Come* (London: Hutchinson & Co., 1933), 395.
12. Ibid, 404.
13. Ibid, 274.
14. Wells, *The Research Magnificent* (London: Macmillan & Co., 1915), 209, 205.
15. Ibid, 315.
16. Ibid, 44–45.
17. Wells, *The Island of Dr. Moreau* (London: W. Heinemann, 1896) 150–51.
18. Wells, *Experiment in Autobiography* (London: Victor Gollancz & Cressett Press, 1934), 2:540.
19. Wells, *Complete Short Stories*, 182.
20. Bernard Bergonzi, *The Early H.G. Wells* (Manchester: Manchester University Press, 1961), 171.
21. *See* Brian Aldiss, "Introduction" to H. G. Wells, *In the Days of the Comet* (London: The Hogarth Press, 1985).
22. Wells, *In the Days of the Comet*, 127–28.
23. Honoré de Balzac, quoted by Anthony Storr, *The Dynamics of Creation* (Harmondsworth: Penguin Books, 1976), 114–15.
24. Ibid, 119–20.
25. Wells, *A Year of Prophesying* (London: T. Fisher Unwin, 1924), 270.

Science and the World State:
Education as Utopia in the Prophetic Vision
of H. G. Wells

W. Warren Wagar

Writing in the summer of 1971, at the close of an era in recent history characterized by fierce commitment to ideas and ideals, Alfred Borrello took stock of the reputation of H. G. Wells. He lamented that "for far too long during his lifetime and after his death, critical and scholarly interest . . . has confined itself to the investigation of his ideas and their application to a world rapidly approaching the madness he predicted." Borrello attributed this unseemly obsession to the hypnotic influence of Wells himself, but he found a parallel betwen Wellsian messianism and the passions of the counterculture of the 1960s. The time had now come to probe more deeply. "Beneath the incrustations of ideas which sound more and more naive as we become increasingly aware of their essential impracticality, lies another, fundamentally more interesting Wells— Wells the literary figure."[1]

Just last year, in a brisk study of Wells for Cambridge University Press, John Batchelor said much the same thing. "If one stands back from Wells," wrote Batchelor (and he stands very far back indeed), "it is not of course, upon the advocate of an Open Conspiracy, the teacher . . . or the Victorian scientist struggling with God that one's attention is focused, but upon the writer."[2]

One gets the sense that the critics—who in the 1940s and 1950s had refused to put their reputations at risk by examining Wells under any rubric—have more or less agreed on a proper niche for him. A few voices have been raised on behalf of a few of the later novels—Batchelor likes *The Bulpington of Blup,* for example, and Robert Bloom is keen on *Brynhild.*[3] But the "best" things, chiefly from the period 1895 to 1910, have all been spotted and sorted out, and a suitable place has been found for them in late Victorian and Edwardian letters. If there are, let us say, 500 significant writers in English, my guess is that Wells is safely established somewhere between numbers 315 and 325. Wellsians need lose no more sleep over the matter. Their hero has survived the cut, and continues his discussions on the art of fiction with Henry James in Valhalla, although—considering the many demands on James's time—no doubt by appointment only.

But from what I hear in other quarters, in philosophy and intellectual history as well as in postmodernist literary theory, the application of timeless canons of criticism to texts is rapidly growing just as old-fashioned and therefore intolerable as our former preoccupation with an author's ideas and what we thought he meant to say. Interest has shifted from author to critic to reader. All at once we are free to read any text however we please, secure in the understanding that we will never grasp what the author meant or what his work "really" means, and that such things are irrelevant anyway. Literary pantheons crumble to dust. Last Judgments between novels quick and dead are reversed, and all texts are cast into limbo for eternity.

I may have got the deconstructionists wrong, but in the meantime I shall use their declaration of the independence of readers to justify a confession. For this one reader, in the case of at least this one author, it is surely beside the point what the author meant to say or what the artistic value of his work in the 1980s may or may not be.

The trouble is simply stated. Although I have produced academic studies of H. G. Wells and taught H. G. Wells in my courses, all my efforts are colored by the belief that H. G. was fundamentally correct. His central conviction, that civilization would collapse unless the right sort of people got hold of it and replaced the system of sovereign nation-states with a secular and socialist world polity, is correct. At the level of interpretation, this may be just one more reading among many. But what if—at the level of future history, at the level of reality—H. G.'s central conviction happens to be true?

Recall Wells's own confession in 1914, when he introduced a new edition of his *Anticipations*. In some ways, this is my favorite Wellsian text. He spoke, for the first time in just these words, of an "open conspiracy." The project of "an open conspiracy of intellectuals and wilful people against existing institutions and existing limitations and boundaries is always with me; it is my King Charles's head." In due course, the conspiracy would unfold, and in its train would come the world commonwealth.[4]

Almost any reader of Wells will grant at least this much, that the vision of an "open conspiracy of intellectuals and wilful people" to build Cosmopolis occurs with laborious regularity in most of his

fiction and nonfiction after 1914, and appears prominently in his
major prophetic writings before 1914, in *Anticipations,* in *A Modern Utopia,* and elsewhere.

But if a reader of Wells takes this message to heart and incorporates it into his own world view, his own construction of human
destiny (whether Wells "meant" what he said or not), it changes
everything. A devoutly Christian critic can subject the sayings of
Jesus to any sort of literary analysis he chooses, but in the final
reckoning his acceptance of Jesus as the Messiah makes it impossible for him to stop at this point, or even to read the words of Jesus
with the detachment possible for the nonbeliever. So it is in my
case. Although I do not believe in the divinity or the infallibility of
H. G. Wells, I am quite sure he was substantially right in his vision
of things to come. The world state is *my* King Charles's head, too.[5]
Because few major writers of our time have shared this vision,
Wells assumes an importance in my mind out of all proportion to
his standing in literature.

This does not mean we should proclaim him our Leader and
establish the First Church of Wells, Scientist. His ashes would
return from their resting place and choke us if we tried! But it
remains inescapably true, for me at least, that H. G. Wells was the
most significant thinker of the twentieth century—not because he
was a great philosopher or scientist or because he was pre-
posterously clever, but because he was right about the future of
mankind.

Or, I should say, right in most respects. No one is ever entirely
right, and I do have one large problem with Wells's vision. The
problem makes its presence felt in almost everything he wrote. It
cannot be dodged. Indeed, evidence of it appears in his introduction to the 1914 edition of *Anticipations.* The open conspiracy,
Wells argued, would not follow the course of the coups and insur-
rections dear to historians. A gang of politicians would not seize
power, much less a cabal of bureaucrats. "It is not by canvassing
and committees, by tricks and violence, but by the sheer power of
naked reasonableness, by propaganda and open intention, by feats
and devotions of the intelligence, that the great state of the future,
the world-state, will come into being."[6]

This is not an isolated sentiment in the inventory of Wells's
foreviews. Time and again, he rejected both Fabian permeation and
Marxian revolution in favor of a broadly conceived program of
research, education, and propaganda that would enable his Open
Conspirators to bypass the political process altogether. Mankind, in
effect, would be *taught* to live as one worldwide community; and

the new world order would consist not of laws and agencies but of minds linked together in a common evolving intelligence as wide and vast as the earth itself. It is not far fetched to define education, in its Wellsian usage, as "mankind in the making," the "mind of the race" learning to live in peace with itself and master the universe. For Wells, education was both a means to the end and the end itself: both revolution and utopia.

Seen in this light, Wells could almost be described as a philosophical idealist. "All the things that men and nations do," he proclaimed in *The Outline of History,* "are the outcome of instinctive motives reacting upon the ideas which talk and books and newspapers and schoolmasters and so forth have put into people's heads. . . . All human history is fundamentally a history of ideas."[7] Or, as Gemini told Stella in *Babes in the Darkling Wood,* "the one and sole *reality* in human life is mental. . . . To live is to think; to act consciously is merely thinking by action; there is no other living."[8]

But of course Wells was not an idealist in his theory of knowledge: in this department, he spent most of his life upholding a positivism more rigid in some ways than that of Auguste Comte, and almost wholly innocent of twentieth-century philosophy of science. He sometimes denied it, but I cannot doubt that for H. G. Wells, the knowledge furnished by science was exact knowledge, hard and true, subject to improvement here and there as research progressed, but solid and trustworthy nevertheless. Science, he believed, rendered not only politics obsolete, but also diversity of opinion, creed, and culture. It was the science he had studied in South Kensington, a Victorian schoolmaster's science, the learning that saved him from a life of commercial drudgery. As Jean-Pierre Vernier once noted, Wells turned to the education of mankind because he could never forget that education had changed *his* world; he concluded that, applied on a global scale, it could change the world of everyone else, too.[9] But education of a particular sort, never education in general! The education that Wells tirelessly preached was always grounded in the liberating certainties of his youth. Man, he wrote in 1939, must be "re-educated as a conscious world citizen. . . . The scientific vision of life in the universe and no other has to be his vision of the universe. Any other leads ultimately to disaster."[10]

Here, I suspect, is where Wells's prophetic imagination fell short, and perhaps even foundered. Knowing enough science to teach it, but not enough to conduct research or enough philosophy to grasp its limits, Wells let himself be drawn into a messianic scientism that short-circuited democracy, menaced civil liberty, and guaranteed that in a Wellsian world order, supreme power would be wielded by technocrats. In a century scarred by the depredations of all-knowing emperors and their samurai, his model of world order—its abundant merits notwithstanding—missed the mark. For the most part, the younger men and women who might have rallied to its banners saw it as a medicine more terrible than the disease it proposed to cure.

So it may be argued that the principal flaw in Wells's prophetic vision was his philosophy of education. He stressed education not only because he wanted to encourage freedom of thought and inquiry but because he was certain of the power of a proper "scientific" education to transform all men and women everywhere into servants of the emerging racial mind. Wellsian education led to a kind of enlightened despotism, analogous to the Western Republic of Comte (ruled by sociology) and the technological utopia of Edward Bellamy.

At a deeper level, I agree reluctantly with David Bleich that utopian visions such as Wells's express fantasies of omnipotence and omniscience originating in early childhood.[11] As long as the ambient culture supports a faith in the possibility of objective and exact truth, well and good. One need not be neurotic to enjoy the prospect of omniscience, if he can believe in it rationally. But rather early in the twentieth century, at least by the 1920s, faith in the possibility of objective and exact truth had faded; and with the passing of that faith, it became quite difficult for anyone to embrace the utopism of a Comte, a Bellamy, or a Wells. In fact many twentieth-century minds encounter Wellsian utopism only as it appears in caricature in such great anti positivist dystopias of twentieth-century fiction as Yevgeny Zamyatin's *We*, Aldous Huxley's *Brave New World,* and C. S. Lewis's *That Hideous Strength.* They would not even recognize the inspiration it supplied to one of the few great twentieth-century utopian visions, Pierre Teilhard de Chardin's *The Phenomenon of Man.* (How a Jesuit mystic came to take instruction from someone like H. G. Wells is another story altogether, too long a story to tell here!)

The point is that Wells seems to have believed, with a credulity approaching religious faith, that modern natural and social science, if properly taught, could demolish the walls separating the various atoms of humanity and inaugurate an age (to use a word favored by Teilhard de Chardin) of unanimity. When all men were of one mind, peace and justice would follow inexorably. Wells would never have understood my favorite line from the essays of Zamyatin: "But fortunately, all truths are erroneous."[12]

One exhibit in evidence of Wells's faith in scientific certainty is the lecture he delivered in 1902 at the Royal Institution, "The Discovery of the Future." Recently reprinted in the journal of the World Future Society,[13] it is one of the first programmatic statements anywhere of the need for a discipline devoted to the scientific study of the future. But it goes still further, invoking the faith of the abbé de St.-Pierre and the *philosophes* of the French Enlightenment that application of the methods of the natural sciences to human affairs will disclose "the laws of social and political development." And since all science "aims at prophecy," nothing prevented us, Wells announced, from building an "ordered picture of the future that will be just as certain, just as strictly science, and perhaps just as detailed as the picture that has been built up within the last hundred years to make the geological past."[14]

A few years later, in *The Future in America,* he pulled back a step or two from his position in "The Discovery of the Future," tempering his positivism with the pragmatism he had learned from William James and the biology he had learned from T. H. Huxley. He now assigned a larger role to "the hearts and wills of unique incalculable men." At about the same time, in *First and Last Things* and his essay on "The So-Called Science of Sociology," he scolded the heirs of Comte and Spencer for assuming that the social sciences could approximate the precision of physics. But he still held that "much may be foretold as certain, much more as possible," and he wavered not at all in prescribing for his open conspirators a firm grounding in the laws, revelations, and worldview of modern inductive sciences.[15]

As his prophetic career unfolded, Wells invested more and more effort in the struggle to extend the methods and worldview of science to an understanding of man and society. The study of history was formally annexed in *The Outline of History,* where it also issued a call for the development of sciences of business, government, and world politics. In *The Work, Wealth and Happiness of Mankind,* which during its earlier stages was known as *The Science of Work and Wealth,* Wells answered his own appeal.

But more revealing than Wells's attempts to bring the study of human affairs under the authority of science was his underlying assumption that science comprised a single body of truth, still incomplete, but destined to light man's way to godlike wisdom and power. The only thing standing between the human present and the

human future was ignorance, or, more precisely, muddle headed-
ness. People refused to think hard, clearly, and straight, in the
manner of good scientists. When they learned to do so, the path to
the godlike future would be obvious, and open conspirators would
take us there with no further delay.

One of Wells's most neglected utopian novels, *In the Days of the
Comet,* states his case unambiguously. Looking back to the pre-
utopian past, the narrator remarks: "In that time of muddle and
obscurity people were overtaken by needs and toils and hot passions before they had the chance of even a year or so of clear
thinking. . . . We were angry and hasty because we stifled in the
darkness, in a poisoned and vitiated air." Perplexed by problems
they never learned to formulate, men and women lacked the resources to solve any of them. "There was no thorough cool thinking
in the world at all." Then came the comet, Wells's metaphor for the
light of science. Its tail mingled with the earth's atmosphere, and
suddenly "the power of thought and restraint had been wonderfully
increased." Heads cleared throughout the world. Warfare, national
rivalry, sexual jealousy, and capitalist greed vanished like smoke
scattered by a fresh wind.[16]

In *New Worlds for Old,* Wells reduced socialism to science. "The
fundamental idea upon which Socialism rests," he contended, "is
the same fundamental idea as that upon which all real scientific
work is carried on. . . . It is an assertion that things are in their
nature orderly; that things may be computed, may be calculated
upon and foreseen." Men working together could learn how to
overcome the accidents and hazards of life and build a planned
social order comparable to the order already achieved in the natural
sciences. Springing out of the "common sanity of mankind," the
principles of socialism "simplify life." Wells continues: "Once they
have been understood they clear away and render impossible a
thousand confusions and errors of thought and practice. They are,
in the completest sense of the word, illumination."[17]

If socialism were actually science, the same could be said for the
political process itself, rightly understood. In the words of Trafford,
Wells's heroic physicist in *Marriage,* all political thought and effort
had thus far amounted to nothing. Politics would continue "until
the spreading certitudes of the scientific method pierced its unsubs-
tantial thickets, burst its delusive films, drained away its folly."[18]
Or, as King Egbert put the matter at the conference unifying mankind after the atomic war in *The World Set Free,* "Science . . . is
the new king of the world." The American president demurred, as
any American president would probably feel obliged to do at such a

time. What about the people? Were the people not sovereign? Egbert swept him aside. The true sovereign of mankind was the mind of the race, "that common impersonal will and sense of necessity of which Science is the best understood and most typical aspect."[19] Forced to choose between Bacon and Rousseau, Wells (as always) chose Bacon.

It also followed that if science and scientific method were clearing away the muddle of human existence and making things plain at last, it should be a relatively straightforward task to collect all knowledge under a single roof. Wells's campaign in the 1930s to bring about world integration through a new encyclopedism, launched in *The Work, Wealth and Happiness of Mankind* and pursued further in *World Brain,* illustrates as plainly as anything his view of the relationship between science, education, and social change. From science came the clear, bright, compatible truths that cognitive synthesists could assemble in a single universal system, which teachers could transmit to students and students could use to manage the world's affairs calmly and efficiently without resort to ballot boxes or barricades.

Unquestionably, Wells believed all this, and had no desire or plan to use science as a Trojan horse to gain for himself or his open conspirators the kind of absolute power analyzed by Orwell in *Nineteen Eighty-Four.* As most Wellsians know, he rejected leadership and despised followership with a passion that bordered on violence. The only followers he ever wanted were willing young women, and his place for them was in bed, not in the council chambers of the world state. As he wrote in *The Common Sense of War and Peace:* " 'Leadership' is entirely incompatible with the clear and critical apprehension of how things are and where things are, which is the natural activity of such a mind as mine. You might just as well expect a chart and compass to steer a ship." Commenting later on his tactics for getting rid of would-be disciples, he added: "The role of the man of science is to show the way and not lead the way."[20]

But personal remarks such as these did not mean, as they seemed to do, that individuals of sterner fiber were necessarily called upon to play Napoleon. Most of the real "leaders" in Wells's utopian and speculative fiction were men of science too. Their function too was to show the way more than to lead it. If a mariner had a good chart and a good compass, why did he need someone to tell him how to get where he was going? Likewise mankind. Equipped with reliable knowledge of the laws of matter, life, history, and social change; why would mankind need leaders, or, for that matter, ballots?

Nothing was required save the knowledge itself, and a resolute
trained elite who could get round the politicians and apply it to the
tasks of global integration and management.

Wells came increasingly in the 1930s to spell out the implications
of his views of science and education for human diversity, and to
speak with a bluntness that his former ties with the Fabians and
various other circles in British public life may have restrained him
from using. His days were drawing to a close. The world he wanted
to save was showing itself more vicious and intractable than ever.
People had to be told, and if necessary, told off, before it was too
late.

One blueprint for the future in these later years, surely the most
elaborate and persuasive, is *The Shape of Things to Come,* not the
priggish film produced by Alexander Korda, but the novel, which
Wells published in 1933. In this scenario of events from 1933 to
2106, H. G. assigned a critical role to education in building Cosmopolis. "Modern education," his future historian reported, "began as . . . the propaganda of the Modern State. It sought to
establish a new complete ideology and a new spirit which would
induce the individual to devote himself and to shape all his activities to one definite purpose, to the attainment and maintenance
of a progressive world-socialism." The open conspiracy, initially a
movement of scientists, technicians, and industrial managers
known as the Modern State Fellowship, "was a trained body
pledged to impose its own type of training upon all the world. It
proposed to be the New Humanity. It would accept no compromise.
It made the whole educational framework militant. No other type of
school and no other system of teaching was tolerated for more than
half a century. Never before was man so directed and so disciplined."[21]

Although Wells allowed a more permissive society to supplant
the puritan regime of the Modern State Fellowship in the second
half of the twenty-first century, *The Shape of Things to Come*
evidenced all his usual impatience with politics. The intellectual
inspiration of the Modern State Fellowship was a path-breaking
work of sociology entitled *Social Nucleation,* in whose imaginary
pages Wells invented support for his suspicion that most differences of opinion were unnecessary. His sociological alter ego
wasted no time condemning the obstructive absurdity of parliamentary democracy with its dogma of a loyal opposition. "About most
affairs," he insisted, "there can be no two respectable and antagonistic opinions. . . . There is one sole right way and there are

endless wrong ways of doing things. A government is trying to go the right way or it is criminal."[22]

Critics might read *The Shape of Things to Come* as proof that Wells was a closet Stalinist or Fascist, but of course he was nothing of the sort. As he wrote of his protagonist in *The Anatomy of Frustration* three years later: "Free enquiry and discussion *must* lead to his own conclusions. . . . Men's minds are very much alike. . . . they differ mainly through differences in experience and training. Under the same conditions and in the presence of the same problems people think alike with only very slight individual divergences—divergences of little or no importance in relation to social and political life." It followed that "men have no right to a thousand contrasted faiths and creeds and that the multitudinousness of people in these matters is merely due to bad education, mental and moral indolence, slovenliness of statement, and the failure to clinch issues."[23]

Wells returned to the same point in *The Camford Visitation* in 1937. A junior reader for "Camford University Press," who advocated a new microfilmed world encyclopedia that would unify religion and philosophy as well as science, argued that conflicting views on the ends of life result only from differences in feeling and rearing. "But sound thinking and sufficient knowledge," he continued, "can dominate feeling. Most of this stuff about incurable differences of opinion is nonsense, brains are as alike as eggs. You can beat them up or boil them hard or scramble them or poach them or let them go rotten. But cook them the same way and they will come out very much alike."[24] Wells repeated the argument in almost every book he wrote thereafter, culminating in *'42 to '44* with the decree: "Only one body of philosophy and only one religion . . . can exist in a unified world state. . . . Chemistry, physiology, botany, are the same for all the world and are continually expanding and correcting themselves, and so it must be with philosophical and religious truth."[25]

Clearly, these are not the sentiments of a classical liberal. Wells was *not* a classical liberal. Nor was he a social democrat. His creeds, as I catalogue them, were positivism (with a dash of idealism), collectivism, and technocracy. Although he believed passionately in the power of education with the faith that only someone touched by philosophical idealism can harbor, it is clear that by education he meant the diffusion of the scientific method, as he defined scientific method, leading to the emergence of a collective mind that would abolish politics, sweep away the greater part of human diversity, and create a unitary world civilization. In this higher sense, education was not only something of immense power: it took the place of class struggle and revolution, it took the place of government, it took the place of religion, and it became the chief activity of Homo sapiens. But because in any educational system some people know more than others, and knowledge in Wells's system was power, his philosophy of education entrained, in future reality if not in future theory, a technocratic model for the management of human affairs.

To cite David Bleich once again, "Utopia as a viable idea depended on a prevailing cultural faith in some kind of workable 'objective' reality, on the belief that social behavior is organizable in such a way that individual experience will be conflict-free."[26] Wells was saying, in effect, that when certain buttons were pushed by certain suitably competent button-pushers, human affairs would more or less arrange themselves, with no need for the give and take of politics. His thesis was plausible as long as one could believe in the power of science to produce hard, clear truths revealing what everyone needed for the good life and how to deliver the goods without fail. Such belief no longer really exists. I do not rule out the possibility that on some far future day the human race may draw astonishingly close to the felicity H. G. had in mind. But not yet. Not for centuries, if ever.

Meanwhile, week in, week out, political decisions have to be made. The war of the classes continues, alongside the wars of nations, creeds, races, sexes, and individuals. Sacrifices are required, commitments are required, compromises are required, to carry on. The critical decisions can be taken by bureaucrats or technocrats, by party bosses or generalissimos, or by whole peoples engaged in democratic struggle for peace and justice. But whoever makes the decisions, they cannot be entrusted to Science, with a capital "s."

The weight of evidence thus far suggests that in the next century power will flow more and more in the direction of the bureaucrats and technocrats, somewhat as in the transition to utopia foreseen by Wells in *The World of William Clissold* and *The Shape of Things to Come* (but without the Wellsian idealism and selflessness). The image of a world run by experts takes on more substance with each passing decade. In the two superpowers, in Japan and post-Maoist China, in the Europe of the Eurocrats, the administrative and technical elites play an increasingly larger role that could well be the prologue to a new (and, let us pray, quite temporary) system of global management. Twenty-five years ago, when I wrote *H. G. Wells and the World State,* I had no inkling of this, because so much of it was still embryonic.[27]

But Wells's naive Victorian scientism and vulnerability to the steel-gray glamor of technocracy do not invalidate the rest of his vision of world order. At least not for me. I remain convinced that his instincts were entirely right on the subject of war and peace: the only practical alternative to the present world system is a world state, and the only possible way thither is a citizen-based world revolution, although the citizen base must be much bigger than Wells himself had in mind. We cannot expect the ruling circles of any modern capitalist or state-capitalist ("communist") regime to lend their support; on the contrary, they are all mortal enemies of world democracy, because they all have much invested in things-as-they-bloody-are.

At the same time, I agree with Wells that no world state worth having can be built or, if it is built, endure without the intellectual, moral, and spiritual support of a unified world civilization. I fully share his dismay at the multitudinousness of mankind in the modern age, dissenting only from his hope that synthesis would come from the "spreading certainties" of science. Modern science, too, is multitudinous. Synthesis will come (if it does) and consensus will come (if it does) because enough of us, the preponderance of Homo sapiens, freely choose to set aside our differences and live together as one family in the House of Earth. In the long run, world history is on the side of synthesis. Arnold Toynbee was essentially correct in arguing that civilizations evolve toward ecumenicity as their various constituent tribes and cultures interpenetrate over the span of many generations, and Karl Marx was essentially correct in his cry that working people, if they only knew it, have no country. We are already halfway down the road to world integration, thanks to technology, the media, market forces, exchanges of ideas and mores, and much more. Whether we will have the time and wits to go the rest of the course before we commit racial suicide, I am not a good enough prophet to say. But as H. G. put the matter in the preface to the omnibus of his scientific romances published in the 1930s, "This is an entirely indifferent world in which wilful wisdom seems to have a perfectly fair chance."[28]

I also heartily concur with H. G. Wells in his view—stated in every one of his utopian and prophetic texts—that research, education, and propaganda are the essential first steps in any movement to integrate mankind, and that when all is said and done, education is the ultimate best use of human life. Of learning, of crafting, of taking new paths and testing new powers, there will be no end in a just world order.

Yet in one essential respect, let me repeat, Wells was dangerously wrong. The sciences, as they flourished in his years in South Kensington, or as they flourish today, give us no wisdom, no justice, no grace. Nor do the experts schooled in their conflicting mysteries. The dream of an automatic utopia that any fool with a modicum of proper training can plainly see and build is nothing but a foolish dream. The sooner we wake from it and get on with the serious business of world democracy, the better.

Notes

1. Alfred Borrello, *H. G. Wells: Author in Agony* (Carbondale: Southern Illinois University Press, 1972), xv–xvi.

2. John Batchelor, *H. G. Wells* (Cambridge: Cambridge University Press, 1985), 159.

3. *See* Robert Bloom, *Anatomies of Egotism: A Reading of the Last Novels of H. G. Wells* (Lincoln and London: University of Nebraska Press, 1977); William J. Scheick, *The Splintering Frame: The Later Fiction of H. G. Wells* (Vancouver: University of Victoria Press, 1984).

4. *The Atlantic Edition of the Works of H. G. Wells* (hereafter cited as AE) (London: Unwin, 1924), 4:278–79.

5. *See* W. Warren Wagar, *The City of Man: Prophecies of a World Civilization in Twentieth-Century Thought* (Boston: Houghton Mifflin, 1963) and *Building the City of Man: Outlines of a World Civilization* (New York: Grossman, 1971).

6. AE, 4:282.

7. H. G. Wells, *The Outline of History* (New York: Macmillan, 1920), II:508.

8. Wells, *Babes in the Darkling Wood* (New York: Alliance, 1940), 400–401.

9. Jean-Pierre Vernier, *H. G. Wells et son temps* (Publications de l'Université de Rouen, 1971), 401.

10. Wells, *The Fate of Man* (New York: Alliance, 1939), 64. [Title in U.K., *The Fate of Homo Sapiens.*]

11. *See* David Bleich, *Utopia: The Psychology of a Cultural Fantasy* (Ann Arbor, Mich.: UMI Research Press, 1984).

12. Yevgeny Zamyatin, *A Soviet Heretic: Essays by Yevgeny Zamyatin,* ed. Mirra Ginsberg (Chicago: University of Chicago Press, 1970), 110.

13. Wells, "The Discovery of the Future," *Futures Research Quarterly* 1 (Summer 1985), 56–73.

14. AE, 4:373–74.

15. AE, 26:12–13; *see* also Wells, *What Is Coming?* (New York: Macmillan, 1916), 1.

16. AE, pp. 10:34, 42–43, 261.

17. Wells, *New Worlds for Old* (New York: Macmillan, 1908), 21, (331–32).

18. AE, 25:277.

19. AE, 21:141–42.

20. Wells, *The Common Sense of War and Peace* (Harmondsworth, Middlesex: Penguin Books, 1940), 8; and "The Greatest Opportunity the World Has Ever Had." *Sunday Dispatch,* 27 July 1941.

21. Wells, *The Shape of Things to Come* (New York: Macmillan, 1933), 398.

22. Ibid., 256–57.

23. Wells, *The Anatomy of Frustration* (New York: Macmillan, 1936), 87, 13.

24. Wells, *The Camford Visitation* (London: Methuen, 1937), 48.

25. Wells, *'42 to '44: A Contemporary Memoir upon Human Behaviour during the Crisis of the World Revolution* (London: Secker and Warburg, 1944), 101.

26. Bleich, *Utopia,* 125.

27. *See* W. Warren Wagar, *H. G. Wells and the World State* (New Haven: Yale University Press, 1961), 201, 61(n).

28. Wells, *Seven Famous Novels* (New York: Knopf, 1934), ix.

Genius Misunderstood: Toward an Asian Understanding of H. G. Wells

Kirpal Singh

It may be useful to begin by quoting a short passage from John Carey's 1982 *Booker McConnell Prize Speech:*

> The basic error of the modernist ethos now seems sadly obvious. For if the function of literature is to foster imaginative sympathy, then should not the writer, of all people, set an example by having enough imaginative sympathy with his audience to gain and keep their attention? Imaginative sympathy is hardly likely to be fostered by someone who feels he is too good to write for the majority of his fellow-men.[1]

A little before this passage, Carey makes another interesting and relevant observation. He says, if you take

> for example, the connection between the movement for social reform in the nineteenth century and the novels in which the imaginative context of that movement was created, you can see a particularly clear instance of the way in which fiction can be dynamic, thought-promoting activity within a culture—not only educating the heart, as great novels always have, but also expanding the capacity of the communal mind.

Two points contained in these quotations are particularly worth bearing in mind: imaginative sympathy with the audience and expanding the capacity of the communal mind.

The late S. Radhakrishnan, world-respected scholar, statesman and president of India, begins the chapter on literature in his book *The Present Crisis of Faith*[2] by stating that "The aim of literature is the good of the world—*visvasreyah kavyem.*" Radhakrishnan goes on to say that literature's purpose is to "redeem the world" and that the writer is not only an entertainer but a prophet. It is the task of the writer to offer constructive visions for a better world in which mankind will be proud of its achievements. The writer must attempt to go beyond himself, leaving aside subjective obsessions for objective goals. While the raw materials will be drawn from personal experiences and personal beliefs, the writings must indicate a desire to put these aside for the more common cause of human betterment. It is difficult to combine sweetness and light, but light is what finally distinguishes the truly great writer from those whose abundant sweetness remains unendingly the gathering point of academic ants in dire want of nourishment.

Carey and Radhakrishnan have been used as convenient frames of reference. They remind us that not everyone would agree with the hard and fast rules concerning literature that trans-Atlantic nabobs like Henry James have laid down and pontificated upon. It is a familiar and an old quarrel: the relationship of life to literature. Remembering Wells and his many polemical statements, it is necessary to note that the position he attacked vis à vis James was one held primarily by western writers. The East has never fully endorsed the doctrine of art for art's sake. Wells has had, and will continue to have for a long time, a receptive audience in places such as India and China and Japan, not because of his having used the concept of the samurai but *for his conviction that what he wrote mattered*. In other words, to the East his significance lies in his unceasing attempts to offer glimpses into other worlds, newer worldviews, fresh visions.

Wells seems unique in this respect. In our own time, Wells remains a prime example of the writer who passionately believed and held the conviction that the pen was powerful, that the written word *was* potent and that all that could be done ought to be done to exploit it. Again and again we confront Wells's attempts to express cogently his unshaken belief that he could change the minds and hearts of people through the sheer brilliance of his wit and force of his literary talent. He did this forcefully, with a vigor that upset many people and hurt some close friends. Perhaps the reason why so many could not accept his apparent optimism was that the prevalent ethos was chiefly one of defeat, at least defeat of the word. For most people then, if the word mattered, it mattered for its glitter rather than its gold. Writers such as James, Joyce, Conrad, adept at the verbal art, wrote for a discriminating and select audience. They were interested in the word, but often for its own beauty or for their personal delectation. When they exploited the word—Joyce more than anyone else—they did so in the belief that the enlightened ones who read them would know what they were about. The unenlightened ones, the common men, did not ultimately matter. They wrote for the converted, the aesthetes. Wells was writing for the whole world.

And so Wells chose to emphasise clarity of purpose and

simplicity of expression. Those who spend years perfecting the
subtle art of indirect statement would naturally become impatient
with Wells and accuse him of lacking complexity. But it is hard to
believe that Wells was altogether mistaken in his mission. There *is* a
difference between attempt and success, and on many occasions
Wells did not succeed, but the attempt was there. Wells begins to
stand out more and more as an example of the man who refused to
compromise his talents and explored all avenues open to him to
push his views forward. He tried to establish that imaginative
sympathy with his audience that Carey alludes to. He tried very
hard to expand the capacity of the communal mind, a task increasingly ignored by modern writers in the West. He tried not only
to mirror the world but redeem it. Unfortunately for him, those who
exercise authority in the world do not take kindly to redeemers.

In short, Wells broke the canon, and the self-appointed pundits
and custodians were distressed. Many have said he was a man
ahead of his time. Orwell has told us how so many were in a sense
Wells's own creations.[3] We have been told and retold that Wells's
astonishing popularity was due to the climate of the years: people
needed someone like him, he echoed intelligent discussions and
gave powerful expression to fearful apprehensions, he marvelously
combined the wonderful with the nightmarish. Brian Aldiss has
stated that because Wells stood so energetically for change, the
establishment could not accept him, because to the establishment
change is anathema.[4] In the same connection, Aldiss cites the
reluctance of people to accept science fiction which is said to be the
thing that Wells did best.

To an Asian mind, these perplexities do not warrant any long-
drawn discussion because the fundamental principle upon which
they operate is faulty. In India the writer falls into the great and
revered tradition of being a seer. In China he occupies the venerable position of a sage. In the West, a writer is a writer. In the West
it would be a serious breach of logical reasoning to ask the question: what is the role of the writer as a *citizen?* The writer is, first of
all, a writer and everything else is secondary. In the East the writer
is *first of all* a citizen, a human being, only second a writer. The
point is clear. One of the great truths about Wells is that he did not
suffer from a failure of nerve, from a deep lack of confidence that
plagued modern writers. Many modern writers mistrust their own
work, apologizing and being defensive, uncertain whether they are
making sense to people, wondering if what they're doing is worth
doing. The beautiful and endearing thing about Wells is that these

doubts almost never troubled him. Because he took himself very seriously, because he took his work seriously, because he took us seriously, we take him seriously too. There are many writers who take themselves seriously, but from a purely subjective perspective, believing that they are god's gifts to us and hence we owe them the sacred duty of worship. The Asian has very little trust and faith in such writers who set themselves up as a select breed of honey-producing bees. Worse, many such writers would have readers take them seriously without returning the courtesy.

Brian Aldiss has drawn attention to another crucial consideration: that Wells was first and foremost a teacher. Wells's teacher-self shows itself everywhere, but never more memorably than in his scientific romances. They are all fables, providing haunting myths of modern man's human condition. As we grow older we realise how terrifying the vision is in *The Time Machine*, in *the Island of Doctor Moreau*, in *The Invisible Man*,. Repeatedly, the mind is cautioned against any easy slide into unthinking prosperity, blind technology. Even at his most optimistic, Wells does not seem to have advocated the pursuit of science and technology for their own sake. Always he wanted these fruits of human knowledge to be harnessed to something larger: how to make us live better, think better. It is very moving to read in his *Autobiography* how awkwardly he struggled to develop his brain, to give it more meaning than gray matter.

Because the West has some curious belief in the undisputed glory of the individual, it has not always welcomed its teachers, its gurus. From within the canon, there is Wordsworth, who wanted to be regarded as a teacher but was consistently attacked as a poet. From outside the canon there is Aldous Huxley, who wanted to popularise the perennial philosophy but was dismissed as a mystifying guru. Why is the West so uncomfortable with writers who are primarily teachers? Asians find in their reading of English literature that if the "teaching" is done through satire (that is, through ridicule and irony) it is more acceptable, more tolerable, even sometimes, glorious. But the English mind does not, it would appear, seem capable of coping with teachers who teach straight, to put it bluntly. The moral must be adorned by a tale. Why? When F. R. Leavis formulated his version of the Great Tradition and claimed a moral vision at the center of those he championed, he still banished those that did not live up to the received expectations of the label "artist". He had severe problems with D. H. Lawrence. And Wells may be said to have paved the way for writers like Lawrence. In the East, pupils very often outshine their teachers but

they rarely betray them. In the West, the better pupils become
embarrassed when reference is made to their teachers; hence Lawrence.

To state the above is to venture on sensitive ground. Maybe there
are cultural differences for these radically diametric viewpoints and
responses. In an age like ours, is it not time that these differences
be brought into the open? Is it really honest to say that Wells's idea
of a world state is thoroughly wrong and ought not to be heeded?
Or does it reflect the questioners' paranoia that something might
change if they took the idea seriously? Are we afraid of becoming
one people, common citizens of the future? Wells's rulers, the
samurai, are ancient figures—in essence they are there in Plato, in
Bacon. In his *Outline of History,* Wells exhibited a synthesis of
thought remarkable for its temerity, candid and bold in its fervour,
honest in its favorites. For Wells, Asoka the Great was, perhaps, the
most exemplary ruler the world ever knew; here was the Little
Man, paying homage to the Big Man. His eclectic mind picked on
an ancient Indian emperor to provide the example; ancient Jap-
anese discipline to provide the image. The Asian mind is moved,
deeply stirred, by this tribute. Would it be totally accurate to say
that this was mere idealism on the part of a naive Wells eager to
promote only his own peculiar brand of utopia?

"I am English by origin but I am an early World-Man," Wells
tells us in *H. G. Wells In Love.*[5] Asians will find it easy to identify
with this conception of the World-Man. It is the vision of all our
prophets and wise men. Asians will also agree with Wells that a
Federal Air Control Board is needed to ensure the safety of international air travel. Asians have experienced the narrowing effects of
nationalism and are in total sympathy with Wells for a world state.
They have benefitted immensely from versions of the Sankey Declaration of Human Rights. They have laughed at themselves for
centuries when contemplating the fate of those lower down the
stream. They need to give women the honor and the courage they
rightly deserve. They are aware of the transforming power of science and technology, know that theirs is a race against catastrophe
and that education is the key answer. In so many ways, Wells
speaks to Asians so directly that he has become a symbol of that
rare *worldspirit* that transcends time and place to make them reflect
on the vicissitudes of human nature, human longing, human
achievement. Wells constantly talked about the possibility of men
like him being destroyed, but he never talked about their being
defeated. The indefatigable strength he showed, even to the very
end when the mind was felt to switch, is all the more impressive for

its singularity. Even if he did not always show too much understanding of such cultures as the Asian or the African, his spirit was
in the right place—and that is of paramount concern to Asian
readers of his work.

A possible explanation for this Asian respect for Wells may be
gleaned through a startling comparison with Wells's Eastern counterpart: Rabindranath Tagore. There are several commonalities, but
only a few need to be enumerated. First of all the dates: Tagore,
born 1861, died, 1941, age, 80 years; Wells, 1866, 1946, age roughly
80 years. Both studied at the University of London, if not in the
same college. Both passionately loved writing and speaking, both
believed in the world citizen, both advocated drastic changes in
educational, social, political, economic, cultural attitudes. Both
wined and dined with the greats of the world, believing that if they
got to the right people they might be able to effect change more
quickly. Both believed in the creative and liberating results of a
healthy and happy sex life, both traveled far and wide giving lectures and talks designed to fashion a new ethic, a new ethos. Both
realized the dangers if science and technology were given complete
freedom of operation, but both also advocated strongly the proper
uses of science and technology to promote human welfare and
lessen human drudgery. Both wrote over a hundred books, embracing various genres. Both were honored in their own lifetimes as
much as they were attacked. Both have now, curiously, come under
some eclipse—Wells perhaps more than Tagore. Of course Tagore
won the Nobel Prize and his poetry gave India her national anthem.

It is amazing to observe and remark on the similarities. Tagore's
biographer, Krishna Kripalani, writes that in 1912 Tagore met
Wells, but does not say anything more.[6] Most biographies and
critical works on these two men do not mention them together at
all. This raises several questions. For example: was it the time in
which they lived that was chiefly responsible for their boundless
energy, commitment, devotion? Or was it their own personality
(unlike Wells, Tagore hailed from an aristocratic background)?
There is a lot of work to be done here because the detailed comparison of these two men will yield insights that would move us
closer to the world vision they both wrote about and embraced.

One factor, however, can be immediately highlighted. In the case
of Tagore, always his writing and his world vision was informed by a
spiritual faith, a central religious tradition that went back to the
Upanishads, the *Vedas.* Wells lacked this center, this abiding spiritual dimension. His attack on Catholicism notwithstanding, his
writings and his reconstructions of the world would have been far

more readily pertinent if he had had such a center. At certain moments—like that magnificent apocalyptic scene in *The Time Machine*—Wells almost did embrace a religious vision. Could Wells have benefitted from eastern spirituality? Tagore openly admitted that the East could learn so much from the West; he even confessed that it was good that a country like India had come under English rule because this made Indians rethink their own future and their own history. Wells had in abundance a sense of the future, but perhaps lacked a more critical sense of the past; or, when he came to acquire one, he converted it into yet another thrust for the future.

Whether or not Tagore and Wells were wrong in having ambivalent sympathy for a country like Russia, or wrong in preaching a freer attitude toward cultural integration, are details that will provide scholars with stimulating fields of further inquiry. In the history of modern times, Wells and Tagore stand out like giants, towering above those hundreds who provoked and challenged them. In Tagore's words, their minds were without fear and their heads were held high.[7] It is a sad comment on our own inability to accept the vision of these men that when, often, we are asked to discuss their work, we make polite, apologetic noises about how literature and life are not to be confused and how these men faltered because they gave us ideas, not characters. Characters may move us, but it is ideas that take hold of us. *Are we afraid to be taken hold of?*

Notes

1. John Carey, *The 1982 Booker McConnell Prize Speech* (London: Faber & Faber, 1983).

2. S. Radhakrishnan, *The Present Crisis of Faith* (Delhi: Hind Books, 1970), 176–84.

3. George Orwell, *The Collected Essays, Journalism and Letters*, (Harmondsworth: Penguin, 1970), 2:170–71.

4. Brian Aldiss, *Billion Year Spree: The History of Science Fiction* (London: Corgi, 1975), 128–51.

5. G. P. Wells, ed., *H. G. Wells in Love*, (London: Faber & Faber, 1984), 235.

6. Krishna Kripalani, *Rabindranath Tagore: A Biography* (London: Oxford University Press, 1962), 220; In this connection I wish to thank Professor David Smith, author of *H. G. Wells: Desperately Mortal* (New Haven and London: Yale University Press, 1986), for some very useful information concerning the Wells-Tagore link.

7. Rabindranath Tagore, *Gitanjali*, (London: Macmillan, 1913), 20.

PART TWO
Wells and the Novel

Introduction

There is general agreement that Wells reached the height of his powers as a novelist with *Tono-Bungay* (1909) and *The History of Mr Polly* (1910). Soon afterwards, he quarreled over the art of fiction with Henry James, and after the First World War he and his contemporaries, John Galsworthy and Arnold Bennett, were scornfully dismissed by Virginia Woolf. Wells went on writing novels until the end of his life, but subsequent responses to his fiction have been framed by the reactions of James and Woolf and by his own self-deprecating comments, such as the passage in his *Experiment in Autobiography* in which he wonders "whether I am a Novelist." When, in the 1950s, the extent and seriousness of his youthful fiction reviewing came to light, this was still viewed as something of a false start in a career largely devoted to using the novel as a propaganda vehicle. Gordon N. Ray wrote of his early reviewing in an article with the condescending title, "H. G. Wells Tries to Be a Novelist"—the implication being that he had either failed or abandoned the attempt and that his later addiction to the novel of ideas would have seemed inadmissible to his earlier self.

In the first essay in this section, J. R. Hammond, the founder of the H. G. Wells Society and a distinguished Wells critic and bibliographer, offers a pugnacious reassessment of Wells's artistic reputation. Though he did himself a disservice by overproduction, Wells as Hammond describes him is a consistently experimental novelist, exploring ambiguity, probing the unconscious, and fracturing the settled view of reality that can be found in the fiction of his Edwardian contemporaries. If not exactly an avant-gardist, Wells is shown as a worthy contemporary of Joseph Conrad, E. M. Forster and D. H. Lawrence. This positive reassertion of Wells's importance in early twentieth-century English fiction is echoed from a variety of standpoints in the succeeding essays in this section.

The thrust of Christie Davies's essay is twofold. On the one hand, as a professional sociologist, Davies endorses the authenticity of Wells's evocations of the "world of work," based on his own experiences as a shopkeeper's assistant. On the other hand, Davies identifies Wells's greatness as that of a comic writer and satirist; his essay is, above all, a celebration of Wells's genius as a humorist. The Wellsian comic hero, according to Davies, is an "economic misfit" who bears the brunt of the contradiction between the social values of thrift and efficiency, and those of individual self-realization—a contradiction that lies at the heart of modern societies. Davies points out how integral the comic form is to Wells's portrayal of the lower-middle class, and he ends up by referring to Wells's influence on two subsequent novelists who shared his fascination with the world of work, George Orwell and Sinclair Lewis.

Maria Teresa Chialant is concerned with tracing the parallels between Wells and his great predecessor in English comic fiction, Charles Dickens. Once again, her essay can be seen as a part of the reaction against James's and Woolf's attacks on Wells's fiction; both James and Woolf disapproved of Dickens in much the same terms as they disapproved of Wells. Where Wells differs from Dickens, according to Chialant, is in his reflection of the imperialist age in which a metropolitan economy is visibly dependent on capitalist initiatives taken all over the globe; hence the importance of the "quap" expedition in *Tono-Bungay*. In other respects, such as his use of the metaphor of social disease and of the framework of the *Bildungsroman,* Wells's "social panorama" novel may be seen as an Edwardian sequel to *Bleak House*. Both Dickens and Wells strain technique to the limits in their attempts to portray the totality of a sick and disintegrating society. Once again, these are not "realist" novels: Dickens wrote in the preface to *Bleak House* that he had dwelt on the "romantic side of familiar things," and the creator of Edward Ponderevo and the "quap" episode might have said so too.

In "Uncle Wells on Women," Bonnie Kime Scott is concerned not with the comic Wells but with the so-called "prig" novels, including *Ann Veronica, Marriage,* and *Joan and Peter,* which attracted both James's and Woolf's particular scorn. There has been a revival of interest in these novels, many of which have been recently reprinted, and once again we find Scott insisting that they should be classed as social "romances" rather than realistic texts. She approaches them by way of their early female readers—including Dorothy Richardson and Rebecca West—and then explores the gender issues raised by their narrative structures. Herself a noted feminist critic of modern literature, Scott is well-placed to offer an authoritative critique of what Freda Kirchwey once referred to as Wells's "very perishable" feminism. Scott reminds us that the "prig" novels all too often have stereotyped romantic outcomes, in which the New Woman succumbs to the attractions of one of Wells's "technical wonder males." At the same time, these novels endorse woman's aspirations to an extent that was controversial in their own time, and they continue to stimulate discussion whatever their artistic failings. Like others of Wells's novels, these have clearly not proved as forgettable as Henry James and Virginia Woolf once supposed. The essays in this section demonstrate how much scope they still offer for fresh readings.

Wells and the Novel

J. R. Hammond

My conviction is that Wells the novelist, not merely Wells the scientific romancer, or Wells the prophet, or Wells the educator, or Wells the anti-utopian utopian, or Wells the thinker, or Wells the saviour, will have his day. If it be not now, yet it will come.

—Robert Bloom, *Anatomies of Egotism*

Circumstances have made me think a good deal at different times about the business of writing novels, and what it means, and is, and may be; and I was a professional critic of novels long before I wrote them.

—H. G. Wells, "The Contemporary Novel"

1

In his influential essay "Technique as Discovery," Mark Schorer observes: ". . . as James grows for us . . . Wells disappears."[1] This assessment is based on current critical attitudes towards Wells as a novelist. During his lifetime, his novels enjoyed wide popularity but since his death, while his science fiction and short stories continue to be widely read, his reputation as a *novelist* has been almost totally eclipsed. Wells himself had no illusions concerning the transitory nature of his fame:

So far as I am concerned I find that thinking about the qualities of my work and my place in the literary world, or the world at large, an unwholesome and unprofitable employment. I have been keenly interested in the discussion of a number of questions, I have been a haphazard and pampered prophet, I have found it amusing and profitable to write stories and—save for an incidental lapse or so—I have never taken any very great pains about writing. I am outside the hierarchy of conscious and deliberate writers altogether. I am the absolute antithesis of Mr James Joyce.[2]

This was written by H. G. Wells in 1930. By that time he had become a world figure, known and respected throughout the English-speaking community as a prophet, historian, educationalist, and seer. As a novelist he had long ceased to command a world audience, his most ambitious effort in that direction—*The World of William Clissold*— having, in his own words, marked "the collapse of an inflated reputation." His heyday as a novelist had been during the years 1900–1914 when, with *Kipps, Tono-Bungay, The History of Mr. Polly, Ann Veronica,* and *The New Machiavelli* he had fascinated and entertained an audience of millions. After the First World War, there was no longer a world readership for his fiction. He was still very widely read—*The Outline of History* and *A Short History of the World* sold more than 2 million copies and were translated into many languages—but as a *novelist,* his influence on the reading public had virtually evaporated. The commanding position he had once shared with Bennett and Galsworthy was now occupied by a new generation of literary idols—Joyce, Lawrence, Aldous Huxley, and Virginia Woolf. At the end of his life, he commented wryly that the novels he wrote in the 1930s did no more "than make his decline and fall unmistakable."[3]

Since his death, there has been considerable critical interest in his science fiction and short stories, but the prevailing attitude towards his novels is one of faint embarrassment. Today he is regarded as a somewhat old-fashioned figure, a writer who continued to repeat until well into the twentieth century the conventions and techniques of the Victorian realist tradition, a novelist who cannot be regarded as in any sense experimental and whose works are in a totally different category to those of Lawrence, Conrad, and Joyce. Thus Bernard Bergonzi in his otherwise excellent study, *The Early H. G. Wells,* states: ". . . I am assuming as axiomatic that the bulk of Wells's published output has lost whatever *literary* interest it might have had, and is not likely to regain it in the foreseeable future, whatever value it may possess for the social historian or the historian of ideas."[4] And Robert Barnard in his *A Short History of English Literature* writes disparagingly of Wells, "whose bouncy, punchy fiction in the realistic tradition has aged badly."[5] The thesis I wish to argue is essentially twofold: first, that despite superficial indications to the contrary, his work has more affinity with the modernists than the realists—that is to say, he was much more consciously experimental in his work than is generally acknowledged and, secondly, that his novels are much more complex and diverse than a first reading would indicate. But to begin with, it will be useful to "set the scene" by offering a concise summary of his novelistic career.

2

Wells graduated to writing novels after a long apprenticeship of producing short stories, essays, and miscellaneous journalism. His first real breakthrough came in 1895, when he was twenty-eight, with the publication of *The Time Machine*. This was quickly followed by a series of "scientific romances" including *The Invisible Man* (1897), *The War of the Worlds* (1898), *When the Sleeper Wakes* (1899), *The First Men in the Moon* (1901), and *The Food of the Gods* (1904). In these he made skillful use of the teeming possibilities of science to create a series of mythopoeic visions and speculations concerning man and his place in the universe. His first realistic novel—as distinct from the romance—was *The Wheels of Chance* (1896), a bicycling idyll notable for its evident nostalgia for the rural peace and beauty he had known as a young man. This was followed by a number of novels in which Wells discussed topical sociological themes—*Love and Mr Lewisham* (1900), *Kipps* (1905), *Tono-Bungay* (1909), *Ann Veronica* (1909), and *The New Machiavelli* (1911). These novels both fascinated and exasperated Henry James who, while admiring their abundant energy and craftsmanship, felt that they offended his canons of artistry. "You must at moments make dear old Dickens turn in his grave, for envy of the eye and the ear and the nose and the mouth of you," he wrote, "you are a very swagger performer indeed."[6] Throughout this first phase of his work, Wells was still feeling his way as a literary artist, uncertain as yet of his direction or his true metier, deliberately trying over a range of styles and themes. Then followed a phase he described as the "prig novels"—novels in which a solipsistic hero (usually the narrator) comments extensively on political, social, and moral questions and in which the quest for a purpose in life is a predominant element.

Marriage (1912), *The Passionate Friends* (1913), *The Wife of Sir Isaac Harman* (1914) and *The Research Magnificent* (1915) belong to this phase. They remain readable and interesting today though inevitably with the passage of time the discussion of contemporary social problems has dated. The finest of this group is probably *Marriage,* if only because it is written with such evident care and its central character, Marjorie Pope, is one of his most vital and convincing heroines. During the middle period of his life—the years from 1916 to 1930—he experimented with a number of novels on topical issues of the day, including *Mr Britling sees it Through* (1916), *The Secret Places of the Heart* (1922), *Christina Alberta's Father* (1925), and *Meanwhile* (1927), stories which, *Mr Britling* excepted, did little to enhance his literary reputation and confirmed many critics in their judgment that he had severed himself from literature. In his final decade he embarked on a series of promising experiments—including *The Croquet Player* (1936), *Brynhild* (1937), *The Brothers* (1938), and *Apropos of Dolores* (1938)—in which he deployed allegory, satire, and irony to ventilate his growing pessimism concerning the human condition and his continuing interest in problems of personality and character. He continued to write fiction until the end of his life. His last novels—*Babes in the Darkling Wood* (1940), *All Aboard for Ararat* (1940), and *You Can't Be Too Careful* (1941)—revealed an abiding concern for humanity and a refreshing willingness—in a writer in his seventies—to experiment with new styles and themes. Critical opinion is sharply divided on the merits of the fiction of his final decade. To some it is simply additional evidence of his abdication of any major role in English literature and further proof of his steadily declining powers. To others the novels of his last period offer extraordinary riches of characterisation and insight and reveal a masterly writer completing "the great imaginative work of a lifetime."[7]

So much is familiar. What is not so familiar is the seriousness with which Wells himself regarded his novels. Despite his statement that "I am outside the hierarchy of conscious and deliberate writers altogether," and the disingenuous aside in his autobiography that "the larger part of my fiction was written lightly and with a certain haste,"[8] the fact is that he regarded his novels with great seriousness and took immense pains over their writing. In a letter to his friend Arnold Bennett in 1901 (Bennett had published a study of popular novelists, *Fame and Fiction,* which omitted reference to Wells), he complained: "For me you are part of the Great Public, I perceive. I am doomed to write 'scientific' romances and short stories for you creatures of the mob, and my novels must be my private dissipation."[9] And to Frederick Macmillan in 1908 he wrote: "As I told you long ago I want to specialise as a novelist. I think now my opportunity is ripe, and that if new novel follows novel without anything to distract people's attention—any other sort of work by me, I mean—it will be possible to consolidate the large confused reputation I have at the present time."[10] What distracted him from his laudable ambition to "specialise as a novelist" was the First World War and the immense social, moral, and intellectual ferment this engendered. But it is significant that during the last thirty years of his life—when he was increasingly obsessed with the need for world unification and for fundamental changes in educational and political ideas—he continued to write fiction, producing no fewer than fifteen major novels between 1916 and 1946 in addition to novellas, sketches, and short stories. The writing of fiction remained one of his primary concerns throughout his literary career and almost his last work, "The Betterave Papers," was an ironic review of his literary achievement in which he looked back with whimsical detachment on his entire corpus as a novelist.

The evidence provided by his manuscripts and letters suggests that, far from having been written "lightly and with a certain haste," his fiction was written and revised with great care. Much more is now known of his creative methods than was apparent during his lifetime. We know from the evidence of posthumously published works and from his correspondence with James, Gissing, and Bennett that the writing of his novels involved a lengthy process of revision during which each work underwent a series of drafts until he was satisfied. In 1960, for example, a critical edition of *The History of Mr Polly* was published containing a reproduction of several pages of the original manuscript. In 1969 a hitherto unpublished novel, *The Wealth of Mr Waddy* (an early version of *Kipps*), was published in a scholarly edition containing much new material on Wells's methods of composition. From these and other sources it is abundantly clear that, whatever else he was, Wells was a painstaking and demanding artist who approached his work with thoroughness and care. Writing apropos *Love and Mr Lewisham,* he observed: "There is really more work in that book than there is in many a first class F. R. S. research, and stagnant days and desert journeys beyond describing."[11] Wells's restlessness—his interest in a wide range of diverse subjects, his tendency to be working on several different projects at any one time, his ability to assume at will a style appropriate to the work in hand—has led to an assumption that he wrote hastily and with little attention to language or aesthetic considerations. It is becoming increasingly clear that this assumption is based on a superficial reading of his work and that the more closely his novels are studied, the narrower the gap between Wells and Joyce becomes. A number of recent studies have demonstrated convincingly that as a novelist, Wells devoted the closest attention to language and imagery and that he is very far from being the careless writer he is so often held to be. Robert Bloom in *Anatomies of Egotism: A Reading of the Last Novels of*

H. G. Wells closely examines the novels of his final period and finds in them no diminution of his powers as a creative artist. David Lodge in *Language of Fiction* discusses in considerable detail the language of *Tono-Bungay* and concludes that it is a coherent and much underestimated work of art. Frank D. McConnell in *The Science Fiction of H. G. Wells* examines the scientific romances and finds ample testimony to their literary and imaginative qualities. The evidence provided by his own writings, then—including his manuscripts, drafts, and letters—belies the view that his works were produced carelessly and suggests on the contrary that most were written with considerable (and in some cases meticulous) attention to language.

In the light of this testimony to his conscientiousness as a writer, some explanation must be found for the widespread critical ambivalence towards Wells and for his perfunctory treatment in so many reference works on the English novel. There are four principal reasons that account for his comparative neglect in modern literary studies. First, he has been taken too readily on his own estimation; that is, his claim to be "the absolute antithesis of Mr James Joyce" has been taken at face value. Second, his prolific work in other fields, what he termed in his letter to Macmillan his "large confused reputation," has militated against his acceptance as a serious novelist. Third, the fact that he lived to be almost eighty and wrote some fifty full-length works of fiction has inevitably weakened his stature as a man of letters. In a word, he lived for too long and wrote too much to be retained readily in critical focus. Fourth, and most significantly, he is still widely regarded as a realistic novelist in the vein of Arnold Bennett and as a writer whose novels have little relevance to the needs and concerns of the latter part of the twentieth century.

3

His own published estimation of his standing and attitudes has been accepted for many years as the definitive statement of his position. Because he insisted again and again that "I had rather be called a journalist than an artist"[12] this has been taken to be a statement of the truth—instead of what it so patently was: a piece of exaggerated false modesty forced from him as a result of his quarrel with Henry James. When involved in an argument, it is a natural human tendency to adopt an extreme position, to assume a defensive posture in the sharpest possible contrast to that adopted

by one's opponent. Faced with James's claim that the novel had to
conform to standards of excellence and purity as defined by himself, Wells felt he had no alternative but to assert the opposite view:
that the novel could be whatever the author chose to make it, and
that he (Wells) was making no claim that his own novels were fully
harmonious works of art. Wells, then, has become a victim of his
own protestations. Because he adopted as his critical stance the
view that all art is essentially anarchic and discounted any claim
that his fiction was of enduring literary merit, this has come to be
accepted as the received attitude to his work. By insisting that his
fiction was of transitory interest—"I wave the striving immortals
onward, and step aside"—he unwittingly did himself a disservice;
for whereas the novels of Joyce, Lawrence, Conrad, and James have
received sustained critical attention, only a small proportion of his
own fiction has received serious study. During the past two decades
his scientific romances have been the subject of increasing scholarly attention, and there is now wide recognition of their literary
and artistic importance. The same recognition has yet to be ac-
corded to his *novels.*

A second reason why he has received comparatively little critical
attention as a novelist is the fact that he diversified (some would say
dissipated) his literary talents over so many different fields. He was
not simply a novelist, nor was he content to express himself solely
in the form of fiction. He was simultaneously a sociologist and
prophet, in works such as *Anticipations, A Modern Utopia,* and
The Shape of Things to Come; a popular educator in *The Outline of
History* and *The Science of Life;* a prolific journalist and commentator on world affairs; and a world figure in his own right, a man
who interviewed Lenin, Stalin, and Franklin D. Roosevelt and who,
at the height of his fame, commanded an audience of millions.
Angus Ross in his article on Wells in the *Penguin Companion to
Literature* writes: "Wells's writings suffer from the restlessness
which kept his astonishing talents from being completely and satis-
factorily effective in any one direction." Thus he is now paying the
price for having been so immensely popular during his lifetime, for
having diversified his skills over so many different areas of intellectual life. He *was* a novelist, certainly. But he was at the same time an
educator, a Fabian socialist, a popular historian, a writer on social
problems, a pioneer of women's emancipation, and a host of other
things. It is precisely this diffusion of his talents that makes it so
difficult to appraise him. Indeed, he was such a prolific writer and
interested himself in so many aspects of human affairs that it is only

now, forty years after his death, that his achievement can be assessed dispassionately and the wheat separated from the chaff.

Wells is now paying the penalty for having written too much and too unevenly over a long period of time. His literary career spanned exactly half a century, 1895–1945, and throughout that time he poured out a seemingly endless flow of novels, short stories, romances, speculations, pamphlets, and forecasts in addition to a very considerable amount of journalism. (It has been estimated that he wrote at least three thousand unreprinted articles.) Inevitably, in such a vast body of work there are considerable variations in quality. Whereas at the height of his powers he was producing work of the calibre of *Tono-Bungay* and *The History of Mr. Polly,* he was also capable of writing mediocre novels such as *The Soul of a Bishop, The Wife of Sir Isaac Harman,* and *The Secret Places of the Heart.* This very unevenness, coupled with the repetitive nature of some of the later fiction and journalism, has done grave damage to his literary reputation. His contemporaries Joyce and Conrad were content to write a comparatively small quantity of fiction of a consistently high standard. Wells was constitutionally incapable of this. Restless and mercurial by nature, he was always eager to be working on the next project, the next idea. New themes, ideas, plans, and speculations poured from him in a never-ending flood— so much so that quite early in his career W. E. Henley warned him of the dangers of over-production:

> You have a unique talent; and—you have produced three books, at least, within the year, and are up to the elbows in a fourth! It is magnificent, of course: but it can't be literature[13]

Had he possessed the patience and determination to concentrate instead on producing a smaller number of novels of a more uniform standard, his literary standing today would probably be considerably higher.

But perhaps the most important single factor militating against his acceptance as a serious and relevant novelist is the dominance of the received view that he belongs firmly with the naturalist school. In the great divide in English literature between "realists" and "modernists," Wells is felt to belong wholly with the realists, that is with the realistic tradition of the novel as exemplified by Dickens, George Eliot, and Arnold Bennett. The tenacity with which this view is held is surprising in the light of the wealth of evidence to the contrary. Since 1960 a number of influential studies have demonstrated that his scientific romances and short stories are extraordinarily rich in imagery—religious, psychological, mythological—and that many are capable of an allegorical interpretation. Yet the view persists that *as a novelist* he was writing in a firmly established nineteenth-century mode and continued to do so until the day of his death. The dominant attitude to Wells is that his novels are to be read at face value; that they possess a surface meaning and no more. The detailed textual, linguistic, and analytical study devoted to such works as *Ulysses, Sons and Lovers,* and *To the Lighthouse* has bypassed Wells altogether. He is simply not regarded as a fruitful field for academic scrutiny.

It is true that some of his early novels—*The Wheels of Chance, Love and Mr Lewisham, Kipps*—bear many of the hallmarks of the realist tradition, but simultaneously with these he was writing *The Time Machine, The Sea Lady,* and *The Food of the Gods:* works which are dense in imagery and rich in allegorical overtones. From the outset his work was consciously experimental in tone and method.

4

Wells was 21 in 1887. The formative years of his life coincided with the breakup of the old order in science and philosophy and the beginnings of modern psychology and sociology. The years of his literary apprenticeship, 1886–95, saw the discovery of X-rays, the publication of the first works on psychoanalysis, the first English edition of Marx's *Capital,* the internal combustion engine, the first electric power station, and the first telephone switchboard.

T. H. Huxley's *Agnosticism* appeared in 1889 and Frazer's *The Golden Bough* in 1890. The year of the publication of *The Time Machine,* 1895, also saw the invention of wireless telegraphy and the cinematograph and the first electrified main line railway. A new spirit of innovation, enquiry, and experiment was abroad. As Malcolm Bradbury has observed: "The communal universe of reality and culture on which nineteenth century art had depended was over."[14] The intellectual climate of uncertainty and questioning—it should not be forgotten that the debate stimulated by the publication of Darwin's theory of evolution was raging throughout Wells's childhood and adolescence—is reflected in changes in literature and the arts. The beginnings of Wells's literary career coincided with the publication of innovative works by Conrad, Strindberg,

and Chekhov and, and in other arts, by Gauguin, Munch, and Ma-
hler.

It would be remarkable indeed if this spirit of experiment was not
evident in Wells's own writings. His earliest significant essay, "The
Rediscovery of the Unique" (1891), drew attention to the
uniqueness of all things, that no two objects of the same class are
exactly alike. He was quick to perceive that a recognition of this
fact has implications in the field of morality:

> We may, however, point out that beings are unique, and that therefore
> we cannot think of regulating our conduct by wholesale dicta. A strict
> regard for truth compels us to add that principles are wholesale dicta:
> they are substitutes of more than doubtful value for an individual study
> of cases. [15]

Years later he described this paper as his "first quarrel with the
accepted logic" and throughout his life he adhered to the view that
logical processes and language shared "the profoundly provisional
character, the character of irregular limitation and adaptation that
pervades the whole physical and animal being of man." [16] From the
outset, his writings reflect this sense of doubt and provisionality, a
deep awareness of the future. In place of a confident faith in social
advance his early novels and stories are notable for their profound
pessimism, their troubled sense of a society in process of fragmentation, a world which is no longer solid. In *The Time Machine, The
Invisible Man* and *The Island of Doctor Moreau,* he questioned the
complacent assumption that human evolution would inevitably lead
to progress, and in such short stories as "The Remarkable Case of
Davidson's Eyes," "The Plattner Story," and "The Story of the
Late Mr. Elvesham," he implicitly cast doubt in the validity of the
accepted framework of reality. In place of belief in a "knowable
world wholly accessible to reasoned and rational enquiry" [17] (which
one would surely expect to find if Wells was indeed a realist writer),
we find the reverse: a novelist obsessed with the unconscious, with
imagery of death and corruption, with themes of alienation and
violence.

Ambiguity is his hallmark rather than assurance. In the preface to
a collected edition of his short stories he obsevered: "I would
discover I was peering into remote and mysterious worlds ruled by
an order logical indeed, but other than our common sanity." [18] This
preoccupation with states of mind and experience "other than our
common sanity" is characteristic of his work. His novels and stories are *disturbing,* not only in the sense that they explore themes

of alienation, apocalypse, and decay, but in their representation of inward states of consciousness. Edward Prendick, the narrator of *The Island of Doctor Moreau,* is obsessed by the sense that he is not a rational creature, "but only an animal tormented with some strange disorder in its brain, that sent it to wonder alone, like a sheep stricken with the gid." The stress on anxiety and isolation we associate with such authors as Kafka and Camus is also characteristic of Wells. Even in the works that are generally regarded as comedies, there is a significant element of violence and disorder. One thinks of the dismissal of Parsons and the battles with Uncle Jim in *Mr Polly,* the "Battle of Crayminster" in *Bealby,* and the spirited destruction that occurs in *The War of the Worlds* and *The War in the Air.* The reader has an impression of a world that has run amok, a society at odds with itself. Many of the novels contain a discordant element, a character who introduces an effect of imbalance into the narrative and deflects the tidy progression of the plot. Montgomery in *The Island of Doctor Moreau,* Marvel in *The Invisible Man,* Chaffery in *Love and Mr Lewisham,* Ramage in *Ann Veronica,* The Tramp in *Bealby*—each acts as an irritant, a dislocating force which compels the reader to acknowledge man's irrationality.

As Wells developed self-confidence as a novelist, he became increasingly aware of the flexibility of his medium and began to experiment more and more openly with the conventions and assumptions of the nineteenth-century realist tradition. Throughout his life, he was fascinated by the relationship between fiction and reality. His scientific training under T. H. Huxley had convinced him of the provisional nature of all forms of life, and, in his early speculations such as "The Possible Individuality of Atoms" and "Another Basis for Life," he questioned the solidity of accepted notions of the physical world. Since his central philosophical belief was to assert "the necessary untrustworthiness of all reasoning processes arising out of the fallacy of classification,"[19] his scepticism is inevitably reflected in his approach to the novel. On entering a Wells novel—even those which on the surface appear to be realistic—one is continually aware of a blurring of the distinction between the fiction one is reading and the world beyond the text. The opening sentence of his earlier "realistic" novel, *The Wheels of Chance,* contains the name of a drapery emporium followed by the words, "a perfectly fictitious Co., by the bye." This reminder that what the reader has before him is a *novel* destroys the illusion of reality: an illusion that the author is at pains to erode at several points in the story. In an early novel, *The Wealth of Mr Waddy*

(1898–99) there is an interesting example of his indebtedness to Sterne:

> Allusion has been made to a Mr. Kipps during the course of this story. He has flitted in a transitory way into quite a number of scenes. At the very outset you saw him at Folkestone, aghast at Mr. Waddy's language, and in the chapter immediately following he appeared again, a younger and simpler Kipps apprenticed at Tunbridge Wells, and as a round eye and a raised eyebrow regarding the noble Chitterlow with reverent astonishment over the edge of an art class easel. Then you glimpsed him at the elopement, flushed and proud, amidst a scandalised circle . . .
>
> The manifest intention of the author has been to arouse interest and curiosity in this person, to provoke the reader to ask, What the devil has Kipps to do with it? I don't see how Kipps comes in. Who *is* this Kipps? Dammy, here's Kipps again! and so forth. Now, manifestly while Mr. Waddy trundles with a steadily accelerated velocity down that steep place upon the Leas, there comes a pause of awful expectation. And in that pause there can be nothing more fitting than two or three intercalary chapters, about this same intrusive Kipps. That mystery disposed of, the time will be ripe for us to return and look for the surviving fragments (if any) of Mr. Waddy.[20]

The jocularity of the style disguises the fact that he is deliberately toying with the reader, arousing expectations that may or may not be fulfilled. The passage calls to mind the scene in *Tristram Shandy* when Sterne interrupts the narrative with a digression and then continues: "But I forget my uncle Toby, whom all this while we have left knocking the ashes out of his tobacco pipe." Similar instances of toying with the reader are scattered throughout his work. In the opening chapter of *Tono-Bungay*, the narrator, George Ponderevo, refers at numerous points to his father, arousing anticipations that his father is to be a significant character in the story. In fact the father plays no part in George's adventures; a deliberate mocking of narrative conventions that is an important element in Wells's overall design. George's failure to discover his roots strengthens the theme of alienation that underlies much of the novel's imagery.

Wells was also testing out approaches in structure and method. *The Invisible Man* and *The History of Mr Polly* both have an unusual structure that on first reading appears to fracture the narrative but on subsequent readings can be seen to contribute in a material way to the unfolding of the story. In *The War of the Worlds*, he employs the device of two narrators: a technique Stevenson had previously used with great effectiveness in *Treasure Island*. In *A*

Modern Utopia, he achieves a hybrid that is neither a realistic novel nor a romance but a fusion of the two, "a sort of shot-silk texture between philosophical discussion on the one hand and imaginative narrative on the other."[24] In *The Dream*, the story begins in the distant future but then becomes a realistic novel with interjections from the standpoint of a future age. In *The World of William Clissold,* which significantly is subtitled *A Novel at a New Angle,* he was seeking to break new ground in the English novel by elaborating a full-scale mental autobiography. Arnold Bennett wrote to him: "This is an *original* novel. My novels never are."[22] Throughout his life, he was an experimental writer, regarding each new novel as a fresh departure and consciously experimenting with a range of styles, themes, techniques, and approaches. Indeed, the closer one studies Wells, the more one is aware of a depth of complexity that deserves careful attention. As B. Ifor Evans observes in *A Short History of English Literature:* "Uneven as he is, the danger is always to underestimate him."[23]

In her influential essays "Modern Fiction" (1919) and "Mr Bennett and Mrs Brown" (1924), Virginia Woolf criticised Bennett and Wells for being "materialists" who were more interested in describing external details than the inner lives of their characters. By using the term "materialist," she explained, she meant that "they write of unimportant things; they spend immense skill and immense industry making the trivial and the transitory appear the true and the enduring."[24] In bracketing Wells and Bennett together, she was unwittingly rendering Wells a disservice, for in doing so she was perpetuating a misconception that is still very widely held. Bennett was an heir to the French realists: a classic example of a writer whose novels are windows on reality. Wells, by contrast, was a novelist whose work implicitly challenges realist conventions. It is precisely because his novels *are* self-conscious and pessimistic, and because they reject the cohesive worldview of the Victorians and focus increasingly on the inner lives of their characters, that he can be regarded, like Conrad, as a transitional figure between realism and modernism.

5

The abiding impression of Wells's fiction is of its ambivalence. From *The Time Machine* to *You Can't Be Too Careful,* it would be difficult to name any of his novels that ends on a note of resolution. The characteristic ending of a Wells novel is of a questioning, a deliberate ambiguity that is at once stimulating and disturbing. To compare the final paragraph of a novel by Austen, Trollope, or Bennett with the ending of almost any Wells novel is to appreciate the contrast between realist fiction and what might be termed the novel of indeterminacy. It is rare in Wells's fiction to find a neat tidying-up of loose ends. It is much more common to find an ending on a note of uncertainty or irresolution: Hoopdriver "vanishes from our ken," George Ponderero cleaves through the sea in a destroyer, Mr. Polly ceases to admire the sunset and announces "we can't sit here for ever." There is an apparent reluctance by the author to arrive at a point of fixity. In place of a symmetrical conclusion, one is left in a state of flux.

Similar instances of ambiguity occur with surprising frequency in his fiction. An interesting example is the conclusion of *Mr Britling Sees It Through,* a novel describing the reaction of a representative Englishman to the First World War. Mr. Britling has been writing in his study until dawn. He gets up from his desk and stands motionless at the window matching the sunrise:

> Wave after wave of warmth and light came sweeping before the sunrise across the world of Matching's Easy. It was as if there was nothing but morning and sunrise in the world.
> From away towards the church came the sound of some early worker whetting a scythe.[25]

The scythe is a patently ambiguous image. It is a well-known symbol of death, shaped like the waning moon before extinction. Father Time is invariably depicted holding a scythe. On the other hand, it is open to an opposite interpretation: that of life and renewal. The scythe is used to mow the old growth to make way for the new. Is the reader to infer that the war represents a new beginning, or is it on the contrary a harbinger of extinction? The drift of Wells's final chapter tends to the former, but the element of doubt remains.

On examination it can be seen that a number of his novels conclude with an ambiguous image—the scythe in *Mr Britling,* the destroyer in *Tono-Bungay,* the withered flower in *The Time Machine,* the fire in *The Wonderful Visit.* This deliberate ambivalence, a seeming reluctance to reach a point of finality, is characteristic of Wells's fiction. It stems from his attitude of mind and his refusal to admit that the world of physical reality is final and definite:

> I find most of the world that other people describe or take for granted much more hard and clear and definite than mine is. I am at once vaguer

and more acutely critical. I don't believe so fully and unquestioningly in this "common-sense" world in which we meet and exchange ideas, this world of fact, as most peole seem to do. I have a feeling that this common-sense world is not *final*.[26]

This view of reality is crucial to an understanding of his approach to the novel. Because he rejected the realist worldview—the notion that the tangible world possesses a unifying logic—and because an awareness of man's provisional nature was central to his philosophy, his approach to literature and to all forms of art was inherently experimental. There could be no finality about man; man was "finite and not final, a being of compromises and adaptations."[27] It followed that all philosophy was provisional and tentative, all political thought, all psychology. The novel no more than any other form of creative achievement could be subject to rules and conventions. It must be provisional, an artifact to be perpetually renewed and reshaped. His sense of man's plasticity led him to write novel after novel in which a relatively stable environment is fractured by the introduction of a catalyst—the angel in *The Wonderful Visit*, Griffin in *The Invisible Man*, Chitterlow in *Kipps*, Trafford in *Marriage*. The arrival of this catalyst sets in motion a process akin to a chemical reaction in a laboratory experiment, with the characters reacting on one another in response to the disturbing agent. The process is analogous to the dropping of a stone into a tranquil pool. Each of the novels ends with the action still in a state of motion, while the water is in a state of agitation.

It is clear, then, that on balance Wells's fiction has more in common with that of Conrad and the twentieth-century modernists than is commonly acknowledged. It shares with their work an emphasis on flux rather than stasis, discursiveness rather than cohesion. It shares with them a richness of symbolism, imagery, and metaphor, and a relationship between author and text that is frequently more complex than appears on first reading. Above all, when studying Wells one is increasingly conscious of an oblique relationship between reader and narrator: the meaning does not reside only in the surface text, but behind it. It is this that distinguishes his work most sharply from that of Bennett and Galsworthy.

Notes

1. Mark Schorer, "Technique as Discovery," *Critiques and Essays on Modern Fiction 1920–1951*, ed. J. W. Aldridge (New York: Farrar, Straus & Giraux, 1952), 72.

2. H. G. Wells, Introduction to Geoffrey West, *H. G. Wells: A Sketch for a Portrait*, (London: Gerald Howe, 1930), 13.

3. Wells, "The Betterave Papers", *Cornhill Magazine* (July 1945), 363.

4. Bernard Bergonzi, *The Early H. G. Wells* (Manchester: Manchester University Press, 1961), 165.

5. Robert Barnard, *A Short History of English Literature* (Oxford: Basil Blackwell, 1984), 149.

6. Leon Edel and Gordon N. Ray, ed. *Henry James and H. G. Wells*, (London: Rupert Hart-Davis, 1959) 122–23.

7. Robert Bloom, *Anatomies of Egotism: A Reading of the Last Novels of H. G. Wells* (Lincoln and London: University of Nebraska Press, 1977), 8.

8. Wells, *Experiment in Autobiography* (London: Victor Gollancz and the Cresset Press, 1934), 2:499.

9. Harris Wilson, ed., *Arnold Bennett and H. G. Wells: A Record of a Personal and a Literary Friendship* (London: Rupert Hart-Davis, 1960), 60.

10. Lovat Dickson, *H. G. Wells: His Turbulent Life and Times* (London: Macmillan, 1969), 164.

11. Wells, letter to Elizabeth Healey, quoted in West, *H. G. Wells: A Sketch For a Portrait*, 137–38.

12. Edel and Ray, eds., *Henry James and H. G. Wells*, 264.

13. Quoted in Norman and Jeanne Mackenzie, *The Time Traveller: The Life of H. G. Wells* (London: Weidenfeld and Nicolson, 1977), 110.

14. Malcolm Bradbury and James McFarlane, *Modernism 1890–1930* (Brighton: Harvester Press, 1978), 27.

15. Wells, "The Rediscovery of the Unique." *Fortnightly Review*, July 1891, 110.

16. Wells, "Scepticism of the Instrument" (1903), reprinted as an appendix to *A Modern Utopia* (London: Chapman & Hall, 1905), 378.

17. Jeremy Hawthorn, *Studying the Novel* (London: Edward Arnold, 1985), 29.

18. Wells, Introduction to *The Country of the Blind and Other Stories* (London: Thomas Nelson & Sons, 1911).

19. Wells, "Scepticism of the Instrument," 384.

20. Wells, *The Wealth of Mr. Waddy*, ed. Harris Wilson (Carbondale and Edwardsville: Southern Illinois University Press, 1969), 56.

21. Wells, *A Modern Utopia*, viii.

22. Bennett, letter to Wells, 27 October 1926, *Arnold Bennett and H. G. Wells*, 236.

23. B. Ifor Evans, *A Short History of English Literature* (Harmondsworth: Penguin Books, 1951), 181.

24. Virginia Woolf, *The Common Reader: First Series* (London: Hogarth Press, 1968), 187.

25. Wells, *Mr Britling Sees it Through* (London: Cassell & Co., 1916), 433.

26. Wells, *The World of William Clissold: A Novel at a New Angle* (London: Ernest Benn, 1926), 1:27–28.

27. Wells, *A Modern Utopia*, 376–77.

Making Fun of Work: Humor as Sociology in the Works of H. G. Wells

Christie Davies

H. G. Wells's early comedies such as *Kipps, The History of Mr Polly,* and *Bealby*[1] make fun of work as Wells had known it. It is a measure of his genius that he was able to transmute the underlying bitterness of his own experience into his skilled comic accounts of Kipps and Mr. Polly working as draper's assistants, of the little shopkeeper of Fishbourne, and of Bealby's rebellion against domestic service. In Wells's comedies, the rationalizing forces of the market place, of competition, of organization—which have marked the service sector of retailing as much as any other branch of a modern economy—are mocked and ridiculed for having shaped the unsatisfactory working lives of Kipps, Mr. Polly, and their colleagues. Indeed, *The History of Mr Polly* is Wells's comic masterpiece, and the adventures of Mr. Polly debunk work as effectively as those of *The Good Soldier Švejk* debunk warfare.

The success of Wells's comedies of work raises two sets of questions. First, how does he depict work, and in particular work as experienced by a particular sector of the lower-middle class in the early years of the twentieth century, and how does he set about arousing the insightful laughter of his readers, not just at individuals, but at an entire social process? Second, how can Wells's levity be related to that of later literary mockers of and scoffers at the pieties of work, and how can the underlying gravity of Wells's comedy be linked to the subsequent evolution of the sociology of work?

In all complex industrial societies, the work of individuals is coordinated and constrained by the forces of the market-place, the interplay of supply and demand, and the edicts, instructions, and regulations of bureaucratic organizations. These are the essential mechanisms of any rational large economic system—rational in the narrow sense of economizing, of endlessly squeezing more out of less to produce greater economic efficiency.[2] The culture of most modern societies is only partly in harmony with these processes, for although efficiency, diligence, productivity, and thrift are central values of these societies, their cultures also tend to stress the values of hedonism, individual self-expression, and self-realization that lead individuals to experience the forces of rationalization as oppressive.[3] It is this cultural contradiction that lies at the heart of Wells's comedies of the life of the English lower-middle class in the early twentieth century. Wells wrote about what he knew, but his was a happy choice for it was the members of this class who were most likely to embody the contradiction between the values of work, thrift, and efficiency and those of individual self-realization and yet whose constrained and precarious economic circumstances left them with little room for manoeuvre.

Wells's comic heroes are lower-middle-class misfits whose vague and inchoate but nonetheless real wish for self-expression is in conflict both with the constraints of their economic position and with the limiting, economizing creed of work held up to them as an ideal even by other members of their own class. Their case is not that of peasants shrugging off the exhortations of a distant landlord, or of factory workers bitterly resentful of the Stakhanovite hectoring of the commissar; but of people uneasily aware of the discordant views within their own group and even within their own minds: "He [Mr. Polly] could not grasp what was wrong with him. He made enormous efforts to diagnose his case. Was he really just a 'lazy slacker' who ought to 'buck up'? . . . He made some perfectly sincere efforts to 'buck up' and 'shove' ruthlessly. But that was infernal, impossible. He had to admit himself miserable with all the misery of a social misfit" (*Mr Polly, Quartette,* 434).

Wells used the position of lower-middle-class misfits such as Kipps or Mr. Polly as a pivot for his comic attack on the organization and mythology of work of his time. It is a mark of Wells's comic talent that he could build comedy out of the twin threats of failure in a market economy—unemployment and bankruptcy—and use them to ridicule the myths of enterprise.

Unemployment for Mr. Polly meant loneliness, frustration, anxiety, and humiliation as he sought to sell himself to a new employer. Yet even as Mr. Polly was squeezed by economic circumstances and tried to squeeze himself even further to fit those circumstances, a part of him, the marvellous phrase-making Mr. Polly, remained free to subvert through humor the forces pressing in on him. In this way, Wells was able to show Mr. Polly in comic conflict not merely with other individuals but with the harsh impersonal constraints of his social and economic world. Given his powerless and precarious situation, Mr. Polly did not dare to assail his competitors and opponents directly to produce one of Wells's characteristically ludicrous individual fights that accelerate into farce and sometimes tragedy. Nonetheless, Mr. Polly's unspoken phrases entangled them as thoroughly as their economic pressures entangled Mr. Polly. In the back of his mind, competitors were labeled "Smart Juniors" full of "Smart Juniosity," devotees of the "Shoveacious Cult," and his own outward demeanour "Obsequies Deference." Behind this servile pose, the irrepressible phrase-making part of Mr. Polly's brain sought to encapsulate the very employer he needed to impress:

"Chubby chops?" Chubby Charmer? . . . Chump chops! How about chump chops? said the phrase-maker with an air of inspiration." (*Mr. Polly, Quartette,* 428).

Phrases were for Mr. Polly as in a later generation hidden grimaces were for Kingsley Amis's "Lucky Jim" Dixon: a secret defence against and defiance of a world outside his control.[4]

Wells was equally successful in his humorous undermining of an uneasily held business ethic in the revealing scene where the shopkeepers of Fishbourne are gathered after the fire started by Mr. Polly had demolished their premises. In theory their shops are a source of livelihood, ambition, identity, and opportunity; in practice an irksome road to inevitable bankruptcy:

"It's cleared me out of a lot of old stock," said Mr. Wintershed; "that's one good thing."
The remark was felt to be in rather questionable taste, and still more so was his next comment.
"Rusper's a bit sick it didn't reach *'im.*"
Every one looked uncomfortable, and no one was willing to point the reason why Rusper should be a bit sick. (*Mr. Polly, Quartette,* 563).

The committing of arson by small shopkeepers seeking to defraud the insurance company has long been a subject of ambiguous ethnic jokes of both Jewish and bigoted anti-Semitic origin,[5] but Mr. Polly alone knew the truth about his own arson. The humor of the other traders' uneasiness lies in the gap between their wish to uphold the conventional view that they were victims snatched from their callings by fire and their own strong but private and unstable sense of having escaped from a commercial trap.

These are the ways in which Wells gets the reader to laugh at the grim and cheerless face of failure in the rational world of the marketplace. His comedies are built on the crushed fate of men who have been "whittled down" (*Mr. Waddy,* 70) and are now "crawling along a drain pipe until (they) die," (*Kipps, Quartette,* 543), "going down a Vorterex," (*Mr. Polly, Quartette,* 493), caught in "the hard old economic world, that enacts work, that limits range, that discourages phrasing and dispels laughter," (*Mr. Polly, Quartette,* 493).

It is perhaps not surprising in the circumstances that many of Wells's comic assaults are directed against small entrepreneurs who had succeeded, or those keen white-collar workers who had allowed the copper to penetrate their souls. Perhaps Wells's best attack on the reduction of work to a "system" is the portrait of that muddled exponent of a kind of proto-Taylorism,[6] Kipps's employer Mr. Shalford. As a satire on the successful, rationalizing entrepreneur, it is something of a cheat for there are more of the slogans than the substance of efficiency about Mr. Shalford. Mr. Shalford may have considered himself "the Napoleon of haberdashers," (*Mr. Waddy,* 71) but it was by means of fraudulent bankruptcy and marriage for money that he had risen in his chosen trade. Mr. Shalford's tour of his store with Kipps in tow and his exposition of his "system" governed by minute rules and heavy penalties, where assistants slave like machines (but only when watched) is a mockery of efficiency rather than the real thing, though this naturally adds to the humor of Wells's observations.

Mr. Shalford's comically oppressive system is easily shown by Wells to be a mere mixture of petty cheeseparing and bunkum. This makes for endless fun at his expense, but it does mean that Wells (here at least) evaded the problem of the residual but very real oppressiveness of a genuinely efficient system run by a more intelligent, numerate, rational, and innovating Shalford. Were Shalford stripped of his vanity, pettiness, muddle, and other all too human weaknesses; he would be a less comic but possibly an even more threatening figure, and Wells would have to distinguish much more clearly than he does between the pains of inefficiency and the pains of efficiency. Shalford and his system are a sham; increased entropy disguised as constructive momentum, "by order" mistaken for order:

> Once a year came stock-taking. . . . Then the splendours of Mr. Shalford's being shone with oppressive brilliance. "System!" he would say, "System. Come! 'ussel!" and issue sharp, confusing, contradictory orders very quickly." (*Kipps, Quartette,* 53).

Some of the successful small businessmen in Wells's comedies show a more genuine gift for rational economy and entrepreneurship than Mr. Shalford. One such figure is the aggressive Mr. Benshaw, the hoe-wielding small-holder in *Bealby* who plays such a major part in the Battle of Crayminster, another of Wells's ludicrous fights between, among, or at least involving the respectable. Mr. Benshaw is a stock comic figure who is placed there only so that Wells can satirize a social type, albeit with great success:

> Mr. Benshaw was considering very deeply the financial side of a furious black fence that he had at last decided should pen in the school children from further depredations. It should be of splintery tarred deal, and high, with well-pointed tops studded with sharp nails, and he believed that by making the path only two feet wide, a real saving of ground for cultivation might be made and a very considerable discomfort for the public arranged, to compensate for his initial expense. The thought of a narrow lane which would in winter be characterized by an excessive sliminess and from which there would be no lateral escape was pleasing to a mind by no means absolutely restricted to considerations of pounds, shillings and pence. In his hand after his custom he carried a hoe, on the handle of which feet were marked so that it was available not only for destroying the casual weed but also for purposes of measurement. (*Bealby*, *Quartette*, 818–9).

Much of Wells's comic portrait of Mr. Benshaw consists merely of the standard established ingredients of old satires of hard joyless tradesmen in the grip of the Protestant ethic and its utilitarian successors[7]—it is the stuff of which ethnic jokes about canny, calculating Scotsmen, Gabrovonians, Regiomontanos or New England Yankees are made.[8] Nonetheless Wells moves with skill between Benshaw's real economic achievements, his joyless personal existence, and his aggressive anger against those who impinge on his domain or the literal fruits of his labor. Benshaw is above all a measuring, calculating, economizing man, whose hoe is a gauge as well as a tool and a weapon, and whose ideal revenge is to cramp his unruly neighbours into a narrow path of "considerable discomfort" from which "there would be no lateral escape". Benshaw's ideal of a completely fenced-in countryside is, of course, the antithesis of Mr. Polly's resentment of a world where all roads seem to be "bordered by inflexible palings or iron fences or severely disciplined hedges" (*Mr. Polly*, *Quartette*, 461).

The idea that a strong commitment to the calculative rationality of work drives out the capacity for the careless enjoyment even of leisure hours is one of Wells's favourite themes. In *Mr Polly* even the elderly golfers of Wimbledon "smite hunted little white balls with the utmost bitterness and dexterity" (*Mr. Polly*, *Quartette*, 461). It is this notion, too, that underlies Wells's use of the well-established comic national stereotype of eager, earnest, hustling American tourists in Europe, always pursuing happiness but never quite catching up with it. When Mr. Polly worked in Canterbury, he was suitably impressed by the American tourists' determined, methodical, hurried attempt to "do" Chaucer and Marlowe in an afternoon, to grasp only the "Broad Elemental Canterbury Prahposition" stripped of its "side-shows" and "second-rate stunts." This attempt to measure leisure as if it were work, a sort of Baedeker productivity drive, Mr. Polly terms "Cultured Rapacacity" and "Vorocious Return to the Heritage" (see *Mr. Polly, Quartette,* 431).

One of Wells's best portraits of a member of the lower-middle-class held fast in a niche is that of Mr. Polly's cousin Harold Johnson, who to his regret was not a small businessman but a railway ticket clerk on a fixed salary. Johnson's life is ruled by gray, distasteful figures and by an obsessive hatred of waste that far exceeds his wish for profit. Like Mr. Benshaw, Johnson is a gardener with a real but also symbolic liking for narrow, waste-free paths. By contrast, Mr. Polly's most vivid, affectionate, and human memory of his recently deceased father was of an angry and violent confrontation with just such a physical constriction, as his father struggled to lug a jammed sofa up a narrow winding staircase:

> A weakly wilful being, struggling to get obdurate things round impossible corners—in that symbol Mr. Polly could recognise himself and all the trouble of humanity. (*Mr. Polly, Quartette,* 438).

Johnson has no such passions, he has become a mere projection of the routine methodical world of the ideal petty bureaucrat, much as the thriving tradesman whom Johnson urges Mr. Polly to emulate—"Rymer, Pork Butcher and Provision Merchant, The World Famed Easewood Sausage"—has become a "distinguished comestible" (*Mr. Polly, Quartette,* 444). To use Max Weber's phrase, the bureaucratic Johnson "is chained to his activity by his entire material and ideal existence . . . a single cog in an ever-moving mechanism which prescribes to him an essentially fixed route of march."[9]

In these various ways Wells's comedies repeatedly caricature the rationalizing work ethic and its deleterious effects on successful and failed alike. However, the cage-like nature of work in Wells's comedies is also indicated by his portrayal of various antitheses to it. The simplest of these is escape, the brief escape of a holiday, or temporary affluent unemployment, the flight of Bealby, the final release of Kipps through chance inheritance, and of Mr. Polly by successful arson and bungled suicide. Holidays are unwork, days free from routine and regularity, compulsion and the clock. Holidays shine "out like diamonds among pebbles" (*Mr. Polly, Quartette,* 407) in contrast to a life dominated by work that has "the hue of one perpetual dismal Monday morning"—"no adventure, no glory, no change, no freedom" (*Kipps, Quartette,* 55) and where even food becomes "the rope of meal-times" (*Kipps, Quartette,* 52). For Mr. Polly, "Holidays were his life, and the rest merely adulterated living" (*Mr. Polly, Quartette,* 459). The contrast is particularly well drawn by Wells at the point where Mr. Polly realizes that his father's insurance money cannot last forever and he is doomed to return to the dismal life of a small draper. Mr. Polly knows that the time has come to "get off his bike":

> The happy dream in which he had been living of long, warm days of open roads of limitless, unchecked hours, of infinite time to look about him, vanished like a thing enchanted. He was suddenly back in the hard old economic world that enacts work, that limits range, that discourages phrasing and dispels laughter. He saw Wood Street [where unemployed shop assistants sought work] and its fearful suspenses yawning beneath his feet. (*Mr. Polly, Quartette,* 493).

For Mr. Polly and Kipps alike, there is a key turning point in their relationship with work—the big escape where they simply walk away from it. In *The Wealth of Mr Waddy,* Kipps on inheriting the fortune of the late Mr. Waddy sees the money above all as the end of work:

> The Emporium was over forever. Forever!. . . . HOLIDAYS! HOLIDAYS! All the year was to be one long Holiday now, the Sundays OF HIS FUTURE, THE EARLY CLOSING AFTERNOONS had spread out and touched one another. (*Mr. Waddy,* 114).

Mr. Polly as a successful arsonist and failed suicide likewise learns that "when a man has once broken through the paper walls of everyday circumstances, those insubstantial walls that hold so many of us securely prisoned from the cradle to the grave, he has made a discovery. If your world does not please you, *you can change it.* He could, for example, "clear out." It became a wonderful and alluring phrase to him—"Clear out!" (*Mr. Polly, Quartette,* 566–7). For the next month, Mr. Polly becomes a wanderer and, instead of working, leads a healthy outdoor life, seeking out the interesting in a timeless, unbusinesslike way.

However, it is significant that Wells does not allow his heroes to take to a permanent life of idle wandering and squandering.[10] Bealby eventually crawls back hungry, frightened, and repentant to the tasks of a steward's room boy at Shonts; Kipps loses most of his first fortune and ends up running a small bookshop in Hythe; and Mr. Polly becomes odd-job man at the Potwell Inn. Only Bealby, though, is really defeated—both Kipps and Mr. Polly enjoy curiously unrealistic happy endings, back once again in the uncertain world of the small businessman. These unreal endings immediately pose the question: why should our heroes feel more content or fulfilled running a bookshop in Hythe or a pub in Potwell than a draper's shop in Fishbourne? The answer is partly an economic one. Neither Kipps's bookshop nor the Potwell Inn are under financial pressure. Kipps is sufficiently well off not to have to worry about the solvency of his bookshop thanks to his lucky investment in Chitterlow's distant theatrical speculations. Wells tells the reader even less about the finances of the Potwell Inn, but one may infer from the final note of fluvial security that closes Mr. Polly's history, as it does that of Kipps, that there is no fear of the Potwell Inn's ever-plumpening landlady losing her shape or her license. Somehow the fictitious Potwell Inn is immune from the kind of memorable slide into debt and disaster that had overwhelmed Wells's own maternal grandfather, George Neal, who had kept the Fountains Inn in Chichester and the New Inn at Midhurst with an equal lack of success.[11] For unexplained reasons, the Potwell Inn, like Kipps's bookshop in Hythe, is exempt from the harsh economic generalizations that Wells put in the mouth a "gifted if unpleasant contemporary" about the slow inevitable slide into bankruptcy and ruin of the small retailer (see *Mr. Polly, Quartette,* 524–6).

Because Kipps's wealth frees him from the economic anxieties and pressures of a small trader with little capital, he is able to survive the collapse of his sponsor (and in effect partner), the Associated Booksellers' Trading Union, and float alone buoyed up by his liquidity. Kipps is depicted as a man able to relax and potter about his shop chatting idly to non-customers disguised as potential customers about matters unrelated to his business.

For Mr. Polly, work at the Potwell Inn was larger, more active, more varied than it ever had been in the cramped little shop in Fishbourne. Although his tasks at the Inn are listed rather than described, the list conveys an impressive disregard for specialization or the division of labor. Mr. Polly runs a small ferry; hires out boats; drowns cats; and looks after poultry, ducks, garden, picknickers, and an orchard as well as the Inn itself.

In addition to these images of ideal work as an activity both relaxed and varied, Wells also briefly shows his readers the joys and perils of work as self-expression. The events that lead to the dismissal of Mr. Polly's close friend Parsons from the Port Burdock Bazaar can be seen as a comment on this aspect of a man's working life. Parsons' manic excitement when dressing a shop window, and his principled but unwise defence of his creation against higher authority lead to one of Wells's characteristically ineffective lower-middle class brawls that accelerate from farce to social rather than physical tragedy. In this way, Wells was able to give comic expression to the inevitable conflict between individual self-expression and the workings of a hierarchical organization designed for more mundane ends. Parsons' fight with his employer Mr. Garvace (and Mr. Garvace's minions) ends in disaster as the frustrated artist, when ordered out of what Parsons sees as, "his" window, smites the "sacred" "autocratic" bald head[12] that symbolizes Mr Garvace's authority with a thin cylinder of rolled huckaback (see *Mr. Polly, Quartette,* 413–9). Parsons is sacked and Mr. Polly also subsequently leaves the tedium of work for the anxious humiliation of unemployment. The fundamental contradiction of the modern world between the "economizing," rationalizing pressures of a hierarchical organization and the limitless anomic individual drive for self-realization (embodied in Mr. Garvace and Parsons respectively) can have no easy or peaceful resolution. It is no wonder that Mr. Polly puzzles about the incident for years afterwards, trying to decide who had been in the right.

Wells's insights into "work and its discontents"[13] may be found today in studies of work satisfaction and dissatisfaction by industrial sociologists and social psychologists. The importance of factors such as variety, job rotation, autonomy, and creativity in improving levels of work satisfaction are repeatedly observed,[14] though it has proved extremely difficult to establish exact relationships between the objective aspects of a task and the subjective assessment of that task by the person performing it. Also the expectations that individuals bring to their work are very varied and modify the degree to which a particular task is found to be rewarding or frustrating.

The widely held view first propounded by Maslow[15]—that as societies become wealthier and more secure, so that in consequence the individual's most basic physiological needs and requirements for safety and security are met, "higher order needs" for autonomy or self-actualization emerge—is intuitively plausible but has not been empirically validated. There have been many studies to test Maslow's hypothesis, but the results of these have been contradictory.[16] There seems to be some truth in Maslow's thesis, but it is difficult to know how much, and much of its popularity is due to the congruence between Maslow's progressive humanist values and those of even the most number-crunching of social psychologists. It can be plausibly argued that the insights into the nature of work to be found in Wells's comedies *are* supported by the later findings of the social psychologists and sociologists—but only with caution, for such people are likely to share many of Wells's values and will shape and interpret their findings accordingly. Also I have of necessity tended to select those aspects of Wells's treatment of work that can be viewed within conventional sociological and social psychological frameworks. To cite the findings of the practitioners of the latter in support of my interpretation of Wells is dangerously close to becoming a circular argument.

One of the most striking of the social psychologists' findings is the insatiable character of the "need" for "self-actualization or growth," "in the sense that the more it is satisfied the more important it becomes."[17] When this finding is placed alongside another seemingly limitless phenomenon that can be readily observed pressing hard on the working individual—namely, the economizing rationalizing drive for efficiency, productivity, and results in order to produce enhanced profitability or the meeting of ever higher quantifiable bureaucratic targets—it is clear that there is ample empirical support for the view of the macrosociologists that our anomic modern societies are characterized by major irresolvable cultural contradictions.[18]

Scientific discoveries, improvements in technology, and the automation of routine tasks lessen the pressures of scarcity and remove obstacles to job enlargement; but they also create—or, more accurately, permit—new pressures for greater standardization and specialization of work roles. Those with power are able to monitor and control certain kinds of work with ever greater precision, and this has led them to attempt to grade and sieve even less easily quantifiable human activities and achievements such as military credibility (a bigger bang for a buck), scholarship (the citation index), or even religion.[19] Those without power are encouraged to assent to this through an invoking of the politics of egalitarian envy by their rulers.[20] In the past, the central ideological demand of the egalitarians was for equality of material resources and possessions, but now it has been extended to cover nonmaterial aspects of satisfaction from work by the imposition of arbitrary bureaucratic rules of accountability on those whose autonomy and self-realization in their work appear higher than average.[21] They should be, must be, made as disciplined and as bored as the rest. Alienation cannot be abolished so it must be universalized. On this point at least the view of work held by both the levelers and the bureaucratic centralizers is consistent with the ideology of their common Jacobin ancestors.

There is one striking weakness in Wells's thinking that he shared with many of the reformers and radicals of his day. They assumed that the painful clashes between the individuals' quasiromantic demands for self-expression and the economizing constraints of the marketplace could be abolished by changing the *forms* through which these clashes found expression. Hence their rejection of the dominant institutions of the nineteenth century: capitalism, voluntary organization, middle-class respectability, and family authority in favour of the fallacies of the twentieth—socialism, enhanced central and local government power, more stringent bureaucratic controls, the politicization of the everyday world, and authoritarian leveling. Wells was in fact wiser than most, as readers can see from his satire of the Webbs as Oscar and Altora Bailey in *The New Machiavelli* or his quarrel with the inanely blind and authoritarian George Bernard Shaw about the true nature of Soviet Russia.[22] His mockery of the Baileys is worth quoting in this context for its accuracy and prescience:

> If [the Baileys] had the universe in hand, I know they would take down all the trees and put up stamped-tin green shades and sunlight accumulators. Altiora thought trees hopelessly irregular and sea cliffs a great mistake.

> [At the Baileys'] you felt you were in a sort of signal-box with levers all about you, and the world outside there, albeit a little dark and mysterious beyond the window, running on its lines in ready obedience to these unhesitating lights, true and steady to trim termini.[23]

Richard Remington in *The New Machiavelli* can dismiss the work of Herbert Spencer much as the narrator in *Mr Polly* shrugs aside Samuel Smiles, even though it is doubtful whether Wells had read either of these prophets of individualism and self-help with any thoroughness or understanding.[24] Indeed Remington clearly sympathizes with his father's diatribe against individual ownership:

> Property's the curse of life. Property! Ugh! Look at this country all cut up into silly little parallelograms. . . . It isn't a world we live in,

Dick; it's a cascade of accidents, it's a chaos exasperated by policemen!
. . . the folly and muddle that come from headlong, aimless and haphazard methods (31).

Remington himself says of the Victorian epoch:

That age that bore me was indeed a world full of restricted and undisciplined people, overtaken by power, by possessions and great new
freedoms, and unable to make any civilized use of them whatever (40).

For Remington this is indeed the essential nature of late nineteenth-century England. Like the Wells who created him, he failed
to recognize that the spontaneous order emerging from the marketplace, from a system of law grounded in precedent, from the
unforseeable process of discovery and invention is as structured
and necessary as the planned order of corporate decision-making,
statute law, or the deliberate design and replication of a machine.[25]
Wells's odd phrase "restricted and undisciplined people" is an
attempt to slide across the essential nature of the contradiction
necessarily at the core of all large-scale urban societies based on
modern technology. It implies that if only they would embrace
science, civilization, and socialism, then in that great ideal of order
and economy, they would become more disciplined and yet, by
some mysterious dialectical alchemy, also less restricted! You will
want to do what they tell you to do. Members of the Progressive
League unite; you have but your parallelograms to lose. Wells's
choice of this regular but unpleasing shape to symbolize people
who are trapped, enclosed, restricted in a confined and inefficient
world that provides minimal space for maximum boundaries is a
shrewd one. If only these randomly shaped and sized parallelograms could become a disciplined lattice of squares or hex-
agons, individuals would have more room to expand! Yet Wells is
wrong both about means and about ends. Planning and Fabian
socialism with their "administrative fizzle and pseudo-scientific
chatter" [see *The New Machiavelli,* 166] have not in the long run
improved the sprawling streets of South London so disliked by
Remington and Wells. They have merely destroyed its human scale
and undermined the involved spontaneous order that Wells failed to
recognize and appreciate in order to build alien tower blocks and
bloated schools, divided by areas of (in both senses) indefensible
space deserted at night save for the vandals and the occasional
mugger or rapist.[26] Even if the "human splendours" of Wells's
"justly organized state" [see *The New Machiavelli,* 13] were possible, individuals would still be trapped in the disciplined grid it

would require. Indeed human beings may well feel more free in and therefore prefer an untidy heap of parallelograms to the square cages of battery chickens or the hexagonal symmetries of the beehive. Even in a properly planned, surveyed, and measured excavation, many a Mr. Polly will cry out: "Hole! . . . 'Ole! . . . Oh! *Beastly* Silly Wheeze of a hole! . . . Roöötten Beëëastly Silly Hole!" [*Mr. Polly, Quartette,* 391, 395].

Indeed, it is Wells's Edwardian holes that have survived and not his brave new worlds; the holes have proved to be greater than the sum of Wells's paths. It is not Wells's utopian rhetoric but the frustrations of his ordinary heroes trapped not by introspective existential doubts but by external circumstances that remain vivid today. Readers laugh at their antics, and rejoice when they escape. Readers are as much moved by their unformed, clumsy but intense sense of beauty and adventure as by any detailed self-conscious account of the exotic sensations of an aesthete or explorer at the limits of human experience. Yet Wells could only have achieved all this within the framework of a comedy. In any other setting Wells's exploration of the feelings and perceptions of a Mr. Polly, a Kipps, or a Bealby trapped in the mundane world of work of the lower-middle classes would risk appearing sugary, mawkish, condescending, and emetic. Wells's greatness lies in his ability to judge exactly the degree of comic distance each situation requires—an achievement that places him alongside Cervantes, Dickens, or Hašek—and not in his flawed and contradictory grand ideas. If Wells's novels were, as is often claimed, but a dustbin for ideas, it is the dustbins that have survived (as any literal-minded person would expect, for that is what dustbins are built to do). It doesn't matter that Wells's bubbling thoughts and images are inconsistent, for the business of the novelist is to explore our contradictory world, not to resolve it.

Wells's comedies have also influenced and inspired other gifted writers of humor. George Orwell is often cited as a savage critic of Wells's later grand schemes,[27] but he was also the imitator of *The History of Mr Polly* in *Coming up for Air* (1939). Orwells's hero George Bowling actually read *The History of Mr Polly*[28] prior to his own failed break through the "paper walls of everyday circumstance." Mr. Bowling experienced but a few days on the other side of those insubstantial walls—to find that his childhood home, Lower Binfield, had become a depressing version of Wells's Bromstead—before returning to his everyday tasks at Flying Salamander Insurance. (Mr. Polly's neighbor little Clamp of the toyshop was insured with Royal Salamander.) The Royal Salamander has flown, and so has the Wellsian joy and optimism of Mr. Polly's escape— George Bowling will become Winston Smith.

The most important offspring of Wells's comedies though is Sinclair Lewis's *Babbitt* (1922), an American version of *Mr Polly*. Babbitt, unlike Mr. Polly, is a successful businessman, but he is rendered equally discontented by the incessant pressures of and for efficiency and productivity, and in his own way he also tries to escape. The contradictions of success can be as disturbing as those of failure and are just as rich a source of comic action, description, and comment. Sinclair Lewis greatly admired Wells and indeed named his eldest son after him.[29] He called *Tono-Bungay* "the liveliest of novels"[30] and found "in the early Wells, especially in Mr. Polly, such a sensational gaiety."[31] It is difficult to believe that the creation of Babbitt was not influenced by the example of Mr. Polly and Uncle Ponderevo.

Lewis, like Wells, wrote too much, and his later work is better forgotten, if only that we may concentrate our attention on his early comedies where he employed his "vigorous and graphic art of description to create, with wit and humour, new types of people."[32] This comment made at the time of the Nobel award to Lewis applies with equal force to the author Lewis so much admired, H. G. Wells.

Notes

1. All three are to be found in H. G. Wells's *A Quartette of Comedies* (London; Ernest Benn, 1928); subsequent quotations from this edition are cited parenthetically in the text. I have deliberately chosen to analyse Wells's *successful* comic writings and to ignore *Love and Mr Lewisham* (of which Wells himself wrote: "The attempts to get comic relief into *Love and Mr Lewisham* certainly failed." *See* Harris Wilson, "Introduction" to H. G. Wells, *The Wealth of Mr Waddy.* (Carbondale: Southern Illinois University Press, 1969), xiv. I have also omitted *You Can't Be Too Careful* (London: Secker and Warburg, 1941), which is a total failure. *The Wealth of Mr Waddy* may be regarded for our present purpose as an early version of *Kipps*.

2. *See* Daniel Bell, *The Cultural Contradictions of Capitalism*, 2nd edition, (London: Heinemann, 1979), 10–11; Frederick Herzberg, *Work and the Nature of Man* (London: Staples, 1966), 1–4; Krıshan Kumar, *Prophecy and Progress, the Sociology of Industrial and Post-Industrial Society* (Harmondsworth: Penguin, 1978), 83–88, 227–28.

3. See Bell, *Contradictions,* 14–18, 53–54, 69–74.

4. *See* comment in Patrick Parrinder, *H. G. Wells* (Edinburgh: Oliver and Boyd, 1970), 81.

5. *See* Christie Davies, "Jewish jokes, anti-Semitic jokes and Hebredonian jokes" in Avner Ziv, ed., *Jewish Humour,* (Tel Aviv: Tel Aviv University, 1986), 59–80.

6. From Frederick W. Taylor, author of *The Principles of Scientific Management* (New York: Harper, 1911), an American engineer who rationalized work so as to produce maximum productivity by rigidly programming the actions of each individual. His system, known as Taylorism, was much admired by Lenin.

7. On the reality behind the satire, *see* Max Weber, *The Protestant Ethic and the Spirit of Capitalism* (London: Unwin, 1930), esp. 181–82, and Bryan Wilson, *Religion in Secular Society* (Harmondsworth: Penguin, 1969), 41–44, 259.

8. *See* Christie Davies, "Ethnic Jokes, Moral Values and Social Boundaries," *British Journal of Sociology* 33 (September 1982): 383–403; Christie Davies, "Folklor, anekdoti i ikonomicheski progres" in *Smekhut vuv folklora, Problemi na Bulgarskiya Folklor,* 7 (Sofia:

Izdatelstvo na Bulgarskata/Akademija na naukite, 1987): 66–77; and Christie Davies, "Stupidity and rationality: jokes from the iron cage" in Chris Powell and George E. C. Paton, eds., *Humour in Society: Resistance and Control* (London: Macmillan, 1988), 1–32.

9. Max Weber, *From Max Weber: Essays in Sociology*, ed. H. H. Berth and C. W. Mills (London: Routledge and Kegan Paul, 1948), 228.

10. Anthony West notes that his father H. G. Wells strongly deprecated the life led by H. G.'s own elder brother, who became a permanent dropout cycling round rural England like Mr. Polly, earning pin-money as an itinerant clock-mender and watch-pedlar. *See* West, *H. G. Wells: Aspects of a Life* (London: Hutchinson, 1984), 196–97.

11. Ibid., 161–62.

12. Wells often uses baldness as both a badge of authority and a mark of pomposity.

13. This is the title of Daniel Bell's classic Essay "Work and its Discontents" (1956), reprinted in Bell, *The End of Ideology* (Glencoe, Ill.: Free Press, 1960) 222–62.

14. *See,* for instance, Robert Cooper, "Task Characteristics and Intrinsic Motivation," *Human Relations* 26 (1973), 387–413; and Lyman W. Porter, Edward E. Lawler III, and J. Richard Hackman, *Behavior in Organizations* (New York: McGraw-Hill, 1975), 277–98.

15. *See* A. H. Maslow, "A theory of human motivation," *Psychological Review* 50 (1943): 370–96, and A. H. Maslow, *Motivation and Personality,* 2nd edition, (New York: Harper and Row, 1970).

16. *See* Leonard M. Kokkila, John W. Slocum Jr., and Robert H. Strawser, "Perceptions of Job Satisfaction in Differing Occupations," *Business Perspectives* 9 (Autumn 1972): 5–9. But *see also* Porter et. al, *Behavior in Organizations,* 35–47. For a review of the literature, *see* Maria Hirszowicz, *Industrial Sociology* (Oxford: Martin Robertson, 1981), 71–97.

17. Porter et al, *Behavior in Organizations,* 45.

18. *See* Bell, *Contradictions,* and for an earlier period Emile Durkheim, *The Division of Labor in Society* (New York: Macmillan, 1933).

19. See Herzberg, *Work and the Nature of Man,* 1–5.

20. *See* Helmut Schoeck, *Envy: A Theory of Social Behaviour* (London: Secker and Warburg, 1969), 105, 134, 207.

21. *See* Schoeck, *Envy,* 93, 175, 191, 234, 308, 379.

22. *See* West, *H. G. Wells,* 135–42.

23. H. G. Wells, *The New Machiavelli* (Harmondsworth: Penguin, 1966), 165, 166. Subsequent quotations from this edition are cited parenthetically in the text.

24. A good introduction to Spencer's work is Herbert Spencer, *The Man Versus the State,* ed. Donald G. MacRae (Harmondsworth: Penguin, 1969). MacRae forcefully indicates Spencer's importance and criticizes those who have condemned him without reading him. A perusal of Samuel Smiles's *The Autobiography of Samuel Smiles,* ed. Thomas Mackay (London: John Murray, 1905), esp. 131, indicates that Smiles is a very different figure from the caricature mocked by Wells.

25. *See* M. Polanyi, *The Logic of Liberty* (London: Routledge and Kegan Paul, 1951), 156, 185; and Norman Barry, "The Tradition of Spontaneous Order," *Literature of Liberty* 5; no. 2 (Summer 1982), 7–58.

26. *See* Christie Davies, "Crime Bureaucracy and Equality," *Policy Review* 23 (Winter 1983), 89–105.

27. *See* George Orwell, "Wells, Hitler and the World State," in *Collected Essays* (London: Mercury, 1961).

28. George Orwell, *Coming up for Air* (1939), (Harmondsworth: Penguin, 1980), 120–21.

29. *See* Sinclair Lewis, *The Man from Main Street: Selected Essays and Other Writings of Sinclair Lewis,* ed. H. E. Maule, M. H. Cane, and P. A. Friedman (London: William Heinemann, 1954), 158.

30. Sinclair Lewis, "Our Friend H. G.," *New York Herald Tribune Books,* (20 October 1946), in Lewis, *The Man from Main Street,* 160.

31. Lewis, "Our Friend H. G.," 161.

32. From the citation for the 1930 prize, quoted by the editors of *The Man from Main Street,* 3.

Dickensian Motifs in Wells's Novels: The Disease Metaphor in *Tono-Bungay*

Maria Teresa Chialant

> . . . here, they lower our dear brother down a foot or two: here, sow him in corruption, to be raised in corruption: an avenging ghost at many a sick-bedside: a shameful testimony to future ages, how civilization and barbarism walked this boastful island together.
>
> —Charles Dickens, *Bleak House*

> It is quaint, no doubt, this England—it is even dignified in places— and full of mellow associations. That does not alter the quality of the realities these robes conceal. The realities are greedy trade, base profit- seeking, bold advertisement. . . .
>
> —H. G. Wells, *Tono-Bungay*

In 1911, two years after the publication of *Tono-Bungay,* Wells wrote "The Contemporary Novel," which is probably his most interesting statement in the field of literary criticism. The essay is important because it touches upon one of the main controversial aspects of the debate on the novel, which developed in the last two decades of the nineteenth century, reaching down to the 1920s. One passage, in particular, is worth underlining, where Wells says: "I rejoice to see many signs to-day that . . . there is every encourage- ment for a return . . . to the lax freedom of form, the rambling discursiveness, the right to roam, of the earlier novel, of *Tristram Shandy* and of *Tom Jones.*"[1] The emphasis is on the writer's right to use the novel as an unrestricted medium of expression, in the true English tradition of Sterne and Fielding—and of Dickens, too. The connection to the Victorian writer is, in fact, made in the same essay when Wells confesses he finds Dickens's novels, "long as they are," too short for him, and wishes they were more intertwined, so as to "flow into one another."

For Wells the novel was to be "not a single interest, but a woven tapestry of interests." This web-like quality, too, sounds very Dickensian to me. Everybody knows how Dickens's novels are skillfully structured, each image, character, and episode carefully linking to a visible pattern or to a hidden design in which apparently disjointed threads of the plot are finally tied together in a vision of unity and wholeness, even when the ultimate meaning is one of fragmentation and chaos.

In his *Experiment in Autobiography,* Wells discusses his idea of the novel, "planned as a social panorama in the vein of Balzac," in which characters are "only as part of a *scene.*"[2] The importance of conveying an overall picture of the social context in which people live is taken up again when, stressing the necessity of always relating character studies to changing values and conditions, he writes: "Impermanent realities are not to be rendered without an abundance of matter. In a changing world there cannot be portraits without backgrounds and the source of the shifting reflected light upon the face has to be shown."[3] The emphasis here is put upon "change," which is a constant concern of Wells's both as novelist and social thinker.

In *Tono-Bungay,* particularly, this idea of change runs throughout the text. It is the moving force of the novel and expresses itself in spatial structures and characters. Towns as well as careers spread and contract, human bodies grow and shrink, loves flourish and fade. Not only the story, the plot, and the descriptive commentary are built around the idea of change; but also the style flows freely and fluently, and the rhythm proceeds in a pressing and urgent movement to the end, like "our mother of change, the Sea," as the narrator says on one of the last pages of the novel.

The necessity of change as social progress and individual improvement was a widespread notion in Victorian and Edwardian England. Both Dickens and Wells fully experienced in their lives this relentless process of upward social mobility that was so typical of their times. The "self-help" myth was also a powerful literary convention in nineteenth-century fiction, and both writers exploited it in their novels. Not only do most of Dickens's heroes rise from a marginal condition to one of respectability and economic stability, but some of his villains (like Bounderby in *Hard Times*) even function as a parody of the Victorian "gospel of success."

Edward Ponderevo in *Tono-Bungay* is an emblematic type of self-made man, who climbs up the social ladder as irresistibly as he dramatically descends it. But in this novel, change does not stand only for social and economic mobility. It is a polysemic word, concerning matter as well as the mind; it implies man's positive dominion over nature (through technological advancement) but also the violence of his intervention (by ecological defilement). Most of all, the idea of change is linked to that of disease and decay.[4] Pathological metaphors impregnate the text at various levels of signification: society is represented as a sick body, contagion spreading through its fibers, corrupting individuals and institutions.

A disease allusion is already contained in the title itself. "Tono-Bungay" is the name of the quack medicine that brings fame and fortune to Edward Ponderevo and "functions symbolically as a false nostrum offered to a sick society."[5] England is described as an organism going through a process of corruption, and change has become a synonym of unnatural growth, malignancy, and cancer. At the end of the novel, the narrator says: "Again and again in this book I have written of England as a feudal scheme overtaken by fatty degeneration and stupendous accidents of hypertrophy."[6] Images of rottenness are referred to London whose expansion is similar to that of a swollen body or to a tissue whose cells anarchically proliferate and bring death. The double process of growth and movement, on the one hand, and of disintegration and decay, on the other, is conveyed in a crescendo of metaphors. London is first compared to a whirlpool, then to a giantess, finally to a monster. The topography and architecture of the town are rendered by the language of social anatomy: suburbs and buildings are described as "disproportionate growths," and everywhere the narrator discerns "the presence of great new forces, blind forces of invasion."[7]

These images recall the science fiction worlds created by Wells and suggest disturbing associations with mutations of the species and with alien beings coming from unknown, threatening planets. In particular, they remind us of the representation of the city in *When the Sleeper Wakes,* with its gigantic size and cinemascopic effects.[8]

Organic deterioration as the expression of moral and social corruption is made even more explicit in the "quap" episode. "Quap" is a neologism Wells creates here to mean a radioactive substance with extraordinary properties, whose employment in the electricity industry would make the fortune of those who were able to exploit it. George is sent by his uncle Edward to get it in West Africa. Like Marlow, Conrad's narrator in *Heart of Darkness,* he has to go back to nature and the jungle and to look at the shameful face of capitalism as well as at the hidden side of himself. George describes his journey to Africa with strongly symbolic words, "It was for me an expedition into the realms of undisciplined nature out of the world that is ruled by men, my first bout with that hot side of our mother that gives you the jungle."[9]

Quap stands for the last stage of the invasion of an invisible energy that brings destruction and leads to a state of inorganicism and indifferentiation. The desire for indifferentiation is close to the instinct that Freud identifies in *Beyond the Pleasure Principle* (1920) and in his late works as the most fundamental drive in man, known as the "death instinct." This condition, where all tensions are reduced, Freud termed a state of "entropy," as opposed to energy and to the erotic and aggressive drives of any organism. Now, the effects produced by quap suggest a return to the original condition of an entropic state. The images are those of death: the landscape surrounding the beach on which it lies is barren; the ship that carries it literally goes rotten; and the sailors catch malaria and mysterious skin sores. The idea of chaos and utter disintegration is reinforced by the pathological imagery:

> . . . there is something—the only word that comes near it is *cancerous*—. . . about the whole of quap, something that creeps and lives as a disease lives by destroying; an elemental stirring and disarrangement, incalculably maleficent and strange. . . . It is in matter exactly what the decay of our old culture is in society, a loss of traditions and distinctions and assured reactions.[10]

The images of invasion, proliferation and decay are all associated with the idea of cancer. In *Illness as Metaphor* (1977), Susan Sontag writes that diseases have always been used metaphorically to reinforce criticism of society. Shakespeare speaks of "infection" of the "body politic." Modern metaphors suggest a "profound disequilibrium" between individual and society, which is seen as repressive towards its members. Since the nineteenth century, the reaction against industrialism has been expressed through the image of an anomalous growth. William Cobbett's famous definition of London as the "Great Wen" (but also Thomas Carlyle's description of the metropolis) was taken up again and again to indicate the contrast between modern civilization and the organic community of the past. By the time that Wells was writing, the sense of alienation produced by the vastness of the city had already become a literary commonplace, but, in discarding an idealized version of a rural order, Wells saw that order as part of the disease of the whole social organism. As Raymond Williams has noticed, he brought a new outlook to the problem when he connected the ruling power of the city to the ruling power of the country houses.[11]

This is made evident in *Tono-Bungay*. Beatrice Normandy, despite her youth and beauty, is secretly decaying; as an heir of the once-landed aristocracy, which has now been compelled to give way to the new commercial class, she has been spoiled by her idle and parasitic way of living. Her malaise is part of the disease of the whole nation, as the old rural order is just part of the social system. Beatrice refuses to marry George because she is aware of her moral and social sterility.

Another major character in the novel goes through the same process of disintegration. It is Edward Ponderevo, who "so obviously represents social decay that his very person organically responds to it."[12] Besides the "Tono-Bungay" enterprise, he acquires other greater corporations, builds new mastodontic mansions and, like them, grows in a degenerative way and collapses in the end, first financially, then physically.

If Wells was certainly doing something new in the narrative treatment of this theme, he was working here within a recognizable literary tradition, that of the "state-of-the-nation novel," in which Dickens had proved such a master. My argument is, in fact, that *Tono-Bungay* not only relates to the so-called industrial novels (and to *Hard Times* in particular, as David Lodge has effectively demonstrated), but that it takes up where *Bleak House* leaves off. In spite of its light aspects of social comedy, *Tono-Bungay* has a fundamentally somber thesis that makes it close to one of Dickens's darkest novels.

A comparative analysis of the two texts shows structural and topical analogies, corresponding images and symbols, all tending towards an identification of the British social system with a diseased body so that the very act of narration works as a sort of anatomy of society.

In *Bleak House,* England's rotteness is shown by the metaphor of contagion: when one part of the social organism is attacked by germs, others are infected too. Corruption touches both the high and the low, regardless of the repressions and divisions of a society based on class.[13] So Esther catches smallpox from "poor" Jo (through her chamber-maid Charley, who functions as an unconscious social mediator), thus dramatizing the principle that the whole community is responsible for the injustices of the few and pays through its innocent members.

The word "infection" recurs, indeed, quite often in the novel. We first read it in an apparently neutral context on the opening page ("in a general infection of ill temper"), as part of the well-known depiction of London in a November afternoon, enveloped by fog, mud and mire. In this first chapter, words like "pestilent," "decaying," "worn-out," "dead," and "ruined,"—referring to the Court of Chancery—describe not only the paralysis of that institution but of the whole nation. The correspondences among social groups and classes are rendered by an intricate web of connections and complicated interweaving of metaphor and metonymy.[14] In this complex fabric of recurrences, resemblances, and cross-references, a main role is played by images associated with decay. The degeneration of England resounds through the text from the Court of Chancery to the miserable district of Tom-all-Alone's, "a black, dilapidated street, avoided by all decent people." And to make it clear that what refers to this unhealthy place applies to the whole country, the narrator ironically comments: "This desirable property is in Chancery, of course."[15] The passage of the novel where this principle of contiguous association is made most explicit by the omniscient narrator is the one known as "Tom has his revenge." Here the idea of social corruption and moral evil is insisted upon by the hammering of such terms as "contagion," "pollute," "pestilential," "obscenity," "degradation," "wickedness," and "brutality."[16]

And yet in *Bleak House,* as in *Tono-Bungay,* the city is not only the symbol of human waste but also the crucible of incessant energy. London becomes the meeting point of contradictions for both Dickens and Wells, who were ambivalent towards it: they were attracted by its vitality as much as they were repulsed by its degenerative processes.

George Ponderevo's contrasting reactions to London emerge in two important passages: when he first discovers it as a young man and then, at the end of the novel, when he sails down the Thames. On both occasions he is struck by the dinginess and poverty, by the congestion of houses, by the confusion and lack of purpose of the metropolis, but he is also fascinated by its stupendous hustle and liveliness. The last pages of *Tono-Bungay,* in spite of the indictment they express of a whole civilization, sound as an homage to London, with its grandeur and its squalor, and with the magic of its ancient river.

In the first chapter of *Bleak House,* too, despite the fog, mud, and mire, the very presence of the London crowd creates an atmosphere of excitement and vitality. But the prevailing mood is one of anger and indignation: the great city is not so much a microcosm of England, but "a malignant part of it threatening to consume and appropriate the whole."[17]

While he was working at this novel, Dickens wrote to his friend Angela Burdett-Coutts about the destructive effects of the growth of London:"If you go into any common outskirts of the town, you will see the advancing army of brick and mortar laying waste the country fields and shutting out the air."[18] It is interesting to notice the word "waste" here, which was to become a keyword in *Our Mutual Friend* twelve years later. But already in *Bleak House*

(1853) it was conveying Dickens's idea of London, anticipating the "unreal city" of T. S. Eliot's *Waste Land*.

In *Tono-Bungay,* too, "waste" and "sterility," referred by George to his own loves and career, recur quite frequently. *Waste* was, in fact, one of the alternative titles Wells had considered and then discarded for this novel. He explicitly mentions it in the last chapter, when the protagonist and narrator underlines the sense of decay around and within himself, and makes clear the connection between fruitless love and social corruption. In doing this, Wells was certainly following Dickens's example, leaving nothing unsaid or only suggested.

So, as we have seen so far, the analogies between these novels can be traced on the levels of both story and discourse, clustering around the description of the British system in terms of disease. Aristocracy—embodied by Chesney Wold and Bladesover—is seen as a parasite in the social body, despite its tradition and culture. The infected organs are located in London, in the very heart of the nation and the very center of the novel. The actual degenerative processes, however, take place at the margins of society and are shown in two peripheral episodes, Krook's death by spontaneous combustion and the quap adventure, which testify to the inventive powers of both authors in combining realistic and fantastic elements, and in conferring scientific plausibility upon incredible fictions.

The connections of these episodes—which, in fact, are only apparently marginal—to the rest of the novel are made clear by both authors. Krook's shop is represented as the "double" of the Court of Chancery by the heaping up of random objects and old papers covered with dust. Being an extension of that institution, the shop has to disintegrate literally, as a homology for the moral disintegration of England. Quap, too, is shown to be related to English society through the choice of words denoting and connoting disease and decay, which recall the description of London.[19]

There is, however, a movement in terms of spatial structures from *Bleak House* to *Tono-Bungay,* which is consistent with the movement in time. In Dickens's mid-Victorian England, the source of infection lies in the very center of London (Tom-all-Alone's and Chancery); in Wells's Edwardian England, instead, the radioactive, deadly matter is to be found at the outskirts of the Empire—Africa, in fact—reflecting the different historical moment (the age of imperialism at the end of the nineteenth century and beginning of the twentieth). The far-off location of the quap proves beneficial, eventually, since the poisonous matter will be sunk in the ocean and disappear. Wells may be suggesting that if England gave up its imperialistic policy, it could be saved from destruction.

The disfigurement of the social body is metaphorically represented in the novels by two terrible diseases, smallpox and cancer. The remedies adopted to cure those sick societies both prove to be fakes: the Court of Chancery and "Tono-Bungay" alike swindle people without bringing any advantages to the organisms they are supposed to heal.

A healing function is performed, instead, by the narrators, Esther and George. In *Bleak House,* Dickens uses a very effective device, the double narrative: there are two voices, the narrator's and Esther's. The former is harsh, ironical, even cynical; his "detached observation of the world leads . . . to a discovery of the essential nothingness of the human spirit."[20] By contrast, Esther's vision includes the presence of a beneficent Providence; while the world around her seems to deny the existence of a purpose, she provides a center of humor, courage, and love. In spite of her own illness, she is the healer in the novel and expresses Dickens's tremendous energy and hopefulness.[21]

A similar role is played by George in *Tono-Bungay.* In a way he reunites the two narrative points of view: he provides the descriptive comment of the traditional third-person narrator, but also, as the main character in the novel, he offers a personal interpretation of the world around him. Energetic and optimistic, he looks for a meaning in society. When he first arrives in London, he tries to "see lines of an ordered structure out of which it has grown" and to find a purpose behind the "confusion of casual accidents." In this, George reminds the reader of Pip in *Great Expectations,* who, with the innocence and enthusiasm of youth, leaves the country for the great city, in search of experience and success. Both characters will be disappointed, and yet, through love and suffering, they will achieve maturity and wisdom according to the *Bildungsroman* pattern.

A note of hopefulness comes out at the end of *Tono-Bungay* and is represented by faith in science and technology. This vital force is embodied by George's passion for inventing sophisticated engines: first, the flying machine, then the destroyer—a warship which, in the final scene of the novel, "sweeps down the Thames cleaving a section through all the strata of English history."[22] The novel concludes on an ambiguous note: "We are all things that make and pass, striving upon a hidden mission, out to the open sea." This ending is very controversial. Critics disagree on the question of Wells's irony in the choice of a destroyer as a symbol of change pointing to the future. The energy emerging from the last paragraph seems, indeed, to suggest "a dialectic of creation and destruction which has its counterpart in Wells's political projects for the future."[23] It could also mean faith in science for science's sake, as already in *The Island of Doctor Moreau.* There, the protagonist and narrator Edward Prendick, after his terrible adventure, is disgusted with mankind and secretes himself in an astronomical laboratory, cutting himself off from ordinary humanity and probably pursuing "a hidden mission," like George.

In the ending of *Bleak House,* too, there is room for hope in the survival of England. A cautious optimism is represented by Esther's marriage to the man she loves, escaping from London and the past, and moving to the industrial north. The machine, again, seems to triumph in spite of the author's criticism of industrialism. But we know how divided Dickens was on this matter, at least as much as Wells was on the question of science.

Both authors concealed a strong element of pessimism beneath the energy of the storytelling, the ebullience of the characters and the verve of the language. And yet in these novels a sense of vitality comes through, despite the panorama of waste and decay. We could say that the tension between chaos and order is acted out in the structural contradiction between the language of images and symbols (which conveys the idea of fragmentation and death) and the handling of the plot (which moves towards unity and life). These contrasts seem to be solved in the reassuring conclusions, which— within the disease metaphor I have been tracing in the texts—have the function of hinting at possible remedies. Love and forgiveness is the Christian answer Dickens seems to offer through Esther; the search for truth, the Positivistic one suggested by Wells through George.

From what we have seen, *Tono-Bungay* can be read as the Edwardian sequel to *Bleak House,* as they are both written in the tradition of what Arnold Kettle has called the "socially-conscious novel."[24] According to David Lodge, Wells solved the technical problem facing the "condition-of-England novelist," that of how "to accommodate within an imaginative structure an abundance of material of a kind which is usually treated discursively."[25] Wells did it by choosing a narrator who explicitly asserts, on the first page of the novel, his intention of describing and commenting upon the story he is telling; a narrator, in other words, who feels free to use the novel according to the principles he would theorize two years later in "The Contemporary Novel."

Tono-Bungay is an example of fiction "saturated in the personality of the author." Wells certainly puts a lot of himself in, so that the novel, in its own structure, enacts its central metaphor: it grows in an anomalous way. Like the London George describes, there is agglomeration and confusion, but it is also possible to detect "lines of an ordered structure out of which it has grown."[26] The author is unable to subject himself to that discipline of restraint he speaks of in the first chapter. His idea of the novel—he says—is "comprehensive rather than austere." Wells is anticipating here the debate he would enter a few years later with Henry James; a controversy which saw the two writers—once friends—on opposite fronts. James's method as a novelist was that of "selectivity," Wells's of "saturation." The disagreement, of course, was not so much over the "intensive" versus "extensive" novel, as over greater issues of literary theory, which were related to the situation of the English novel at the turn of the century.

The main aspects of this literary quarrel were taken up again by Virginia Woolf ten years later in her essay "Mr Bennett and Mrs Brown" (1924). Here, among other things, she criticizes Wells for giving a false picture of Mrs. Brown, in spite (or because) of "his passion to make her what she ought to be."[27] There is a clear connection between Woolf's argument and James's criticism of Wells for filling his novels with too much material, organized in a confused, random way. And these were also the kinds of objection that both James and Woolf made to Dickens. We find them summarized in an entry in Woolf's diary (13 April 1939) in which she comments upon Dickens's method of writing, in words that she could have equally applied to Wells:

> I read about 100 pages of Dickens yesterday, and see something vague about the drama and fiction; how the emphasis, the caricature of these innumerable scenes, forever forming character, descend from the stage. Literature—that is the shading, suggesting, as of Henry James, hardly used. All bold and coloured. Rather monotonous; yet so abundant, so creative: yes, but not *highly* creative: not suggestive. Everything laid on the table. Nothing to engender in solitude. That's why it's so rapid and attractive. Nothing to make one put the book down and think.[28]

I don't know if Virginia Woolf is right here, but, certainly, neither *Tono-Bungay* nor *Bleak House* is a book that can be put down without making one think—and a lot too.

Notes

1. Patrick Parrinder and Robert M. Philmus, eds., *H. G. Wells's Literary Criticism* (Sussex: Harvester Press, 1980), 195.
2. H. G. Wells, *Experiment in Autobiography* (London: Victor Gollancz, 1966), 2:503.

3. Ibid, 2:504.

4. *See* David Lodge, *Language of Fiction* (London: Routledge & Kegan Paul, 1966); Kenneth B. Newell, *Structure in Four Novels by H. G. Wells* (The Hague: Mouton, 1968); Patrick Parrinder, *H. G. Wells* (Edinburgh: Oliver & Boyd, 1970).

5. Bernard Bergonzi, *The Turn of a Century* (London: Macmillan, 1974), 73.

6. Wells, *Tono-Bungay* (London: Pan Books, 1975), 327.

7. Ibid, 81–82.

8. Wells himself underlined this connection in the preface to the 1921 edition of *The Sleeper Awakes.*

9. Wells, *Tono-Bungay*, 274.

10. Ibid, 278.

11. Raymond Williams, *The Country and the City* (Frogmore: Paladin, 1973), 277.

12. Newell, *Structure,* 77. According to Anthony West, Wells was "bringing something new into consideration when he described the wild growth and proliferation of the new superbusiness and conglomerates as being comparable to the spread of cancer through a living body." *H. G. Wells: Aspects of a Life* (Harmondsworth: Penguin, 1985), 310.

13. Steven Connor, *Charles Dickens* (Oxford: Basil Blackwell, 1985), 61–62.

14. J. Hillis Miller, "Introduction" to *Bleak House* (Harmondsworth: Penguin, 1981), 14.

15. Ibid, 273.

16. Ibid, 683.

17. F. S. Schwarzbach, *Dickens and the City* (London: The Athlone Press, 1979), 131.

18. Edgar Johnson, ed., *Letters from Charles Dickens to Angela Burdett-Coutts 1841– 1865* (London: Jonathan Cape, 1953), 199 (18 April 1852).

19. Lodge, *Language of Fiction,* 238.

20. J. Hillis Miller, "*Bleak House* and the Moral Life," in *Dickens: "Bleak House" A Casebook,* ed. A. E. Dyson (London: Macmillan, 1983), 182.

21. A. E. Dyson, "*Bleak House:* Esther Better not Born?", in *Bleak House. A Casebook,* 270–72.

22. Parrinder, *H. G. Wells,* 68.

23. Ibid, 84.

24. Arnold Kettle, "The Early Victorian Social-Problem Novel", in *From Dickens to Hardy,* ed. Boris Ford (Harmondsworth: Pelican, 1963), 159–70.

25. Lodge, *Language of Fiction,* 221.

26. Wells, *Tono-Bungay,* 79.

27. Virginia Woolf, *Collected Essays* (London: The Hogarth Press, 1966), 1:327.

28. Virginia Woolf, *A Writer's Diary,* ed. Leonard Woolf (London: Triad Grafton, 1985) 297–98.

Uncle Wells on Women: A Revisionary Reading of the Social Romances

Bonnie Kime Scott

H. G. Wells was already "under revision" in the 1920s, and as John Batchelor has noted,[1] he did not particularly relish the process. If I regard Wells as a somewhat avuncular Edwardian, I am perhaps betraying a historical bias, influenced as I am by my reading of women writers of the modernist period—modernist mothers, one might call them. Specifically, I have in mind their reactions to his romantic fiction of 1900 to 1918. Wells and Wells scholars have devoted more attention to his self-proclaimed differences with the realist master craftsman, Henry James, than to Wells in relation to women writers and modernists.[2]

The "Uncle Wells" title comes from Rebecca West, who quipped in an article named for one of his closest colleagues, "Uncle Bennett": "All our youth they hung about the houses of our minds like Uncles, the Big Four: H. G. Wells, George Bernard Shaw, John Galsworthy, and Arnold Bennett."[3] The Edwardian designation for Wells comes to me from Virginia Woolf's well-known essay, "Modern Fiction," another work that features Galsworthy and Bennett as well, though I think Wells's Edwardian penchant for blue-book ideas fares better with Woolf than the forms of materialism Bennett is indicted for in that essay; and Wells is a dated man once again in Woolf's *Jacob's Room,* where twenty-year-old Jacob Flanders considers with some scorn the books of the "elderly" Wells and Shaw on the bookshelves of his Cambridge don.[4] Published in 1922, *Jacob's Room* was Woolf's first sustained experiment in modernist form, and Jacob's visit to the don would have occurred in 1906, making him passé to youth in the first decade of the century. In 1928, Freda Kirchwey, editor of *Nation* and another representative of the younger generaton, offered a comparable designation. In an open letter to Wells, she adopts him as a "secondary parent"—an "ideal father" to be disagreed with by her more skeptical generation.[5] She recalls reading *Ann Veronica* almost as if she had been Ann herself. Kirchwey was seated on a train as a young woman (a progressive setting she shares with the novel's young heroine). "You offered us all the world in tempting cans with lovely labels: Socialism, Free Love, Marriage, Education, World Organization, and H. G. Wells's Patented Feminism—Very Perishable."[6]

Wells had made memorable travels himself, arriving in London from early residence in servants' and apprentices' quarters[7] at a time when young women had begun to make a similar move out of fathers' quarters. The education and access to literary circles and publication that opened to him, opened to them as well. The assumption of a slightly elderly identity helps Wells take on the position of authority in a historical situation that put him on a par with many women of his day.

West's selection of "uncle" for Wells in her "Uncle Bennett" essay was probably a means of addressing Wells's sexual ego—an element which certainly affected his relations with, his perceptions of, and his representations of women—as she recognized from the time that she took him on in her review of his novel *Marriage*. Its most challenging lines feminized Wells and suggested that he was inexperienced sexually, and elderly to boot: "He is the old maid among novelists." Sex was not an accomplishment, but an "obsession that lay clotted on *Ann Veronica* and *The New Machiavelli* like cold white sauce." She also implied that Wells was more successful with scientific subjects—an opinion that critical history has borne out. He had "a mind too long absorbed in airships and colloids."[8]

Dorothy Richardson satirizes a discourse of male authority assumed by members of the Wells circle, apparently on the model of Wells himself. In one scene, Miriam Henderson focuses upon a young male follower of Hypo Wilson, the Wellsian character in *Pilgrimage*. He is engaged in "young men's talk and arguments." She is amused by the "certainty of rightness and completeness" in the group.[9] The existence of rightness and completeness was to become more dubious to modernists, and particularly alien to the rhetoric of Woolf as well as Richardson. Indeed, the modernist predilection for open endings, fragments, and questions may be taken as a shift toward more "feminine" discourse. I use "feminine" here in a sexually non-determinist sense. Wells approaches such open-endedness in *Tono-Bungay*—probably his most successful experimental romance.

Wells's typical male narrator is unable to resist educating a readership of bright young nieces concerning their prospects in the world of trains and scientific study that he has helped to bring about. He tends to have his central male characters do the same, emphatically and repeatedly offering barrages of pedantic facts and worldly wisdom. He is not uncritical of this role. In calling attention to his "male narrator,"[10] he concedes that he has limited descriptive powers. We might object, though, that the subject he cannot describe—a woman's hat—would hardly provide the material for great literary success by a woman narrator. Wells also developed the designation "prig" to criticize an all-knowing male character type in his romances. The prig encourages amused distance in readers. Take, for example, this narrative intrusion in *The Wife of Sir Isaac Harman*. It comes on the occasion of Lady Harman's first rebellion against her husband's patriarchal authority, and hammers home its doctrine of planning ahead:

> In spite of my ill-concealed bias in favour of Lady Harman, I have to confess that she began this conflict rashly, planlessly, with no equipment and no definite end. Particularly I would emphasise that she had no definite end.[11]

Though engaged in a modern world—its problems of waste and its potential for invention—Wells does not strike us as a modernist in philosophy or style; and, as Kirchwey suggests, what feminism he offered was suspect to the next generation, not to mention our own.[12] His "Niagara of ideas"—Woolf's phrase in a review of *Joan and Peter*[13]—and his affinity to realist expression generally prevail over his occasional psychological probes and stylistic leaps. His belief in science and his verve for social reform are late Victorian to Edwardian in nature. Wells's comments on West's style suggest an anti-modernist attitude:

> She prowled in the thickets and I have always kept close to the trail that leads to the World State. She splashed her colours about; she exalted James Joyce and D. H. Lawrence, as if in defiance of me—and in despite of Jane and everything trim, cool and deliberate in the world.

Commenting on *The Judge,* he wished that West had reached the original event that inspired it, instead of lingering in "the steamy rich jungle of her imagination." Wells finds West's stream of consciousness experiment in critical analysis, *The Strange Necessity,* "pretentious and futile."[14]

Although the woman question was certainly one that interested Wells, science at times replaces the feminine in his fictional men's lives. Trafford of *Marriage* finds the height of beauty in science. George of *Tono-Bungay* makes science his "mistress."[15] In offering the story of his love life as a postscript to *An Experiment in Autobiography,* Wells places women in the psychological role of his "Lover-Shadow." He explains, "My innate self conceit and the rapid envelopment and penetration of my egotism by socialistic and politically creative ideas was too powerful ever to admit the thought of subordinating my *persona* to the Lover-Shadow."[16] The scientific theories of eugenics and biological determinism certainly affected his view of woman's role in production. It is an esthetic rejected by Stephen Dedalus in James Joyce's *A Portrait of the Artist as a Young Man:* "It leads you out of the maze into a gaudy lecture room," says Stephen, who fantasizes his activist, socialist friend, MacCann, "with one hand on *The Origin of the Species* and the other hand on the new testament," explaining female beauty in terms of a woman's physical potential for "burly offspring" and "good milk."[17]

Wells does have useful liberal feminist and socialist ideas about the inhibitions patriarchy places on women. Somewhat less successfully, he tries to improve upon the relations of the sexes, including marriage, as represented in fiction. The novels I review here began appearing in the Edwardian era and the last few overlapped with modernism. They are *Love and Mr Lewisham* (1900), *Tono-Bungay* (1908), *Ann Veronica* (1909), *Marriage* (1912), *The Wife of Sir Isaac Harman* (1914), and *Joan and Peter* (1918). In my approach, I shall be practising what Elaine Showalter has termed "feminist critique" to assess Wells's "very perishable" feminism.[18] This essay also uses recent feminist work on narrative, and takes up the lively issues of socialist feminism and biological determinism, as appropriate to Wells's encounters with Fabianism and his interpretation of the biological doctrines taught by T. H. Huxley.

In her recent work on narrative, Rachel Blau DuPlessis calls attention to the traditional ending of the romance in the marriage or death of the female hero; the potential of a female *Bildungsroman* at mid-novel is typically subordinated in novels through the nineteenth century. In the work of early twentieth-century women writers, she detects a writing beyond this ending.[19] Where does Wells fit among these paradigms? Wells insists that significant problems lie beyond the marriage ceremony, and does not assign it the conclusive position that nineteenth-century novelists did. Wells is apt to inform us about the man's faith in and high expectations from marriage to a physically alluring, feminine woman, or to his proper social choice. But, even if he attains such a match, none of Wells's central male protagonists can maintain it. Sir Isaac Harman's plans depend on the acquiescence to a patriarchal scheme by his proper choice of wife; her awakening to a desire for autonomy makes the design impossible. Soon after marriage, Mr. Lewisham encounters deceit in his partner, a young woman whose mere appearance and movements had inexplicably evoked his love. Interestingly, Lewisham's choice of irrational love over ambition in life gives his story the traditional ending we have come to expect for female protagonists in fiction. But, in making this choice, Lewisham rejects a more modern female as option and ending—his alliance to Miss Heydinger. A well-educated and committed fellow-traveler, she provides him with intelligent discussions, a need Lewisham's beloved cannot meet. Lewisham's choice can also be seen as a biological triumph, a survival of the prettiest. In *Tono-Bungay,* George Ponderevo divorces a woman very like the one Lewisham marries; despite the power of physical attraction, bourgeois domestic materialism and intellectual inequality prove over time too stultifying for Wells's more complex hero. In *Marriage,* it is necessary for the couple to go off to the woods to find Thoreauvian simplicity after marriage has become a materialistic society-bound institution. Wells deals deliberately though briefly with the falling off of the romance of the parents in *Joan and Peter.* I haven't much space for Wells's marital and extramarital history in this essay. But we should recall that, with his second wife, Jane Wells, he first defied and then expanded the freedoms of the institution, experimenting further with his relationship to Amber Reeves, who like Jane was his student as well as his lover. By his own account, the most immediate fictional counterpart of these relationships exists in *Ann Veronica,* the novel which so severely shocked Wells's contemporaries.[20] Stymied for some time by Capes's first, unsuccessful marriage, the couple eventually go off to Switzerland where it is implied that they find physical and mental, though unmarried, bliss. Though marriage is somewhat differently situated and handled in the plots of these novels, the effect is not revolutionary. The arrangements and understandings reached by the couples, and the arrested *Bildungsroman* of the central female characters are reminiscent of the outcomes of nineteenth-century novels, as described by DuPlessis.

Wells was clearly looking for new types of male and female romance heroes as early as 1895, when he satirized contemporary fiction for offering three female types: (1) submissive wives, with a resultant production of ten to fourteen children; (2) rebellious young women who become trapped by fast-talking blackguards; or (3) anaemic females. The three corresponding fictional male types were no better. One could choose from: (1) "nincompoop," (2) egotist, or (3) the clearly preferable " 'good,' man, [a sort] generally educated but endowed with insufficient virility to save the female type (2) from the male type (2)" and so reduced to "hanger-on, guardian angel, and consummate prig."[21] Wells thought better things could be expected from writers of sounder intellect and physique than his predecessors.[22] He may have been talking about himself, as the improved inventor of fictional female types.

As suggested in the brief summaries just given, Wells offers his maturing male and female protagonists some variations in selection of a mate. Mr. Lewisham might have chosen an intellectual, activist woman. He seems unlikely to have been oppressive or a blackguard to the woman he did marry, and biological attraction remains. In most of his romances, Wells describes non-anaemic young women who are developing their minds and their society as students and social workers. They begin two of the novels as the central subjects of the *Bildungsroman*. They ride on modern trains to "the eternity of bliss" as the unconvinced Woolf put it in "Modern Fiction."[23] But while they may ride off from papa, and resist the conventional middle-class provider as mate, all too often they discover a virile prig scientist—a fantasy versions of Wells himself. In two novels, *Tono-Bungay* and *Marriage,* these technical wonder males fall out of airborne craft, immediately requiring the traditional role of nursing from the aspiring young women who happen to wait, not otherwise occupied, below. Wellsian heroes have the inconsiderate habit of taking over the novels where women have some prospect of a completed *Bildungsroman,* or at least equal treatment at the start. Capes and Trafford do this, respectively, in *Ann Veronica* and *Marriage.* In *Joan and Peter,* Dolly (Peter's mother) dies just as she gets interesting, and has as her substitution Oswald, a post-imperialist Huxleyite more capable of enunciating Wells's ideas on education.

The Wife of Sir Isaac Harman is exceptional for its central female character's final resistance to remarriage, and the romantic disappointments of its well-intentioned, comic male character, Mr. Brumley. Widowhood achieved, Ellen Harman dares not risk her autonomy and her sense of purpose in directing a set of working women's hostels, by taking up marriage again. Brumley finds himself very deliberately kissed, but unwed. But what Wells creates in Brumley is what he scorned in the novels of predecessors, the "guardian angel" and a decidedly unvirile prig.

Wells's satire of the institution of marriage is probably harshest on the patriarchal despot—Mr. Stanley of *Ann Veronica,* Mr. Pope of *Marriage,* or Sir Isaac of *The Wife.* Her father *is* law to Ann

Veronica, according to her own interpretation. That law is alien to woman is clear from Beatrice Normandy's statement in *Tono-Bungay,* "No woman respects the law. . . . it is too silly." (414). Wells's defeat of the patriarch would be more remarkable if it did not fit so neatly into an Oedipal paradigm. The Wellsian young man all too soon steps into the position of an authority on relationships in most of the novels we are dealing with.

Wells would also release society from the aimless consumerism of traditional domesticity, which victimizes both members of a marriage, though the most offensive spendthrift is typically the young wife. The perception is hardly new. Representation of world plunder for the sake of the tea table goes back at least to Alexander Pope's "Rape of the Lock" and his "Epistle to a Lady." During the period of Wells's romances, Rebecca West was expressing her socialist objection to middle-class female parasitism in *The Clarion.* Though the theme of domestic waste endangers relationships in *Love and Mr Lewisham* and *Tono-Bungay,* Wells's most carefully developed spendthrift is Marjorie of *Marriage*, a character who infuriated West. Not only did she dislike Marjorie, but West was indignant that Wells should have considered such "scoundrelism" as the normal condition of women.[24]

Wells is much more keenly interested in young, educable, potentially childbearing women than in older ones. He typically satirizes the values of older women and wants to relieve young characters of their influence. Virginia Woolf's review of *Joan and Peter* suspects special irritation at certain female types may lie behind Wells's uncharitable treatment of the two suffragette aunts, one of them an aspiring poet. She finds this prejudice working to the detriment of the novel. Wells is not particularly positive in his renditions of the suffrage movement. Here again West shared his reservations and expressed them in her novel, *The Judge,* and in her essays on the Pankhursts, which appeared in *The New Freewoman,* and *The Clarion.* Miss Miniver of Wells's *Ann Veronica* is attributed with a "weakly rhetorical mind" that can only influence a young woman briefly.[25] In *The Wife,* he would seem to represent the narrowness of the suffragettes' aims when Miss Alimony fails to see a common cause in marriage reform, and refuses to harbor the fugitive Lady Harman (187–92). Wells represents the suffragettes' window-smashing tactics in two of the novels considered here, but only to serve the development of the female heroes, Lady Harman and Ann Veronica. Wells also mocks older women as educators in his descriptions of Miss Murgatroyd's school in *Joan and Peter.*[26] George Ponderevo's mother is shown to be an uncomprehending parent, and is far less influential than his surrogate father in *Tono-Bungay,* though some readers may find in her a remarkable survivor.

Wells's background as a biologist also limits his vision of women. While he admits that women like Lady Harman may not take naturally to their children, Wells has no other solution for childrearing than a heavy dependence upon the mother. Though he resists her, mother nature lurks behind the personal interactions of men and women. Ann Veronica may recklessly leave home to live life, but her scientific lover, Capes, explains her flight biologically as an unconscious search for a mate. When citing forms of waste in the modern world, *Tono-Bungay* notes the failure of several women characters to produce children. Wells's earlier prose works, *Mankind in the Making* and *Socialism and the Family,* both take motherhood as an essential and central female role. The ideal Wellsian baby has its mother's primary attention, a situation of nurture supported by monogamy, and inferentially by marriage.[27] *Socialism and the Family* recognizes motherhood as a "public duty" worthy of wages, if done well, and finds "spare-time" mothering undesirable. The proffered wages would liberate women from "contributing some half mechanical element to some trivial industrial product."[28] The formula is difficult for women who aspire to more than mechanical forms of work, and are satisfied by these pursuits. It is worth remarking that West's solution for Marjorie's defects of character is work: "Women ought to have a chance of being sifted clear through the sieve of work."[29] While Wells's fathers are deeply moved by the birth of offspring, there is no labor-sharing in child-rearing. In *Mankind in the Making,* Wells as prig is ready to dictate how much fresh air and what sorts of stuffed animals a baby should have, but it is not he who wheels the perambulator to its ideal situation—a site offering visual stimulation to the baby, but, a sense of sitting on the sidelines to the mother. The formulas are not restricted to his early essays; Rebecca West got more than what she might have deemed an ideal amount of fresh air as the birth of Anthony West approached.[30]

In the novels, there is an admission of something lost to this nurturing situation. As motherhood approaches, Ann Veronica's best days of love are over, and she knows it. Wells's most daring rebel against the patriarchal family is encountered later in life in a brief reference in *Marriage.* Ann Veronica has "subsided . . . into a markedly correct and exclusive mother of daughters."[31] The commitment of motherhood weighs heavily even with Lady Harman, who would have fulfilled her motherly functions, sacrificing her own socialist interests, had Sir Isaac not conveniently died.

Wells's men usually end up with a sense of utopian, ameliorative mission, whether it be writing plays (*Ann Veronica*'s Capes) or—with telling irony—designing destroyers (*Tono-Bungay*'s George Ponderevo); few of his women find meaningful work aside from motherhood. Trafford of *Marriage* returns to civilization with a series of book titles to write. Marjorie, on the other hand, is determined to free him from supporting her and "to be his squaw and body-servant first of all, and then a mother."[32] Rebecca West could not excuse "Uncle Wells" for this sort of thing. She offers what seems a mélange of *Love and Mr Lewisham* and *Marriage* in the following parody (ellipses, hers):

> You know perfectly well what I mean: the passages where his prose suddenly loses its firmness and begins to shake like blanc-mange. "It was then I met Queenie. She was a soft white slip of being, with very still dark eyes, and a quality of . . . Furtive scufflings . . . Waste . . . Modern civilization . . . Waste . . . Parasitic, greedy speculators. . . . "Oh, my dear," she said, "my dear . . . darn your socks . . . squaw. . . . "[33]

Joan of *Joan and Peter* looks forward to a project of building "cottages with sensible insides" (581) , but this is unprepared for in her character development and comes at the very end of the novel, and thus goes untested and undeveloped. Too often, the clever young woman serves the male intellect in the framing of his socially advanced world. This is what Miss Heydinger was prepared to do in *Love and Mr Lewisham*. Alma Wilson (Dorothy Richardson's stand-in for Jane Wells), presides over the Wellsian court. She agrees with the men she speaks with and "told him nothing or only things in the clever way he would admire."[34] Her cleverness, in other words, is a male evocation.

In the novels I have been treating, there were occasional moments of utopian projection. One charming one, not told or meant to be taken too seriously by its speaker, is the planned "City of Women" proposed by Ewart, an artist friend of George Ponderevo in *Tono-Bungay* (202–3). He suggests a separate walled garden as women's domain:

> Dozens of square miles of garden—trees—fountains—arbours—lakes. Lawns on which the women play, avenues in which they gossip, boats . . . Women like that sort of thing. Any woman who's been to a good eventful girls' school lives on the memory of it for the rest of her life. It's one of the pathetic things about women—the superiority of school and college to anything they get afterwards. And this city-garden of women

will have beautiful places for music, places for beautiful dresses, places for beautiful work. Everything a woman can want. Nurseries. Kindergartens. Schools. And no man—except to do rough work, perhaps—ever comes in. The men live in a world where they can hunt and engineer, invent and mine and manufacture, sail ships, drink deep and practise the arts, and fight—"

. . . .

The homes of the women . . . will be set in the wall of their city; each woman will have her own particular house and home, furnished after her own heart in her own manner—with a little balcony on the outside wall. . . . And there she will go and look out, when the mood takes her, and all round the city there will be a broad road and seats and great shady trees. And men will stroll up and down there when they feel the need of feminine company; when, for instance, they want to talk about their souls or their characters or any of the things that only women will stand. . . . The women will lean over and look at the men and smile and talk to them as they fancy. And each woman will have this; she will have a little silken ladder she can let down if she chooses—if she wants to talk closer."

Should sons result from this closer talk, they would be "turned out" when they reach the age of seven. It is the stuff of separatist feminist utopias—Charlotte Perkins Gilman's *Herland* (1915) or Sally Miller Gearhart's *The Wanderground* (1978), though both of these utopias go one step farther in the removal of males, through parthenogenesis. Though it has some appeal and a good deal of humor at the expense of both sexes, the most obvious flaw in Ewart's utopia is that it is strongly deterministic in its division of interests along gender lines.

A more practical and workable idea develops from Lady Harman's hostels for women factory workers. The original institution was really Mr. Brumley's idea, providing him a means of being in regular contact with his beloved Lady Harman. But she suggests expanding the idea to married couples. The notion both infuriates and fascinates the despotic Sir Isaac:

He began to expand the possibilities of the case with a quite unusual vividness. "Double beds in each cubicle, I suppose," he said, and played for a time about this fancy. . . . (sic) "Well, to hear such an idea from you of all people, Elly. I never did."

He couldn't leave it alone. He had to go on to the bitter end with the vision she had evoked in his mind. He was jealous, passionately jealous, it was only too manifest, of the possible happinesses of these young people. He was possessed by that instinctive hatred for the realised love of others which lies at the base of so much of our moral legislation. The bare thought—whole corridors of bridal chambers! made his face white and his hand quiver. (270)

It was a socialist vision that awaited the death of patriarchal capitalism, for which Sir Isaac had emitted the last gasps.

In closing, I should like to consider whether Wells's romances ought to be brought to the attention of students today. I wish I felt that I had discovered a lost text worthy of canonization in *The Wife*.[35] But Sir Isaac is a stick figure, stereotypically assigned a Jewish identification to go along with his industrial successes and his materialist focus. While Lady Harman's *Bildungsroman* culminates the novel, we do not get to know her mind nearly so well as we do the minds of Wells's male heroes. And though he has tried to improve on the male character types he inherited, priggishness and virility creep into his most successful men, who in turn dominate his women. Women are attractive only if desirable to men, and they lose in identity what they gain in love.

The women of modernism who chided Uncle Wells gained a sense of purpose from the flaws and fissures of his romances. They worked at some of these. Their characters needed sensibilities as well as ideas. Their women could be elderly and interesting, and need not be subsidiary to men. Instead of being deterministic, gender itself might be deconstructed, especially in renderings of human psychology. Gender might also be seen in relation to creativity and language. Still, I think Wells has a great deal of practical value. We continue to probe the problem of the relation of the sexes, of course. But there are new demands in what has become everyday life. What are the political and rhetorical problems of male-authored feminism? How is the two-career couple to manage domestic demands of home and family? Where do nature and biological instinct reside in urban, intellectual life? Wells set out seeking solutions to problems like these, though I am not sure he ended thinking them possible. He still is good matter for discussion. And good discussion, rather than rigid canons of achieved success, may be what he sought after all.

Notes

1. John Batchelor, *H. G. Wells* (Cambridge: Cambridge University Press, 1985), 127.

2. Lucille Herbert offers a brief comparison with the narrative experiments of Lawrence and Woolf in "*Tono-Bungay:* Tradition and Experiment" *H. G. Wells: A Collection of Critical Essays*, ed. Bernard Bergonzi (Englewood Cliffs, N.J.: Prentice-Hall 1976). 140–56. Wells and modernism was a recurrent topic at the 1986 Wells Symposium, where this essay was presented.

3. Rebecca West, "Uncle Bennett," *The Strange Necessity: Essays* (Garden City, N.J.: Doubleday, Doran, 1928), 215. Jane Marcus reported to me that West told her she wrote "Uncle Bennett" to deliberately evoke a libel suit from Bennett, describing this as an income-producing strategy in the days when her status was that of the single working woman. Marcus is also keenly aware of West's ability to fashion a tale.

4. Virginia Woolf, "Modern Fiction," *The Common Reader* (New York: Harcourt Brace Jovanovich, 1953), 150–58; Woolf, *Jacob's Room* (San Diego: Harcourt Brace Jovanovich, 1978), 35.

5. Freda Kirchwey, "Freda Kirchwey on Wells as the Ideal Father," *H. G. Wells: The Critical Heritage*, ed. Patrick Parrinder (London: Routledge & Kegan Paul, 1972), 308, 309.

6. Ibid., 308.

7. Rosalind Miles calls this opening of literary circles to many more men from unprivileged backgrounds the "H. G. Wells Syndrome" in *The Fiction of Sex* (New York: Barnes & Noble, 1974), 89 and notes its conjunction with the flourishing of women writers.

8. West, "Marriage," *The Young Rebecca*, 64. In his report on this essay contained in *H. G. Wells in Love*, Wells suggests that he was most interested in her label of him as "pseudo-scientific," and says that it was to discuss this that he arranged a meeting; thus he denies any arousal of sexual pride.

9. Dorothy Richardson, *Pilgrimage IV: The Tunnel* (London: Virago, 1979), 122.

10. H. G. Wells, *Love and Mr. Lewisham* (Oxford & New York: Oxford University Press, 1983), p. 63.

11. Wells, *The Wife of Sir Isaac Harman* (London: Collins, 1930), 137. Subsequent quotations from this work are cited parenthetically in the text.

12. Wells was less consistently attractive to feminists of the next generation, I think, than David Smith suggests in his recent biography, *H. G. Wells: Desperately Mortal* (New Haven: Yale University Press, 1986).

13. Virginia Woolf, "The Rights of Youth: Review of *Joan and Peter*, by H. G. Wells," *Contemporary Writers*, ed. Jean Guiguet (London: Hogarth Press, 1978), 93.

14. Wells, *H. G. Wells in Love: Postscript to An Experiment in Autobiography*, ed. G. P. Wells (London: Faber and Faber, 1984), 101–2.

15. Wells, *Tono Bungay* (New York: Duffield, 1914), 324. Subsequent quotations from this work are cited parenthetically in the text.

16. Wells, *H. G. Wells in Love*, 56.

17. James Joyce, *A Portrait of the Artist as a Young Man* (1916) (New York: Viking, 1964), 208–9.

18. The approach used in this essay might also be described as feminist reader-response criticism. Patrocino Schweikart has suggested that "*certain* (not all) male texts merit a dual hermeneutic: a negative hermeneutic that discloses their complicity with patriarchal ideology, and a positive hermeneutic that recuperates the utopian moment—the authentic kernel—from which they draw a significant portion of their emotional power." While I would not describe Wells's power as emotional, certainly he had utopian designs. Feminist reader response theory suggests that "immasculation" of the female reader can be the result of an androcentric canon. Certainly Wells's criticisms of West show an immasculating design.

19. Rachel Blau DuPlessis, *Writing Beyond the Ending* (Bloomington: Indiana University Press, 1985). William Bellamy has suggested that *Tono-Bungay* is structured around the release of the narrator from an ending process. He associates this narrative of cultural disintegration with the Edwardian period, *see* "Wells as Edwardian," *H. G. Wells: A Collection of Critical Essays*, 100.

20. See Wells, *H. G. Wells in Love*, 83.

21. Wells, "Woman and Primitive Culture," ed. and attributed to Wells by Robert Philmus, *Science Fiction Studies*, vol. 8, no. 1 (1981), 35–37.

22. Ibid., 36.

23. Woolf, "Modern Fiction," 157. Woolf has some fun with the Edwardian love of the train, both in "Modern Fiction" and "Mr Bennett and Mrs Brown," though less at Wells's expense than Bennett's, who is suspected of being enamored of its material aspects.

24. West, "Marriage," 66.

25. Wells, *Ann Veronica* (London: Virago, 1980), 28. Subsequent quotations from this work are cited parenthetically in the text.

26. Wells, *Joan and Peter* (New York: Macmillan, 1921), 112, 123. Subsequent quotations from this work are cited parenthetically in the text.

27. Wells, *Mankind in the Making* (New York: Scribners, 1904), 109–13.

28. H. G. Wells, *Socialism and the Family* (London: A. C. Fifield, 1906), 58.

29. West, "Marriage," 69.

30. Though there are dangers in consulting West's approved version of the story (as there are in crediting *H. G. Wells in Love*), Wells certainly takes on the role of dictator of what is best for couple, mother, and baby in the letters contained in Gordon N. Ray, *H. G. Wells and Rebecca West* (New Haven: Yale University Press, 1974). *See* esp. 44–55.

31. Wells, *Marriage* (New York: Duffield, 1912), 431–32/

32. Ibid., 507.

33. West, "Uncle Bennett," *The Strange Necessity: Essays* 216.

34. Richardson, *Pilgrimage IV,* 132.

35. Wells would not have claimed this himself. He said of books written during 1910–13, including *Marriage* and *The Wife*, "None of them are among my best work. . . . They have less sincerity and depth than anything else that I have written," *H. G. Wells in Love*, 93.

PART THREE
Wells and Science

Introduction

Wells's first book was *A Textbook of Biology;* his first profession was that of a biology teacher. In discussions of Wells's scientific thought, it has long been assumed that he remained a faithful disciple of his own biology teacher, T. H. Huxley. Critics have frequently asserted that there is a direct continuity between the views that Huxley set out in his 1893 Romanes lecture, "Evolution and Ethics," and Wellsian thought. In "Applied Natural History," the first essay in this section, Leon Stover claims that the intellectual relationship between Wells and Huxley was far more adversarial than has commonly been supposed. Stover—himself a polymath of Wellsian dimensions, being at once a leading sinologist, a science fiction writer, and a professor of anthropology—argues that Wells reverted from Huxleyan beliefs to the more optimistic philosophy of Winwood Reade's *The Martyrdom of Man.* Where Huxley believed that humanity must oppose the "cosmic process," Wells and Reade argued that by cooperating with it our species could eventually take control of this process. Such a belief in "Applied Natural History" was, Stover argues, the reverse of Huxley's humanist ethics. This brief but deeply researched and challenging study is a remarkable instance of revisionist scholarship.

In *Evolution and Ethics,* Huxley opposes human law—what he calls the "ethical process"—to the so-called natural laws of cosmic and biological evolution. There is a close link between Stover's essay and John R. Reed's study of the *Island of Doctor Moreau,* since Reed forcefully argues that Wells's scientific romance can be read as an exploration of the dilemmas of law. Recent historians of science have shown just how fundamental is the concept or metaphor of the "laws of nature" in nineteenth-century scientific thought. In Dr. Moreau, Wells created a hero who denounced not only the arbitrary laws of human society but the "fixed laws" of the cosmos as well. This project is doomed, and Prendick, Wells's narrator, becomes the sole survivor of the island that is the scene of Moreau's terrible experiments. Reed's essay offers a subtle account of the relationship between the position of the narrator in this Swiftian satire and Wells's own scientific thought.

W. M. S. Russell's starting-point, in "Wells and Ecology," is Sir
Julian Huxley's dismissive account of Wells's qualifications in the
study of ecology. Russell, who is a vice-chairman of the British
Social Biology Council, defends Wells's grasp of ecological issues,
showing that his views could serve as a welcome corrective to the
errors of popular ecologists today. It is significant that Russell turns
to Wells's scientific romances, notably *The Food of the Gods* and
Men Like Gods, for evidence of the nature of his thought.

Wells's science fiction, however, was not only a vehicle for his
ideas; it was itself generated by his deep and intuitive engagement
with contemporary scientific and epistemological developments.
Such, at least, is the burden of Romolo Runcini's essay on *The Time
Machine*. Runcini, one of two contributors to this volume from the
University of Naples, explores the parallel between the Time Traveller's commitment to the discovery of the future and the twentieth-
century doctrine of scientific planning, with which the later Wells
was so closely identified. The Wellsian type of science fiction plot,
Runcini observes, is a response to the breakdown of the nineteenth-
century doctrine of inevitable progress. The future, in Wellsian
science fiction, is a free space in which we may hope to escape from
the determinism of the society around us; at the same time, our
contemplation of it is overshadowed by fear and foreboding. In an
arresting and boldly speculative essay, Runcini unfolds some little-
explored connections between the nature of modern scientific
thought, the crisis of narrative realism, and the structural originality of Wells's early fiction.

Applied Natural History: Wells vs. Huxley

Leon Stover

In 1884, Wells began at what was to become the Royal College of Science with a study of biology under T. H. Huxley. In 1901, Wells wrote in the college journal he had founded, that "I believed then that he was the greatest man I was ever likely to meet, and I believe that all the more firmly today."[1] In his 1934 autobiography, he repeated the claim. "That year I spent in Huxley's class was, beyond all question, the most educational year of my life."[2]

From these remarks, the critics infer that Wells is the ideological disciple of Huxley. But does it follow that just because he worshipped Huxley as man and teacher, Wells stuck to the man's teachings?

The "yes" answer to that question is such a fixture of Wellsian studies that to doubt it is almost unseemly. But as this is the year of "Wells under Revision," it is at last time to reopen the case.

The issue in question is how far Wells goes or does not go in supporting Huxley's ideological thesis, given out in his famous Romanes Lecture of 1893, "Evolution and Ethics." This paper holds that, far from adhering to it, Wells contradicts it.

Huxley's thesis states:

> Social progress means a checking of the cosmic process at every step and the substitution for it of another, which may be called the ethical process; the end of which is not the survival of those who may happen to be the fittest . . . but those who are ethically the best.[3]

The cosmic process is Darwinian natural selection, natural law. The ethical process is a uniquely human thing, moral law; going against man's animal heritage, it has elevated him above the beasts and made possible human social evolution from savagery to civilization.

Or as Huxley says:

> Let us understand, once and for all, that the ethical progress of society depends, not on imitating the cosmic process . . . but in combating it.[4]

And again he says, human morality

is opposed to that which leads to success in the cosmic struggle for
existence. In place of ruthless self-assertion it demands self-restraint; in
place of thrusting aside, or treading down all competitors, it requires
that the individual shall not merely respect, but shall help his fellows; its
influence is directed, not so much to the survival of the fittest, as the
fitting of as many as possible to survive. It repudiates the gladiatorial
theory of existence.[5]

For Huxley the law of nature, red in tooth and claw, is harmful to
the human cause. Social progress is advanced rather by leaders of
the ethical process, given to a "total renunciation of that self-
assertion which is the essence of the cosmic process."[6] Darwin
himself had said, in concluding his *Origin of Species* (1859), "As
natural selection works solely by and for the good of each being, all
corporeal and mental endowments will tend to progress toward
perfection. . . . Hence we [humans] may look with some confidence to a secure future of great length." Going against that
conclusion, Huxley has it that "cosmic nature is no school of
virtue, but the headquarters of the enemy of ethical nature."[7]

" 'Live according to nature' " is a dictum of the strict Darwinists
he hates. To imitate cosmic nature and take it as "an exemplar for
human conduct" is to reduce ethics to a case of "applied natural
history."[8]

What a finely derogative phrase that is—"applied natural history." It expresses everything Huxley repudiated in the wrong
lesson to be learned from Darwin. He rejects evolution as an
undevout name for divine Providence. In this he is a confessed
"agnostic," his own term, after all.

At the same time, he holds to the residual values of Christian
charity. For Huxley, there is a duality to man, a natural creature yet
endowed with a mysterious motive to overcome his animal heritage.
The nineteenth-century American poet, Waldo Emerson, versified
it this way in his "Ode" of 1847.

> There are two laws discrete
> Not reconciled,—
> Law for Man, and law for thing:
> The last builds town and fleet,
> But it runs wild,
> And doth the man unking.

"Law for man" is moral—the ethical process. "Law for thing" is
naturalism—the cosmic process.

To be sure, Wells like Huxley is agnostic. But there the resemblance ends. Wells by contrast is a moral relativist: "there is no morality in the absolute," he says. "Morality is made for man, and not man for morality."[9] Rather, it is relative to social conditions as they evolve from one stage of human history to another. Morality "is as much a natural adjustment to needs and environment as a claw or a skull or a swimming bladder; it is a thing of the same kind [and] is subject to the same ecological laws."[10]

This is a far cry from Huxley's ethical nature, opposed to the cosmic nature of things. For as Wells has it:

All things are integral in the mighty scheme. . . . All things are integral, but it has been left for men to be consciously integral.[11]

Unlike Huxley, he views "the whole social and political world as aspects of one universal evolving scheme."[12] There is no dualism here, between ethical and cosmic process.

Wells may have worshipped Huxley as man, teacher, and militant scientist. But in his philosophy of nature he followed someone else. His true discipleship on this head belongs to Winwood Reade, "that great and penetrating genius," as Wells called him, for his authorship in 1872 of The *Martyrdom of Man*.[13] This book, the all-time bestseller of the nineteenth century, is addressed to "you blessed ones who shall inherit that future age of which we can only dream," we who are "ignorant of Nature which yet holds us in our bonds." Those "pure and radiant beings who shall succeed us on the earth" will be united in global harmony "for the conquest of creation," when "famine, pestilence, and war are no longer necessary for the advancement of the human race." So shall the future profit from these woes of ours, and man's martyrdom to nature be ended. That much is promised, whatever the price. "The supreme and mysterious Power by whom the universe was created, and by whom it has been appointed to run its course under fixed and invariable law . . . has ordained that mankind shall be elevated by misfortune, and that happiness should grow out of misery and pain."[14]

Indeed, Wells credits this book with setting the example for his *Outline of History*.

Remarkably few sketches of universal history by one author have been written. One book that influenced the writer is Winwood Reade's *Martyrdom of Man*. This *dates,* as people say, nowadays, and it has a fine gloom of its own, but it is still an extraordinary presentation of human history as one consistent process.[15]

And what is this "consistent process" that Winwood Reade looked into with such "fine gloom" if not the cosmic process? For Wells as with Reade, its miseries and pains are destined to lead on to world peace and harmony. But not automatically by the self-running of the cosmic process; it has to be directed. All natural conflicts are to be resolved by natural means, yes; but only insofar as the powers of creation are made known and mastered for the purpose of conscious evolution.

This mastery is to come about with the advent of the Wellsian world state, prophesied in the *Outline*'s last chapter, "The Next Stage of History," given to the coming "Struggle for the Unification of the World." It is the same struggle novelized in *The Shape of Things to Come*. Its future historian says, now that all is accomplished, "The Martyrdom of Man is at an end." At last, "The world is all before us to do as we will."[16]

The revolutionaries of the Modern State Movement, who made this possible, had manipulated the rivalries of nations to end them. War itself was a progressive tool in their hands, fought in *The War that Will End War* (1914), to cite the title of Wells's most famous phrase-making political pamphlet. They understood the utility of human conflict in resolving the clash of national wills by merging them with the collective will of the one-world state. Indeed, says its future historian, "The stars in their courses were pointing our race towards the organized world community, the Modern State."[17]

The struggle to unify the world thus is imminent in the nature of things. As Wells explains elsewhere:

> All our modern imperialisms are this: the more or less conscious efforts of once national states to become world-wide.[18]

Made more conscious by insight into the cosmic process, what is this outcome but the work of applied natural history? Huxley's ethical bad makes for a good result when cosmic nature is imitated and given direction in the name of human destiny. In setting their goals, the Modern State Revolutionaries deal "with the primary, inexorable logic of natural laws." They come on "with all the inevitableness and patience of a natural force."[19]

The key to ending the martyrdom of man is the mastery of nature, and this means working with it, not fighting it. As Winwood Reade says:

> We can conquer nature only by obeying her laws, and in order to obey her laws we must first learn what they are. When we have ascertained by

means of Science, the methods of nature's operations, we shall be able to perform them for ourselves. . . . Finally, men will master the forces of nature; they will themselves become architects of systems, manufacturers of worlds. Man then will be perfect; he will then be a creator; he will therefore be what the vulgar worship as a god.[20]

This is exactly the prospect Wells gives out in his utopian novel, *Men Like Gods*. These radiant beings of the future have at last come to perform nature's operations for themselves, now they understand them. Or as these utopians themselves like to say of Mother Nature, "We have taken over the Old Lady's Estate."[21]

Huxley notwithstanding, humans make no progress by combating cosmic nature on any front, only by learning from it and bringing it in by calculation. Or as Wells explains,

You cannot change the nature of anything. You cannot change nature. But in the last hundred years we have learned to do ten thousand things with nature we never knew how to do before, and in the coming centuries we shall learn to do ten thousand things with human nature that we cannot do now.[22]

Such is human destiny, because "the universe is impelled to express itself and has seized upon man as its medium of understanding."[23]

"The Process," as Wells tags Huxley's cosmic nature in shorthand, is ours to command.

We learn what we can about it and make what is called practical use of it, for that is what the will in the Process requires.[24]

And that will is none other than the intelligence and courage to act on behalf of Huxley's repudiated applied natural history.

Now it is true, as Wells admits with Huxley, that The Process does not play "the part of a Providence for our comfort and happiness."[25] Left to itself, evolution is a blind, hit-or-miss affair. It "might lead anywhere; order came into things only through the struggling mind of man."[26] All the more reason, according to Wells, to gain mindful control over it, thereby to "escape from the accidental and the chaotic."[27] The cosmic process is amoral, to be sure. But it's "the malign drift of chance"[28] in nature man must struggle against, not nature itself as with Huxley's ethical process. When the rules of applied natural history are obeyed, as they are in the Wellsian utopia informed by Darwinian science, "There are no absolute rights and wrongs, there are no qualitative questions at all, but only quantitative adjustments."[29]

The need for quantitative rather than ethical adjustment follows from a naturalistic view of social and political reality. "The primary issues of human association are biological," says Wells. What this comes down to is man's "competitive pressure upon the means of subsistence, which has been the lot of every other animal species." Man is "the creature of a struggle for sustenance," but unlike the rest of creation, we are now aware of the problem (thanks to Darwin) and can adjust to it by means of "directed breeding."[30]

Otherwise, the Darwinian process of natural selection runs blind, electing the fit and unfit at random with no regard for the human future. Just because the civilized man of today, in advance over the savagery of his Paleolithic ancestor, "fights with . . . legal process instead of with flint instruments, is life any less a battlefield?" Besides, men still "fight in masses after the fashion of the ants."[31] Nothing can alter "the fact of lethal violence that underlies all life."[32] There is no remedy but directed breeding to replace by design what is done woefully by chance.

The sadness of a Darwinian universe run wild was impressed on Wells by that "fine gloom" he found expressed by Winwood Reade. In that mood, the author of *The Martyrdom of Man* says,

> In all things there is cruel, profligate, and abandoned waste. Of all the animals that are born a few only can survive; and it is owing to this law that development takes place. The law of Murder is the law of Growth. Life is one long tragedy; creation one great crime.[33]

Wells reflects on these words when he says, "Nature is not a breeder, she is a reckless coupler—and she slays." As with the other animals, man's tragedy is his "reckless parentage."[34]

The law of murder is indeed the law of natural selection, yet it brought forth man, the medium of its understanding through Darwinian science. Now all that remains is the will to act on that science. Meanwhile,

> Man is still but halfborn out of the blind struggle for existence and his nature still partakes of the infinite wastefulness of his mother Nature.[35]

But in the future it will be the business of utopian planning to reduce that waste by regulating the law of murder for progressive ends.

This is possible to do because man is "the rebel child of Nature," who has in him the will to turn himself against the harsh and fitful hand that reared him. He sees with growing resentment the multitude of suffering ineffectual lives over which his species tramples in its ascent. In the Modern Utopia he will have set himself to change the ancient law. No longer will it be that failures must suffer and perish lest their breed increase, but the breed of failure must not increase, lest they suffer and perish, and the race with them.[36]

In the Modern Utopia (the Modern World State), man will do his own elimination of the unfit lot of ineffectual lives by means of "social surgery."[37] In the course of directed breeding, judicious killings will do away with nature's law of random murder to no point.

This is the eugenic meaning of applied natural history. Man's martyrdom to the unmanaged crimes of creation comes to an end, so soon as "directly one sits down in a businesslike way to apply the method of elimination instead of the method of selection."[38]

Quite apart from Darwin's bio-optimism, Wells agrees "that the scheme of being in which we live is a struggle of existences," so that even in his Modern Utopia "there must be a competition in life of some sort to determine who are going to be pushed to the edge, and who are to prevail and multiply." There can be no relaxing from the "drama of struggle."[39] This Huxley failed to appreciate. In repudiating the cosmic struggle for existence, he overlooked the essential truth of Darwinism, which is, "The race flows through us, the race is the drama, and we are the incidents."[40]

The difference between nature and applied natural history is the difference between "the aimless torture of creation"[41] and the will "to substitute aim for that aimlessness."[42] It is the difference between the mutual cruelties of animals and the saving cruelty of intelligent human purpose. The power of science to regulate cosmic nature is equally harsh, but it is not fitful.

At last, man will perform the operations of nature for himself; "presently he will take his body and his life and mould them to his will."[43] By means of Applied Natural History, "He will bring his solvent intelligence to bear upon the . . . control of his own increase, select and breed for his embodiment a continually finer and stronger and wiser race."[44]

To conclude, it is fairly evident that Wells is no follower of Huxley's evolution and ethics thesis. Yet both overstate the meaning of Darwinism for human life.

It matters little, in this regard, that Huxley would combat the cosmic process and Wells ride it. The one says that cosmic nature must be overcome, the other that it must be harnessed, each to his different view on how to improve the human future. One says that the conquest of nature means doing away with the heritage of natural selection, the other that it means intelligent guidance of that force. Huxley thinks man is a different kind of animal because he gave rise to the ethical process, Wells because he now understands how to control the cosmic process.

All the same, both overlook Aristotle's truth that man is different because he is a *zoon politicon,* a political animal. This normative wisdom of the ages, Darwinism notwithstanding, is restated for us in that modern classic of political science by Gaetano Mosca, published in 1895, the year in which Wells brought out his first great novel of Darwinian science fiction, *The Time Machine.*

In his *Elementi di Scienza Politica,* Mosca says, addressing the question of reductive naturalism:

> To put the situation in a few words, the struggle for *existence* has been confused with the struggle for *preeminence,* which is really a constant phenomenon that arises in all human societies, from the most highly civilized down to such as have barely issued from savagery.[45]

Notes

1. H. G. Wells, "Huxley," *Royal College of Science Magazine,* (13 April 1901), 209–11.
2. Wells, *Experiment in Autobiography* (New York: Macmillan, 1934), 161.
3. Thomas H. Huxley, *Evolution and Ethics* (New York: D. Appleton, 1894), 81.
4. Ibid., 88.
5. Ibid., 82.
6. Ibid., 68.
7. Ibid., 75.
8. Ibid., 73f.
9. Wells, "Morals and Civilization" (1897), in Robert Philmus and David Y. Hughes, eds., *Early Writings in Science and Science Fiction by H. G. Wells* (Berkeley: University of California Press, 1975), 221, 226.
10. Wells, *The Fate of Man* (New York: Alliance, 1939), 29.
11. Wells, *Anticipations* (New York: Harper's, 1902), 316.
12. Wells, *Mankind in the Making* (New York: Scribner's, 1904), 16.
13. Wells, *'42 to '44* (London: Secker & Warburg, 1944), 167.
14. Winwood Reade, *The Martyrdom of Man* (1872), 20th edition (New York: John Lane, 1912), 538, 543f.
15. Wells, *The Outline of History* (London: Cassell, 1920), vi.
16. Wells, *The Shape of Things to Come* (New York: Macmillan, 1933), 377.
17. Ibid., 254.
18. Wells, *After Democracy* (London: Watts, 1932), 111.
19. Wells, *Anticipations,* pp. 108, 284.
20. Reade, *Martyrdom,* 513, 515.
21. Wells, *Men Like Gods* (New York: Macmillan, 1923), 107.

22. Wells, "Gifts of the New Sciences," in *The Atlantic Edition of the Works of H. G. Wells* (New York: Scribner's, 1924–27), 27:516.

23. Wells, *'42 to '44*, 17.

24. Wells, *The Undying Fire* (London: Cassell, 1919), 154.

25. Ibid., 154.

26. Wells, *The New Machiavelli* (London: John Lane, 1911), 113.

27. Wells, *First and Last Things* (New York: Putnam's, 1908), 27.

28. Wells, *The War in the Air* (London: George Bell, 1908), 357.

29. Wells, *A Modern Utopia* (London: Chapman & Hall, 1905), 37.

30. Wells, *The Open Conspiracy* (London: Victor Gollancz, 1928), 39, 37.

31. Wells, "Bio-Optimism" (1895), in Philmus and Hughes, *Early Writings,* 208.

32. Wells, *The War in the Air,* 171.

33. Reade, *Martyrdom,* 520.

34. Wells, *The New Machiavelli,* 47; Wells, *Mankind in the Making,* 92.

35. Wells, *The Open Conspiracy,* 44.

36. Wells, *A Modern Utopia,* 137.

37. Ibid., 142.

38. Wells, *Mankind in the Making,* 48.

39. Wells, *A Modern Utopia,* 137.

40. Wells, *First and Last Things,* 102.

41. Wells, preface to *Seven Famous Novels by H. G. Wells* (New York: Alfred A. Knopf, 1934), ix.

42. Wells, *The Undying Fire,* 206.

43. *Ibid.,* 211.

44. Wells, "The Human Adventure," in *Social Forces in England and America* (New York: Harper's, 1914), 415.

45. Gaetano Mosca, *The Ruling Class,* trans. Hannah D. Kahn from the 1923 edition of *Elementi di Scienza Politica* (New York: McGraw-Hill, 1939), 28. First Italian edition 1895.

The Vanity of Law in *The Island of Doctor Moreau*

John R. Reed

About his inspiration for *The Island of Doctor Moreau,* Wells wrote: "There was a scandalous trial about that time, the graceless and pitiful downfall of a man of genius [understood to be Oscar Wilde], and this story was the response of an imaginative mind to the reminder that humanity is but animal rough-hewn to a reasonable shape and in perpetual internal conflict between instinct and injunction."[1] *Injunction* is another word for *rule* or *law,* and Wells's novel is largely concerned with dilemmas of law. The first few pages of the novel question the rules men use to create order, and by its ending, even the abiding laws by which men judge themselves have been called in doubt. *The Island of Doctor Moreau* is an elaborate examination of three basic orders of law: human law, natural law, and the law of nature. By anatomizing each order of law, Wells forces his reader to consider the ground of his or her own moral code.

Anyone who has studied the early version of Wells's novel, or who has read Bernard Loing's detailed account of it, knows how radically Wells transformed what promised to be a rather commonplace adventure tale into a satirical examination of the human need both to establish laws and to violate them. I have no time to explore differences of text here, but one significant change involves the story's beginning.[2] In Wells's original manuscript, Moreau rescues Prendick and takes him to an island where he lives with his family. The revised version introduces the wreck of the *Lady Vain* and the threatened cannibalism among its survivors in the dinghy. The action of this sequence, though familiar both in adventure literature and in fact, acquired a greater resonance in Wells's tale because of the relatively recent precedent-setting decision in the case of *Regina v. Dudley and Stephens* (1884), which determined that, despite the acknowledged necessity for seamen to survive even through cannibalism, human—which is to say British—law would not endorse murder to permit such survival. The law declared that even where men were beyond the protection and the rule of the state, they were obliged to respect human life. It declared survival a secondary concern.[3]

If attempted cannibalism presents one dilemma of the human law opposed to human need, Prendick's experience on the *Ipecacuanha* epitomizes another. The captain of this ship is a brute with little human compassion or reasoning power, but he is an absolute authority. His word is law on his ship. He has the power of life and death over Prendick, and ultimately exiles him—potentially to his death. Whereas the cannibal sequence and the case of *Regina v. Dudley and Stephens* refer to the imposition of a reasoned law upon the rudimentary human urge to survive, the captain represents authority's arbitrary application of law that endangers human life.

These major events at the narrative's outset establish the equations of law/power and impulse/powerlessness, equations that are more firmly established once Prendick reaches Moreau's island, which is, in fact, populated by outlaws. Prendick has been set adrift from the *Ipecacuanha,* Montgomery has fled from England fearing reprisal by the law for an unspecified offense, and Moreau has chosen exile to avoid enemies who hounded him because his scientific experiments violated their social mores. Prendick is an outlaw by mere chance, Montgomery by virtue of an impulsive act, and Moreau by reasoned choice.

Prendick gradually comes to realize that Montgomery has no inner code to govern his behavior and that Moreau's rules are absolute. Prendick is initially very confident about his own moral values, though he has evidently never before been pressed to examine their roots. He is quick to condemn Moreau even before he understands his experiments. When he learns that Moreau is not torturing humans, but humanizing animals, he is relieved, but his moral sensibilities are not appeased. Yet Prendick shares many traits with Moreau. Unlike the self-indulgent Montgomery, he resembles Moreau in his abstemiousness and self-control, though he lacks Moreau's intelligence and will. Prendick thus falls between irresponsibility and absolute authority and is an appropriate average type to undergo an education in the nature of law, which he seems always to have taken on trust. His experiences on the island develop the theme of law and power stated in the opening sequences of the story. Moreau is as arbitrary an authority in his intellectual way as was the brutish captain of the *Ipecacuanha;* and Prendick's struggle for survival with the recidivist animals resembles the miniature version of that struggle acted out in the dinghy of the *Lady Vain*.

Scholars have given attention to those sections of *Moreau* where the beast-men mimick mankind in their hypocritical veneration of law. Although the notion of law was clearly in Wells's mind throughout his novel, the chapter in which the beast-men indulge themselves in chanting their law that includes a series of prohibitions with the refrain "Are we not men?" was a late addition, perhaps designed to emphasize the theme of law as well as to parody Kipling's presentation of the Law of the Jungle in his *Jungle Books* (1894–95).[4] Kipling's Law of the Jungle, presented by the bear Baloo, is chiefly an anthropomorphization of animal instincts. To a certain degree it is also an imposition of human morality upon animals, the final admonition of which is "Obey."[5] Kipling was himself not without irony in presenting his Laws of the Jungle. In "Mowgli's Brothers," the narrator explains that the Law "never orders anything without a reason," though the reasons are flexible. For example, the real reason wolves should not kill men is that more men will come with weapons to kill wolves, but the animals' reason for this prohibition is that "man is the weakest and most defenseless of all living things."[6]

Kipling satirizes human behavior in his jungle stories, but in a marginal, innocuous way. Wells's criticisms are more trenchant. Thus his chapter, "The Sayers of the Law," is a significant axis in his narrative where the three orders of law come into open conflict. The social laws of the beast-men (which they cannot keep) are based upon Moreau's strictures, but they appear to derive from a Natural Law that the "reasoning" beasts now "discover" in themselves. In fact, the only "invariable" law is that of instinct, or biological necessity.

Moreau's declared aim is "to find out the extreme limit of plasticity in a living shape" (94). He has not stopped at that objective scientific experiment, however, but has gone on to instill a sense of right and wrong in his creations. His fixed ideas of moral law are the psychological—one might even say spiritual—equivalent of the physical transformation he has attempted. Ultimately both fail, but it is unclear to what degree they are related. Moreau's experiments epitomize certain intellectual quandaries of his time.

By the end of the nineteenth century, the simple Newtonian world was gone. Newton's precise laws were being blurred and reduced simply to the law of nature, a metaphorical statement of a belief in determinist cause and effect.[7] With the gradual devaluation of providential and miraculous explanations for order in the universe, some new principle of order had to be proposed. Laws were being declared in many areas. Spencer assumed that the laws of nature as described in his theory of evolution (development from homogeneity to heterogeneity, etc.) applied to all existence, human and nonhuman. Henry Thomas Buckle and the scientific historians who endorsed his view perceived laws operating in human history. In *Social Evolution* (1894), Benjamin Kidd enumerated laws governing the development of societies, including the movements of peoples and their ascent to political preeminence. Law, in short, was a term and a concept that fell easily from the lips and pens of thinking men in the late nineteenth century. With the increasing prestige of scientific method, laws of nature were confidently substituted for the laws of God, but William Paley had long before noted the danger of this substitution.

> It is a perversion of language to assign any law, as the efficient, operative cause of any thing. A law presupposes an agent; for it is only the mode, according to which an agent proceeds: it implies a power; for it is the order, according to which that power acts. Without this agent, without this power, which are both distinct from itself, the *law* does nothing; is nothing. The expression, "the law of metallic nature," may sound strange and harsh to a philosophic ear; but it seems quite as justifiable as some others which are more familiar to him, such as "the law of vegetable nature"—"the law of animal nature," or indeed as "the law of nature" in general, when assigned as the cause of phaenomena, in exclusion of agency and power; or when it is substituted into the place of these.[8]

Paley's illustrations of the mechanisms of the human eye and ear as proofs that an intelligent agent lay behind all laws remained significant through Darwin's time.

Replacing the deity with a law of nature was not uncomplicated because many who wished to abandon the notion of an anthropomorphic agent, nonetheless hoped to retain a moral teleology. Herbert Spencer and Auguste Comte, for example, while championing the scientific objectivity of their worldviews, assumed a developmentalism that suggested purpose. In short, to give up God did not mean giving up morality. But on what foundation could morality then be based? Only upon nature. And here an old dilemma, going back at least to Aristotle and carried forward by way of Aquinas into our own day, surfaced. A certain class of philosophers argued that man need only look to nature to find a law of right and wrong. John Stuart Mill, with his customary acuteness, pointed out the confusion implicit in this belief. Several times in his *Three Essays on Religion* (1874) he defined the laws of nature. Here is one example.

When we say that an ordinary physical fact always takes place according to some invariable law, we mean that it is connected by uniform
sequence or coexistence with some definite set of physical antecedents;
that whenever that set is exactly reproduced the same phenomenon will
take place, unless counteracted by the similar laws of some other
physical antecedents; and that whenever it does take place, it would
always be found that its special set of antecedents (or one of its sets if it
has more than one) has pre-existed.[9]

In former times, Mill says, the so-called Law of Nature was the
foundation of ethics, though he assumes that no one would make
that assumption in his own day. But he points out that unwittingly
many persons confuse the two "laws" of nature, forgetting that one
notion applies to what *is,* the other to what *ought to be.* Mill was
stipulating the dangerous confusion between law of nature and
natural law, an equivocation that remains a problem among moral-
ists.[10]

In his introduction to *Natural Law and Modern Society* (1962),
John Cogley summarizes the concept of natural law.

Fundamentally, the idea of natural law (also traditionally called the
unwritten law) is based on a belief that there exists a moral order which
every normal person can discover by using his reason and of which he
must take account if he is to attune himself to his necessary ends as a
human being. Three propositions, then, are included in the definition:
(1) there is a nature common to all men—something uniquely human
makes all of us *men* rather than either beasts or angels; (2) because that
"something" is rationality, we are capable of learning what the general
ends of human nature are; and (3) by taking thought we can relate our
moral choices to these ends.[11]

It should be immediately apparent from this description that the
theory of evolution is opposed to natural law because it conceives
of human nature, like all the rest of nature, as malleable. Natural
law requires that man be consistent and always capable of reason so
that he be able to perceive that law. It is inevitably teleological.
Darwin was the chief proponent of the nineteenth-century belief in
the mutation of species, though he did not use the term "evolution"
to describe his theory. The only alternative Darwin knew of to this
theory of mutable species was the theological doctrine of creation,
and this he rejected.[12] He avoided any teleological or even neces-
sitarian developmentalism in his theory, though many of his disciples were more zealous and less cautious in importing the notion of
progress into biology.

Wells was a thorough evolutionist, but even from his earliest days as a writer, not easily duped by theory. In his remarkable essay, "The Rediscovery of the Unique" (1891), Wells asserts his position with a good deal of flair, declaring that the Rediscovery of the Unique

> shows that those scientific writers who have talked so glibly of the reign of inflexible law have been under a serious misconception. It restores special providences and unverified assertions to the stock of credible things, and liberty to the human imagination.

Simply put, this new notion is the revival of an old fact, that "*All being is unique,* or, nothing is strictly like anything else."[13] The atomic theory, which assumes a universe of similar atoms, as well as the world of morality, which assumes human beings conformable to a limited set of principles, must go. Darwin and Wallace first clearly asserted the uniqueness of living things, and science must advance with this knowledge to explore the "fathomlessness of the unique mystery of life."[14] A few years later, in "The Limits of Individual Plasticity" (1895), Wells theorized that, once granting the possibility of vivisection, we may anticipate unlimited physical modifications of living beings. And he adds that the metamorphosis does not stop with the physical. "Very much indeed of what we call moral education is such an artificial modification and perversion of instinct; pugnacity is trained into courageous self-sacrifice, and suppressed sexuality into pseudo-religious emotion."[15]

Many years later, in *The Science of Life* (1929), Wells stated clearly the basis for his much earlier fancies about Moreau's Island. Explaining the change from systematist or creationist to evolutionary thinking, he declared:

> We know that living things are a slice through a tree, showing every imaginable degree of cousinship, and not falling tidily and infallibly into "kinds." We know that their forms are not constant but changing. And in classifying this assembly, in trying to reduce it to some sort of order and describe it in unambiguous terms, we may choose what conventions we please. [Therefore,] a species, in particular, is no longer a unit created by God, nor is it a natural unit at all like an atom, or a quantum; it is an arbitrarily defined grouping set up by Man for his own convenience.[16]

Moreau's position is a complicated one. He has seen through the falseness of certain "laws" according to which he has been required to live. Social objections, resembling those of the antivivisection movement active at the time Wells was writing his novel, prevented

Moreau from carrying on his experiments.[17] Conservative scientific colleagues would have found his ideas outrageous. Moreau's resistance to these outmoded constraints appears heroic. But in his revolt he has himself tried to revise the laws of man and of nature. Moreau may transform animals into something new and strange, but he cannot make them men. A superficial transformation cannot replace the shaping work of eons. In breaking through the old systematist and creationist views of species, Moreau assumes that he can transcend evolutionary limitations as well.

In his essay "Applied Natural History: Wells vs. Huxley," Leon Stover demonstrates that a major difference between Wells's and Huxley's world views about human destiny was that the one saw man conquering nature through the intelligent guidance of its forces, whereas the other urged mankind to overcome its animal heritage through the perfecting of a moral order. Huxley wanted men to do away with natural selection; Wells wanted to substitute "the method of elimination [through eugenics, or directed breeding] instead of the method of selection."[18] Moreau's position resembles Huxley's because he wishes the human will to triumph over refractory nature. He wishes to impose his law in place of the law of nature. Wells clearly felt that a more gradual approach to the modification of nature's processes was required—for example through the slow effects of eugenics. Though he may be courageous in ignoring the uninformed and reactionary complaints against his research, Moreau is foolish in assuming that he can excise inherited instincts. His great error is to ignore time. Time alone can bring about the kinds of changes Moreau anticipates. Time is a law that Moreau cannot break.

The narrator of *The Food of the Gods* (1904) intrudes upon his story to pass a judgment upon the foolish politician Caterham, who believes that he can establish a political reality simply by mustering a sufficient number of votes. "He did not know there were physical laws and economic laws, quantities and reactions that all humanity voting *nemine contradicente* cannot vote away, and that are disobeyed only at the price of destruction. He did not know there are moral laws that cannot be bent by any force of glamour, or are bent only to fly back with vindictive violence."[19] Moreau suffers from an arrogance like Caterham's, though on a grander scale. He has enforced Fixed Ideas in the Beast-men to make them behave according to a Law. "This Law," Prendick says, "they were ever repeating, I found, and—ever breaking" (102). The Law of the beast-men is a law of prohibition designed to keep them from behaving in a way unacceptable to Moreau. There is punishment for everyone's "want that is bad," and it is assumed that all have such bad wants (75). But all bad wants are defined by Moreau. There is nothing wrong with an animal running on all fours or lapping water, but Moreau has proscribed these natural drives to his creations because he does not want them to *be* animals. By resisting nature, he has called into being the need for a law; in doing so, he has set one law against another.

At this point, Wells's reader is forced to recognize that any law without a natural source is a false law. There is a place in human society for legal, moral, and social "laws," but these laws are not to be confused with laws such as the law of gravity or the second law of thermodynamics. As Mill demonstrated, human beings have a tendency to confuse arbitrary with fixed law. This confusion was institutionalized by Sir William Blackstone in his *Commentaries on the Laws of England*. Blackstone wrote that the will of man's "Maker is called the law of nature." He continues:

> For as God, when he created matter, and endued it with a principle of mobility, established certain rules for the perpetual direction of that motion, so, when he created man, and endued him with free-will to conduct himself in all parts of life, he laid down certain immutable laws of human nature, whereby that free-will is in some degree regulated and restrained, and gave him also the faculty of reason to discover the purport of those laws."[20]

Blackstone merely repeats what had often been argued from St. Thomas Aquinas onward—that all laws, insofar as they partake of right reason, are derived from the eternal laws established by God. In *The Island of Doctor Moreau,* Wells tries to sever the concept of natural law, in which a deity has ordained that an immutable code of moral and physical conduct exists to be discovered by man, from that of the law of nature that does no more than assert the invariability of consequence. He grounds his story in the experiments of a man who, though understanding this critical difference, ignores it out of vanity.

Wells introduces us to the world of Moreau's experiment through a sequence of events showing the falseness or inapplicability of human "laws"—the dinghy and *Ipecacuanha* scenes. Though told cannibalism is wrong, men will nonetheless try to eat one another when they are the only food available. The brutish captain of a ship may impose a rule upon those who serve him, though the function of that rule depends not upon immutable authority but upon present force. All those who cannot make such distinctions are doomed. Prendick survives because he understands the principles of science yet has no desire to make them serve his ends. He is not an outcast, but has willingly left a social world where he was at home. On Moreau's island Prendick becomes fully aware of what it means to be human. He can see that men, like beasts, have impulses and instincts that are difficult to control, but which it is wise to control. Men need not become the slaves of nature. As Huxley stated in *Evolution and Ethics,* they may instead labor to turn the wilderness of this world into a garden. But, as Leon Stover has indicated, Wells felt they could do so by guiding nature, not opposing it. Wells presents Prendick's realization of his unique human power iron-ically. After Moreau's death, Prendick controls the animals by warning them that Moreau and his House of Pain will come again. "An animal may be ferocious and cunning enough," he observes, "but it takes a real man to tell a lie" (157). Although an obvious dig at human duplicity, this statement also asserts Wells's abiding con-viction that man's power to conceive what does not exist enables his self-development. In *The Bulpington of Blup* (1932), Wells has his ultimately unadmirable figure Theodore Bulpington defend his habit of lying by declaring that Religion, Mythology, and History are also forms of lies, but grand lies. In fact, lying characterizes man from his primordial condition. "One gift that poor ape had to help it in its hideous battle with fact. It could lie. Man is the one animal that can make a fire and keep off the beasts of the night. He is the one animal that can make a falsehood and keep off the beasts of despair."[21] But man must also know when he is lying and when he is not. He must know which "laws" he has concocted and which ones he has accepted through observation. At the end of *The Island of Doctor Moreau,* Prendick returns to England, but cannot escape the feeling that the people he sees around him are merely beast-men a few degrees above Moreau's. He tells himself that they are really "perfectly reasonable creatures, full of human desires and tender solicitude, emancipated from instinct, and slaves of no fantastic Law," but he cannot shake his sense of dread (171). At the end of his narrative, Prendick explains that he has withdrawn from society and spends his time reading "wise books" and studying chemistry and astronomy. "There is, though I do not know how there is or why there is, a sense of infinite peace and protection in the glitter-ing hosts of heaven. There it must be, I think, in the vast and eternal laws of matter, and not in the daily cares and sins and troubles of men, that whatever is more than animal within us must find its solace and its hope. I hope, or I could not live. And so, in hope and solitude, my story ends" (172).

Prendick learns that one law abides—the law of matter. The

stars, because they seem to change so little, are the best symbol of that law. But that law, too, is open to new interpretations by men. Man's imagination would conceive new structures for physical conditions—mechanical physics would give way to quantum physics, regularity theory would yield to probabilistic theory—but the conditions themselves would endure.[22] Oscar Wilde, who had to some degree inspired Wells's novel, declared that Art was an attempt to teach nature its place, a clever way of saying that the human imagination created the models by which natural events could be conceived.[23] His failure was to misunderstand the workings of all those laws—moral or natural—that he opposed. Like Moreau, Wilde believed he could shape the world to his own taste. Both were destroyed by the schemes they begot. For Wells, man's hope was to abandon the vanity of imposing human desires upon matter and to reverse the procedure, humbly applying the discoverable laws of matter to man's nature. Man did not, through his God-given reason, decipher the natural law in the material world; instead, through his evolved reason, he applied the very laws that made him to his evolving being.

Notes

1. H. G. Wells, "Preface," *The Island of Dr. Moreau* (New York: Charles Scribner's Sons, 1921), The Atlantic Edition, 1:ix. Subsequent quotations from this work are cited parenthetically in the text.
2. Bernard Loing, *H. G. Wells à l'oeuvre: les débuts d'un écrivain (1894–1900)* (Saint-Jean-de Braye: Didier Erudition, 1984).
3. A. W. Brian Simpson's *Cannibalism and the Common Law* (Chicago and London: University of Chicago Press, 1984) examines the *Regina v. Dudley and Stephens* case in great detail, but also provides elaborate additional information on numerous other cases involving similar circumstances.
4. *See* Robert L. Platzner, "H. G. Wells's 'Jungle Book': The Influence of Kipling on *The Island of Dr. Moreau,*" *Victorian Newsletter* 36 (1969), 19–22.
5. Rudyard Kipling, *The Second Jungle Book* in *The Jungle Books and Just So Stories* (New York: Bantam Books, 1986), 158.
6. Kipling, *The Jungle Book* in *The Jungle Books,* 7.
7. In his *James Clerk Maxwell: A Biography* (Edinburgh: Canongate, 1981), Ivan Tolstoy states that before Maxwell the world of physics was Newtonian and mechanical, but after, Maxwell's equations transcended mechanics and viewed electricity and magnetism in terms of space-filling fields (128). What Maxwell offered "was a completely new outlook, replacing the Newtonian universe of particles and action-at-a-distance forces by a world of fields, an abstract world beyond the ken of our senses. It was a true *scientific revolution,* and it signalled the birth of modern physics" (4). In *Order Out of Chaos: Man's New Dialogue with Nature* (New York: Bantam Books, 1984), Ilya Prigogine and Isabelle Stengers detail the change from Newton's classical mechanical physics, through the revolutions brought about by the statement of the second law of thermodynamics, to present-day attempts to question current physical assumptions about the limits and nature of physical laws. James A. Colaiaco calls attention to James Fitzjames Stephen's description of natural law as metaphorical in *James Fitzjames Stephen and the Crisis of Victorian Thought* (New York: St. Martin's Press, 1983), 69.

8. William Paley, *Natural Theology; or Evidences of the Existence and Attributes of the Deity* 11th edition (London: R. Faulder and Son, 1807). 7–8.

9. John Stuart Mill, *Three Essays on Religion, Collected Works of John Stuart Mill,* (Toronto and London: University of Toronto Press and Routledge & Kegan Paul, 1969), 10:473–74.

10. Mill, *Three Essays,* 377–78.

11. John Cogley, "Introduction," *Natural Law and Modern Society,* ed. John Cogley, et. al. (Cleveland and New York: World Publishing Company, 1962), 19–20.

12. Etienne Gilson stresses this point and observes that Charles Bonnet's notion of "e-volution," which assumed the gradual unfolding of traits in preformed creatures, might not have been entirely objectionable to Darwin, in *From Aristotle to Darwin and Back Again,* trans. John Lyon (Notre Dame, Ind.: University of Notre Dame Press, 1984), 59, 50.

13. Wells, "The Rediscovery of the Unique," *Early Writings in Science and Science Fiction,* ed. Robert Philmus and David Y. Hughes (Berkeley: University of California Press, 1975), 22–23.

14. Wells, "Rediscovery," 29–30.

15. Wells, "The Limits of individual Plasticity," *Early Writings,* 39.

16. H. G. Wells, Julian S. Huxley, and G. P. Wells, *The Science of Life* (New York: The Literary Guild, 1934), 387–88.

17. Richard D. French examines the history of the antivivisectionist movement and its attempts to put its principles into law, along with its struggles to stop the activities of medical experimenters whose work it found offensive, in *Antivivisection and Medical Science in Victorian Society* (Princeton: Princeton University Press, 1975).

18. Leon Stover, "Applied Natural History: Wells vs. Huxley," supra, pt. 3.

19. Wells, *The Food of the Gods* (New York: Scribner's Sons, 1925), The Atlantic Edition, 5:80–81. One wonders how firmly Wells would stand by the assertion that there are fixed "moral laws" that cannot be controverted with impunity.

20. Brendan F. Brown, ed., *The Natural Law Reader* (New York: Oceana Publications, 1960), 104–5.

21. Wells, *The Bulpington of Blup* (New York: Macmillan, 1933), 408.

22. *See* D. M. Armstrong's *What is a Law of Nature?* (Cambridge: Cambridge University Press, 1983) for a sophisticated examination of the alternate theories currently under review in scientific and philosophical circles.

23. Oscar Wilde, "The Decay of Lying," *Complete Works of Oscar Wilde,* introduction by Vyvyan Holland (London: Collins, 1966), 970.

H. G. Wells and Ecology

W. M. S. Russell

The career of H. G. Wells spans three generations. He learned biology from Thomas Henry Huxley, and he taught the art of popular science writing to Thomas Henry's grandson Julian. It is with this second relationship, and with a comment by the later Huxley, that I begin this discussion of H. G. Wells and ecology. In his *Memories,* published in 1970, Sir Julian wrote as follows about H. G. Wells as he was in the year 1927: "He had forgotten much of his biology and what he remembered was by now old-fashioned . . . with little study of . . . ecology."[1]

In the previous year, 1926, Wells had published *Mr Belloc Objects to "The Outline of History."* The account of evolution by natural selection in this book could hardly be bettered until, some three years later, Fisher and Haldane created the modern genetical theory.[2] This hardly suggests Wells had forgotten much of his biology. But was Sir Julian right about Wells and ecology? Let me first put his remark in context. It opens the chapter in which he describes the composition of *The Science of Life.*[3] Essentially, Huxley and G. P. Wells produced material on the various branches of biology, which H. G. Wells then edited and stamped with his genius for popular science writing, to create the wonderful book that appeared in 1930. The remark about Wells applies to the beginning of this collaboration in 1927. It was a gruelling but formative experience for Huxley. He was a competent popular science writer already,[4] but he was a much better one after the collaboration. It was, however, a rough ride. He quotes from the stream of letters Wells wrote him during the composition of the book. They include maxims that every science writer should have before him in letters of gold. But they also include brutal demands for haste, and merciless sarcasms at Huxley's expense. "Look at this letter!" wrote Wells at the end of one ferocious screed. "If it was an article I could get 1500 dollars for it. Look at the waste of time and attention, Oh my collaborator!" Huxley's account is scrupulously fair, and we can see Wells's point of view when we learn that Huxley produced a draft on insect behavior more than twice the planned length of the whole book.

Obviously Wells knew plenty about ecology after editing all the material Huxley and G. P. provided for *The Science of Life;* more than one-eighth of the book is on this subject.[5] Curiously, it does not figure much in his later writings, which are concentrated on human behavior and social organization. Even when he uses the word, as in *The Outlook for Homo Sapiens* or in *'42 to '44,* he turns out to be writing about human behavior and cultural evolution, with little ecology as usually understood.[6] In the *Experiment in Auto-biography,* published in 1934, he called for the establishment of chairs for a new way of teaching history, which he called Human Ecology.[7] In 1967, I published *Man, Nature and History,* which I believe to be the first systematic ecological history of mankind, and for some time I thought I was carrying out his wishes.[8] But again, closer inspection of the passage shows he is thinking of cultural evolution, without any special concern for ecology as such.

But in any case, the question I wish to address is whether Huxley was right in asserting that Wells had made little study of ecology by 1927. So I come back to the Huxley-Wells relationship. In 1941, long after *The Science of Life,* Huxley was chairing a meeting at the British Association and had to prevent Wells from speaking for twice the allotted time, at the expense of the other speakers. Wells never forgave him. The following year, Huxley was being forced out of his post as Secretary of the Zoological Society. Wells offered his flat for a meeting of Huxley-sympathizers, and withdrew the offer at the last minute, nearly preventing the meeting.[9] Huxley's references to Wells are remarkably fair and good-humored. But the experience may have colored his memories of Wells in earlier times.

In the course of their collaboration on *The Science of Life,* Huxley and Wells only had one factual disagreement. Huxley, so humane and progressive in practice, had a curious fantasy of genet-ically determined differences in behaviour and intelligence between social classes, and even of a slum genotype. Wells quite rightly denied this, but Huxley finally insisted on their leaving the question open.[10] So on the one occasion they disagreed on a biological point, Wells was right and Huxley wrong. This hardly inspires confidence in Huxley's view of Wells's knowledge of biology.

More important, the science of ecology really had advanced rapidly in the 1920s, and in animal ecology this was largely due to the work of Charles Elton, who is quoted in *The Science of Life,* which draws considerably on his work.[11] Huxley was understand-ably proud of having taught Elton, among other distinguished pupils, and refers to their pupil-teacher relationship six times in the two volumes of his *Memories*.[12] Now Wells was preoccupied with many other things during the 1920s, and he may well not have kept up with such recent specialist work as Elton's until he was briefed by Huxley and G. P. Wells for *The Science of Life*. But does that mean he knew little of ecology before 1927?

Elton himself began his book *Animal Ecology,* published in that very year, with the words: "Ecology is a new name for a very old subject."[13] The world "ecology" itself was used by Thoreau in a letter in 1858, and well defined, in its German form, by Ernst Haeckel in 1870.[14] The best book ever written on conservation is *Man and Nature,* which was published by George Perkins Marsh in 1864.[15] Major ecological surveys were already being carried out in the 1890s,[16] and by 1900 Sir Ray Lankester was meeting the representatives of other colonial powers to discuss the creation of large nature reserves to protect the wildlife of Africa.[17] So Wells could have known more than a little about ecology while he was still a student of Sir Julian's grandfather, and plenty more long before 1927. That he did know plenty is shown, I believe, in two of his great scientific romances, and it is to these that I now turn.

Men Like Gods was written in 1921–22, and published in 1923.[18] Wells rightly thought this superb romance "got a dull press."[19] If it had no other merits, the book would be memorable for the splendid portrait of Winston Churchill. He is thinly disguised as Rupert Catskill, one of the group of human beings pitch-forked into a parallel-universe Earth, where utopia has been achieved.[20] Catskill, who is even an Old Harrovian, is depicted as a very intelligent, very imaginative overgrown schoolboy, with his head full of military fantasies, which can find reactionary and destructive expression in action. And this is exactly how Churchill would be remembered by posterity, if he had died before the world needed just such a person to help dispose of something totally unintelligent, totally unimaginative, totally reactionary, and totally destructive. In 1913 Violet Asquith recorded in her diary a visit to Churchill with her father on the Admiralty yacht *Enchantress*.[21] She and Churchill were leaning on the taffrail, "gliding past the lovely, smiling coastline of the Adriatic, bathed in sun." "How perfect!" she said. "Yes," replied Churchill, "range perfect—visibility perfect—if we had got some six-inch guns on board how easily we could bombard . . ." And yet Churchill always had some qualities of human feeling, rare among politicians, which made him impossible not to like. This, too, is faithfully depicted in Wells's romance. The outrageous Catskill tries to effect a coup d'état and conquer Utopia, causing three Utopians to be shot in the process. When the hero, Mr. Barnstaple, warns the Utopians, Catskill condemns him to death as a traitor. Nevertheless, when it comes to the point, he is unable to shoot him in cold blood, and gives him a chance to escape. Barnstaple tells him: "I've never borne you any ill-will. . . . Had I been your schoolmaster everything might have been different."[22] No doubt this is just how Wells felt about Churchill.

But of course the main point of the romance is the description of Utopia, and it is the ecological aspect of this, the planned and landscaped environment of utopia which would, I believe, bear study by conservationists today. Conservation is so important that it is very unfortunate the modern conservation movement is often vitiated by two aberrations. The first is the notion that virtually all vertebrate species should be conserved in their natural habitats, or even reintroduced there, irrespective of any threat they may present, as predators, competitors, or disease vectors to man and his livestock. Tiger reserves in India, for instance, are cited as a conservation success story. But there are now so many tigers that some stray out of the reserves and kill livestock or even people.[23] This dangerous development can probably be traced to a distortion of the ancient system of totemic beliefs, far removed from its ecologically appropriate origins.[24]

Recently this idea has taken the form of a belief that animals should be restricted to their native continents. In 1984 an extraordinary fuss was made at an international conference in Africa about the acquisition of some gorillas by a Dutch zoo, experienced in the care of primates. This new fetish deserves some discussion, since it could result in unintended extinctions. Gorillas in most of their native habitats are in serious danger from poachers. The fate of the two breeding colonies of White Rhinoceros is instructive. The northern colony was moved to Murchison Park in Uganda, where all were killed for their horns under the Amin dictatorship. The southern colony was moved to Whipsnade, where they bred enough to supply zoos all over the world.[25] The Père David deer became extinct in the wild in China in the nineteenth century. The only survivors were kept in the Imperial Hunting Park south of Peking. In 1866, a French missionary, Père David, managed to ship two skins to Europe. As a result, European zoos obtained live specimens through diplomats. In 1893–96, the Duke of Bedford bought eighteen of these, and bred them at Woburn Abbey, where their numbers had risen to 242 by 1949. Meanwhile the zoo deer had died out, and those in China had been eaten by starving peasants or killed by European troops suppressing the Boxer Rising. Had it not been for Woburn, the species would be extinct. As it is, breeding stock has been widely dispersed from Woburn, and in 1985 the Marquess of Tavistock returned twenty-two of the deer from Woburn to China at his own expense.[26] In our less-than-utopian world, valuable endangered species should be diffused to as many places and continents as possible.

The second aberration is more serious. Modern rational conservationists are well aware that the major threat to world wildlife and world ecosystems is the excessive growth of world human population, and that unless this is reduced by voluntary birth control all other conservation measures are futile. But popular articles and programmes on conservation habitually fail to mention human overpopulation. This leads to secondary misconceptions, such as the tendency to attribute deforestation in the tropics to slash-and-burn farming, which conserves the forest when practised at low population densities.[27]

After such aberrations, it is a relief to turn back to the saner perspectives of Wells's romance of 1923. Wells realized that man must now take active responsibility for ordering and improving life on earth. His Utopians had no interest in conserving dangerous or destructive species in the wild or any species on their own continents. They eliminated undesirable animals and plants. But first each species was carefully examined for its function in the ecosystem, with due allowance even for ecological changes within the life cycle. "Certain insects, for example, were destructive and offensive grubs in the opening stage of their lives . . . and then became either beautiful in themselves or necessary to the fertilization of some useful or exquisite flowers. . . . And even when the verdict was death . . ., a reserve would be kept . . . in some secure isolation, of every species condemned." What we should nowadays call a gene bank.[28] For the rest, it was all "sweeping schemes of conservation" and improvement.[29]

But above all, Wells realized that the starting point for any improvement in human society *or* its environment is the use of voluntary birth control to end "the overcrowding of the planet." Thus overpopulation was, "these Utopians insisted, the fundamental evil out of which all the others that afflicted the race arose." In the bad old days, they told their visitors, man "spent the great gifts of science as rapidly as it got them in a mere insensate multiplication of the common life. At one time . . . the population . . . had mounted to over two thousand million."[30] Wells's concern with birth control was not, of course, utopian in the inert negative sense; he was active in promoting it. He was a vice-president of the

Malthusian League, of Marie Stopes's Society for Constructive
Birth Control, and of the National Birth Control Council.[31] He was
thus a staunch supporter of voluntary birth control, the pivot of any
rational conservation policy.

The ecological scheme of *Men Like Gods,* however far-sighted,
was little more than a sketch. But in an earlier romance he had
presented some ecology worked out in beautifully fine detail. *The
Food of the Gods* was written and serialized in 1903, and published
as a book in 1904.[32] The food of the gods is, of course, a man-made
growth-promoting substance, called by its creators Herakleophorbia IV, and first tried out on chickens in an experimental farm.
Wells assumes, for his purpose, that it can be absorbed by all plants
and metabolized by all animals, including man. Much of the story
concerns the spread of Herakleophorbia IV through regional wildlife, and Wells describes in detail the English floras, faunas, and
landscapes and their gradual transformation by the spread of the
growth-promoting compound. He invokes "what naturalists call a
centre of distribution," and after the first escapes from the farm
there are soon a number of such centers.[33] This conception of a
man-made substance spreading through an ecosystem is, at least in
such detail, original with Wells. The spread is not only by physical
agents, such as water. The ecological concept of the food-chain
goes back at least to Linnaeus.[34] But it was surely Wells who first
showed that an escaped synthetic compound could pass up a food
chain, with drastic consequences. Grains of Herakleophorbia IV
slip from a cracked pipe into a pond, where they are eaten by
tadpoles, themselves eaten by Dytiscus larvae, which duly absorb
the drug.[35] Precisely such a sequence of events was to become an
urgent problem for ecologists studying the effects of pesticide resi-
dues on wildlife after the Second World War.[36]

These two romances amply refute Huxley's assertion that Wells
had made little study of ecology before 1927. His unique scientific
imagination was applied no less to ecology than to other sciences,
both long before and shortly before 1927. The utopian vision of
Men Like Gods deserves careful consideration by modern conservationists; and *The Food of the Gods* shows all Wells's powers of
prediction, focussing on a problem that arose more than forty years
later, and that remains, more than eighty years later, one of the
most urgent concerns of the modern science of applied ecology.

Notes

1. Julian Huxley, *Memories* (Harmondsworth: Penguin, 1972), 148.
2. W. M. S. Russell, "Evolutionary Concepts in Behavioural Science," pt. 2 *General*

Systems 4 (1959): 45–73; "The Origins of Social Biology" *Biology and Human Affairs* 41, (1976): 109–37; "Biology and Literature in Britain, 1500–1900," pt. 3, *Social Biology and Human Affairs* 45, (1980): 52–71.

3. Huxley, *Memories,* Chap. 12.

4. *See,* for instance, Huxley's *The Stream of Life* (London: Watts, 1926), or even, much earlier, *The Individual in the Animal Kingdom* (Cambridge: Cambridge University Press, 1912).

5. In the edition I have consulted, Book 6 (concerning ecology) occupies 119 pages of the whole volume's 880 pages, but there are other sections concerned with ecology as well. *See* H. G. Wells, Julian Huxley, and G. P. Wells, *The Science of Life: A Summary of Contemporary Knowledge about Life and Its Possibilities* (London, Cassell, 1931).

6. *See* H. G. Wells, *The Outlook for Homo Sapiens* (1942), chaps. 2 and 5; *'42 to '44* (1944), appendix (one) Two.

7. Wells, *Experiment in Autobiography* (London: Victor Gollancz & Cressett Press, 1934), 2 : 646–48.

8. W. M. S. Russell, *Man, Nature and History* (London: Aldus Books, 1967).

9. Huxley, *Memories,* 165–66, 249–51.

10. Ibid., 160–61. On this fallacy, *see* A. H. Halsey, "Genetics, Social Structure and Intelligence" (reprinted from *British Journal of Sociology,* 1958), in A. H. Halsey, ed., *Heredity and Environment* (London: Methuen, 1977), 187–200.

11. Wells, Huxley, and Wells, *The Science of Life,* 592.

12. Huxley, *Memories,* pp. 119, 122, 205; Julian Huxley, *Memories II* (Harmondsworth: Penguin Books, 1978), 75, 230, 243. *See also* Editor's Introduction (by Huxley), C. Elton, *Animal Ecology* (London: Sidgwick and Jackson, 1927), xiii.

13. Ibid., 1.

14. E. J. Kormondy, *Concepts of Ecology* (Englewood Cliffs, N.J.: Prentice-Hall, 1969), viii.

15. W. M. S. Russell, "The Man who Invented Conservation," *The Ecologist,* 2 no. 2, (1972), 14–15.

16. C. S. Elton, *The Pattern of Animal Communities* (London: Methuen, 1966), 29; C. Elton, *The Ecology of Animals,* 3rd ed. (London: Methuen, 1950), 10.

17. Sir Ray Lankester, *Diversions of a Naturalist* (London: Methuen, 1915), 20.

18. J. R. Hammond, *An H. G. Wells Companion* (London and Basingstoke: Macmillan Press 1979), 47, 111.

19. Wells, *Experiment in Autobiography,* 2 : 501.

20. Ibid. Wells admits the novel "frankly caricatures some prominent contemporaries." Cecil Burleigh is linked by both his names to the political Cecils, but is generally thought to represent Arthur Balfour. About Catskill, there is no doubt. *See* Hammond, *Companion,* 113.

21. Lady Violet Bonham Carter, *Winston Churchill as I Knew Him* (London: Eyre and Spottiswoode, 1965), 262.

22. Wells, *Men Like Gods* (London: Cassell, 1923), 204.

23. *Survival Special: 25 Years of Survival,* ITV (Thames/LWT, British Television), 28 March 1986.

24. W. M. S. Russell and Claire Russell, "The Social Biology of Werewolves," in J. R. Porter and W. M. S. Russell, eds., *Animals in Folklore* Ipswich and Cambridge: (D. S. Brewer for the Folklore Society, 1978), 143–82, 260–69, especially 157–59, 162–64, 178–79.

25. *Gorilla and rhinoceros: Survival Special* ITV (Thames/LWT, British Television). For gorillas, *see also* D. Fossey, *Gorillas in the Mist* (London: Hodder and Stoughton, 1983). Diane Fossey courageously organized an active scheme of protection for her gorilla group in Rwanda until her murder in December 1985 (*see Radio Times* 22–28 February 1986).

26. W. Ley, *Dragons in Amber* (London: Sidgwick and Jackson, 1951), chap. 6; *The Times* (London) 12 November 1985, 8, includes a photograph of the Marquess, his Chinese hosts, and one of the deer in the formerly Imperial Hunting Park near Peking.

27. W. M. S. Russell, "The Slash-and-Burn Technique," *Natural History* 77 no. 3, (1968): 58–65, 76; "Population, Swidden Farming and the Tropical Environment" *Population and Environment* (in press); Russell, *Man, Nature, and History,* Chaps. 3, 4.

28. Wells, *Men Like Gods,* 85–86.

29. Ibid., 242.

30. Ibid., 63; *see also* 155–57.

31. P. Fryer, *The Birth Controllers* (London: Transworld Publishers, 1967), 266, 254, 297; *see also* R. Hall, *Marie Stopes: a Biography* (London: Virago, 1978), 116–17.

32. Wells, *Experiment in Autobiography*, 2:654.

33. Wells, *The Food of the Gods*, Atlantic Ed. (London: T. Fisher Unwin, 1925), 137.

34. R. W. Burkhardt, *The Spirit of System: Lamarck and Evolutionary Biology* (Cambridge, Mass.: Harvard University Press, 1977), 73.

35. Wells, *The Food of the Gods*, pp. 133–34.

36. *See*, for example, D. J. Kuenen, ed., *The Ecological Effects of Biological and Chemical Control of Undesirable Plants and Animals* (Leiden: Brill, 1961); J. Sheail, *Pesticides and Nature Conservation* (Oxford: Clarendon Press, 1985).

H. G. Wells and Futurity as the Only Creative Space in a Programmed Society

Romolo Runcini

TRANSLATED BY FERNANDO PORTA

1

H. G. Wells's *The Time Machine* was published in London in 1895. It tells the story of a strange machine and of a scientist, expert in three-dimensional geometry (to which he adds a fourth dimension, time), who uses the machine, to general surprise and incomprehension, to project himself into the future. The Time Traveller's destination is an upside-down version of Victorian England, or, perhaps—denying the advantages obtained from Disraeli's "democratic experiment"—an England that the middle classes are no longer able to acknowledge as the chosen nation, feeling that they have been excluded by the advent of modern monopolies and the consequent social struggles between capitalists and the working classes.

Indeed, it is an England which, with the fall of liberalism, reflects a society with no moral principles. Here the Eloi (that is, the entrepreneurial class) live hedonistically among the green hills of an archaic Surrey, steeped in the luxurious and indolent outlook of a decadent aristocracy. The savage Morlocks (the working classes) are enslaved in subterranean industries and unwillingly submit to their fate while they await their opportunity for revenge.

The idea of a machine moving through a fourth dimension reflected both Wells's own scientific interests and the widespread "marvels" of technology which had appeared in popular books since 1870. In that year, Parliament passed an education act promoting primary education for the masses, which in turn helped the development of new methods of industrial production.

The rise of a mass reading public caused fiction to divide into several different types. This was particularly true of the novel, which separated into different genres catering for the varying interests, tastes, and degrees of education of their readers. In this sense, H. G. Wells can be considered the effective founder of modern science fiction. He exemplifies the humanist throwing himself eagerly into the search for new themes more appropriate to the changing society of the age.

In *The Time Machine,* the prophecy—or rather, the sense of prediction—is carried out on two different levels at once: on the social level, where the author definitely proves to be a pessimist, and on the scientific where, on the contrary, he is optimistic. We can see the importance of these two separate but related aspects when examining how deeply they affect the characterization of the Wellsian hero. Through his personal participation in the technological adventure, this character becomes a sort of collective witness to the contemporary failure of the "mythic horizon" of progress.

2

Now it is on the scientific level that we can verify the positive and negative effects of projecting man into the future. The dimension of time—passing from the great cosmological systems to regulation by machine or, as Koyré says, "from a world of 'thereabouts' to a universe of precision"—had already become a determining factor in the control of energy and the development of new productive processes. When time (*la durée*) is understood in terms of the individual's experience—according to Bergson, this is affected by the expansion or contraction of the subject's visual or auditory space corresponding to his degree of sensory perception—the whole epistemological framework of science is radically changed. The lack of an absolute point of reference in space and time (which Einstein's theory was to deny forever) severs every link with the methodology of the past. The crisis of science, with which the phenomenology of Husserl and Heidegger was concerned, while demonstrating the complexity of the laws of change in space and time, gives to every experiment the unpredictability of an adventure undergone, but still unfolding. Thus, the availability of new categories of knowledge matching the concerns of the ever-changing present opens new horizons to methodologies of prediction. "Prophecy" then becomes the planning of the future in economic, political, and social terms. Planning the structure of society—as in the Russian "Gosplan" and the American "New Deal" of the 1930s and later in the British "Welfare State"—reveals the impact of the mobilization of the masses necessary for the development of production.

The act of planning is always an intervention in time. On the social level, the progressive reduction of the stages of production allows technology to manipulate time, to reproduce its patterns, to elevate its power of concentration and adaptability; that is, it allows the regimentation of men, as in the case of the Morlocks, into factory cadres trained to the rhythms of production. On the other hand, the reduction of the time required for production creates the conditions necessary for a wider and more democratic spreading of well-being and, where possible, a mediation of social control. "Human history," Wells writes in *The Outline of History,* "becomes more and more a race between education and catastrophe."

3

The Time Traveller in his role of inventor of technologies seems a bizarre, but always positive, embodiment of the man of science. Conversely, in *The Island of Doctor Moreau* published in the following year, the figure of the mad scientist emerges amid a succession of monstrous transplants of beasts into men.

A year later (1897), in another scientific romance entitled *The Invisible Man,* Wells's commitment to scientific planning is replaced by man's eternal dream of power, a dream that seeks to escape the confines of nature for purely personal ends. Here we have the archetypal scientist split into two separate characters: on the one hand, the ambitious and ruthless Dr. Griffin, who accidentally discovers—by experiments very similar to those of Stevenson's Dr. Jekyll—a peculiar strychnine-based drug capable of giving his body the optical quality of air. On the other hand, Griffin's old university friend, Dr. Kemp, has wisely spent his own secluded life as a researcher who sees science as an end in itself. Therefore, while Griffin seems to be the last dangerous incarnation of the medieval alchemist, Kemp embodies, in his self-sacrifice and serious-mindedness, the true modern scientist. Unlike the central character of *The Time Machine,* Griffin is sympathetic neither by virtue of his scientific research nor of his style of life; he is, however, the main device of a plot introducing elements of the "marvellous" into a world besieged by banality.

In this story, not without pathos in itself, the conflict between good and evil seems established as a polarity of fixed extremes and does not achieve tragic intensity (in spite of Griffin's catastrophic end) because of the weak psychological characterization of the

protagonist and the exaggerated stereotyping of his alter ego, Dr.
Kemp. We are some distance from the tragic dimension of the
relationship between Jekyll and Hyde.

Thus, while the Time Traveller has captivated the reader with his
profusion of technical information and through the exciting prospect of a future (or a past) at hand, Griffin is presented from the
beginning as nothing but a crafty mystifier, a maniac, a dangerous
man. With the discovery of invisibility (implicit, if only marginal in
the story of *The Time Machine*), the reader is faced with a defined
menace, namely the state of anarchy that will follow if scientific
methodologies are employed without adequate social control. In
The War of The Worlds (1898), the menace coming from the outside—the Martians' invasion of London—is transformed into a kind
of fear that permeates every level of the community and is far more
dangerous than the extraterrestrials' presence in itself. Only the
good sense of the ordinary people, such as the Artilleryman and
Miss Elphinstone, indicates the right moment and the right place to
face both dangers. But here the main character is the narrator
himself, that is, a sort of collective character, a witness of his own
kind.

With the end of the laissez-faire economy, the disappearance of
the private entrepreneur from the horizons of the market, and the
advent of advertising and the new joint-stock companies, socio-
economic space for the individual was preempted by the rise of
more powerful industrial and financial organizations that would
lead to the complete control of production. Consequently, personal
enterprise became socially and ideologically impracticable; in the
age of imperialism, the only possible enterprise was collective.
Wells, like Kipling, had understood this change.

4

Prediction in the scientific and social fields is neither an arbitrary
nor an improbable operation, as futurologists well know. A famous
essay entitled *On the Epistemology of the Inexact Sciences,* published in 1958 by the Rand Corporation, opens the way to a distinction between exact sciences (whose inferential methods are based
on logical and mathematical premises) and inexact sciences (where
the inductive and deductive methods of research are informal), the
latter being the only ones available for the prediction of the future.
Here we should concentrate particularly on the human sciences

since they deal with the cultural, social, and historical laws of evolution.

Such a methodological perspective appears to derive from the familiar Diltheyan distinction between the natural and the cultural sciences. The point is, however, that in studying the process of cultural evolution, individually or collectively, the relevant science must use an interpretative model sufficiently open to the requirements of the phenomenon that is being examined. The study of human history, for instance, can't be entirely objective because so many people are involved.

When in 1901 H. G. Wells published a volume of sociological essays entitled *Anticipations of the Reaction of Mechanical and Scientific Progress upon Human Life and Thought*—predicting a car for everyone, trucks, motorways, military and civil airplanes— he not only offered some general notes for a quantitative account of the services offered by technology, but also outlined a sort of "twilight threshold" beyond which the dangers caused by the concentration of such great energy would grow. But, with the publication of *The Shape of Things to Come* (1933) he passed from a technological prediction to a political one, pointing out the imminent fall of the capitalist system and the urgency of an international agreement between parliamentary, soviet, and fascist states (a rather strange bunch, only conceivable by a Fabian like Wells). This is no longer a prophecy, even though Wells predicted that the Second World War would break out in 1940, considered the old League of the Nations insufficient, hoped for a larger association (the United Nations Organization), and was able to anticipate the political and economic strategies of the superpowers and the great multinationals. No, this is not a prophecy but a chronicle of the future.

In the 1930s, as the effects of the Wall Street crash spread to the most industrialized countries of Europe, the great depression subverted all the individual values once consolidated in the universal myths of progress, order, and well-being. The crisis was not only a living situation but a new universal idea: the fear of the rise of the masses. In the wake of Oswald Spengler, this idea would be further explored by Ortega y Gasset's *La rebelion de las masas* (1930), Keyserling's *Die Neuentstehende Welt* (1933), Picard's *Die Flucht vor Gott* (1934), Huizinga's *In de Schaduwen von Morgen* (1935), and also by such writers as Georges Duhamel, W. H. Auden, and Aldous Huxley, who would turn the crisis into the main concern of their antiutopias. Wells feared the spectre of the crisis: the importance and the involvement of the modern middle classes are reflected in his stratified utopia.

Reality, however, may be no longer ordered according to the old categories: space and time are not absolutes, rather they have been taken to pieces by the industrial system. The evolution of mass society has reduced the possibility of any direct understanding of contemporary history. In these circumstances it is easier to predict the future than to be aware of the present.

5

On the literary level, the writer became aware of a semantic crisis in language that had now become—as a result of the birth of the mass media—a medium of information on a vast scale. With the evolution of the press, photography, cinema (and later, in the thirties, of the radio), the world was explored and represented in various familiar and unfamiliar states; images and ideas could now be reproduced for a mass audience, whereas in the past they could only circulate among the intellectual elite.

Thus, as the modern representation of society reached a wider public, its cultural domain receded from a subjective space determined by the elaboration of hegemonic groups to an objective process of communication worked out from the patterns of production of the ruling system. The first kind of narrative to be found insufficient from this point of view was realism, as the most accessible perspective for a direct use of verisimilitude. With the decline of the laissez-faire spirit, the fictional plot no longer had the function of dramatizing the adventure into the unknown, which since the eighteenth century had characterized the role of the lonely protagonist, the bourgeois hero (the private entrepreneur) dealing with the problems of a developing society. In the novel, these problems had to be solved by the hero's deliberate will to achieve and maintain his supremacy.

Indeed, during the great epoch of nineteenth-century realism (from Balzac to Manzoni, from Dickens to Tolstoy), the plot entered into a mimetic synchronism with the external world, in this way leading the reader into the reassuring space of "mimesis." Even in the fantastic literature of the romantic age—once the supernatural has been let into the every day world through some mechanism of surprise or trickery—the plot requires us to acknowledge a superior and stable order of things to register the depth of any deviation from the norm. The protagonist, as individual and as hero, is the psychological core of the plot. By contrast, the traditional plots of fables, legends, and other stories stopped short of any complex psychology, and the act of storytelling implied following the reassuring linear time of a whole developing society, based on the conflicts and resolution of human needs.

So the plot found in linear time the ontological and spatial foundation of its own principle of imitation. The actions, passions, thoughts, and movements of the characters were measured on the temporal scale as an element indicating causality. Time, objectively considered in its mechanical function (the clock) and productive regulation (the arts and crafts), gave to every action sufficient space for individual or multiple expression at the different levels of narration. This enabled the writer to adopt a mimetic perspective as the necessary analogy for a metaphorical reconstruction of the social order. The plot represented the point of mediation between the social order and the symbolic order, between history and culture, and thus between reality and fantasy.

The plot, from the romances of chivalry to the *Bildungsroman*, had always represented the simple development of an action and a feeling connected to a narrative system that takes human experience as a paradigm for communication. However, what is a plot and what is its function in Wells's fiction? It is an adventure into the realm of possibility, where everything that happens is explained not by the evidence of reality (the real world)—available to the protagonist as a test of his striving—but by a series of technological and political hypotheses.

It is on the basis of these hypotheses that prediction—as a framework for innovation in a world whose values have been rendered obsolete by the glut of information—became the very "clustering core" of the story. In Wells, indeed, prediction was elaborated on the basis of current tendencies in a changing society which was transforming itself into a programmed and totalizing industrial system. His meetings with Stalin and Roosevelt in 1934, debating the political need for serious national planning by the industrialized nations, revealed a Wells who had moved from the confused technocratic vision of *A Modern Utopia* (1905) to something approaching the theory of "the managerial revolution" proclaimed by James Burnham in the 1940s and later reflected in the functionalism of Talcott Parsons.

Wells's two-fold activity as narrator and sociologist set out to bridge the gap between the "Two Cultures" and to link science and literature as two items representing a common social evolution—an evolution that the writer would not fail to recognize, when faced with the technological and imperialistic expansion that was changing the world order. This was indeed the aesthetic perspective of the twentieth-century avant-garde. With this engagement in the assertion of the radical change arising from the now collective human destiny (rather than from the previous individual one), Wells's assimilation of technology can be said to approach that of the Futurists. Moreover, this is what differentiates him from the airy industrial allegories of Jules Verne, with whom he is often confused. In fact, while Verne's scientific fantasies had been an expression of bourgeois optimism based on the superhuman illusion of a free enterprise economy; Wells's fantastic predictions specifically originated in the crisis aroused by the advent of the monopoly system. For this reason, his kind of prediction seems to be more pessimistically inclined, as it is preoccupied with the problems of controlling the new energies stemming from current technology.

Conversely, in Verne the epic of science dominating nature was based on a progressive evolution of mankind, such as was foreshadowed in the machines shown at the great exhibitions of the late nineteenth century with their promise of the technological conquest of the globe. For Verne the appropriation of reality became the principal theme of a theological discourse including in itself the principle of evil, that is, of negativity considered as a residue of economic failure that only the acquisitive outlook and values of the "homo faber" could successfully overcome.

Verne's realism was the literary expression of this ideology. In Wells, on the contrary, realism has given way to a problematic view of the world: his writing is not realistic but hypothetical. Absolute truths are held at a distance. His scientific and political predictions are not founded on the assurance of the present but on the possible balance to be established in the future. It is not certainty that inspires his fiction but uncertainty: its specific genre is the romance. The Wellsian plot, then, does not derive from an intuitive act, but from the piecing together of elements fulfilling the two main functions of concealment and discovery, of the extraordinary case and its explanation.

Therefore, Wells reveals the form of the unknown, the unusual, the evil, not as a temporary fault, but rather as an autonomous and negative force that, in time of crisis, threatens to be a troubling factor in a world socially and technologically too complex. It is this strategy of otherness, with the traps and surprises it holds in store, that enters the direct prose of the Wellsian plot like a ghostly vision of the dangers that man, too proud and confident of his power, is going to face.

The crisis of science and the instability of "petit-bourgeois" ideology initiated this perspective, but it is certainly the use of fear—well achieved in Poe's hallucinatory and mysterious style or with the haunting evocation of the Gothic romance—that provides Wells with the opportunity for an immediate verification of futurity, as the dimension in which we are already immersed.

In short, the impersonality of power occurring with the advent of monopoly capitalism has canceled any possible identification between the hero of the novel and his society: the common man replaces "homo faber." The process of reification definitely subverts the customary order of things: use-value is superseded at all levels by exchange-value. The artificial and omnidirectional time of the machine no longer provides us with a convincing reproduction of reality, and the object is no longer seen as a stable essence but in the never-ending movement towards its total consumption. This has caused modern fiction to follow two main paths: either the symbolic introspection of a character with his "stream of consciousness" (Proust, Joyce, Musil) or the fragmentation of character by means of multiple points of view, intellectual self-division, or the representation of a collective self-awareness (Aldous Huxley, Gide, Malraux), including the consequent vertical or horizontal changes in plot structure.

H. G. Wells belongs to this last perspective; he realized that the only creative space in the history of a programmed society is the future; that is, not a vision obtainable from the present but an event we are all waiting for.

PART FOUR
Educationalist, Utopian, and Visionary

Introduction

The essays in this section offer a composite (but far from exhaustive) picture of a writer who was, as John Huntington puts it, "probably the most significant utopian voice of the twentieth century." Wells's utopianism has its place in the spectrum of socialist politics, but it was also the expression of a visionary dreamer whose idea of human betterment is as often expressed in his imaginative writings as in his nonfiction. Several of the essays that follow move very freely between Wells's discursive social thought and his novels, between argument and image.

John Huntington's title is a reminder that the writer who was so inspiring in his own time is also problematic today. "Problems of an Amorous Utopian" could only have been written after the recent series of fully frank biographies of Wells and after his own apology for his colorful sex life in *H. G. Wells in Love*. What is there to be learned, Huntington asks, from the contrast between Wells's own conduct and the ethics of personal restraint and austere self-discipline characteristic of his utopians? In a fascinating study of works as diverse as *The War of the Worlds, A Modern Utopia,* and *Apropos of Dolores,* Huntington suggests that, if Wells's intellectual consistency is harmed by such contradictions, his art is strengthened by them. Throughout his work, both early and late, there is a more profound representation of the conflict between the rational and irrational in human life than Wells, as a conscious propagandist, was perhaps able to grasp.

One less than fully rational element in Wells's thought was his intense hostility towards two thinkers, Comte and Marx, who figure prominently among his intellectual precursors. Many commentators have taken his animadversions on Comte and his followers at face value, but Martha Vogeler, in an illuminating paper, stresses the complexity of the relations between Wells and the positivists. On the one hand, there is some evidence that Wells, as a self-confessed philosophical carpetbagger, was more deeply influenced by Comtean ideas than he was willing to admit; on the other hand, there are genuine differences between Positivism and the Wellsian emphasis, despite their common insistence on a future based on industrial planning. Our understanding of the course of Wells's utopian development is enriched by Vogeler's account of the ambiguous Positivist responses to his work, including the comically guarded personal relationship between Wells and the leading English Comtean, Frederic Harrison.

Krishan Kumar also takes up the argument between Wells and the Positivists, finding in Wells's 1906 essay, "The So-Called Science of Sociology," a wholesale rejection of the concept of a social science that had animated sociology's Victorian founders. In a striking close reading of Wells's essay, Kumar finds in it both an agenda for its author's life work as a social thinker and a radical intellectual model for today's sociologists to ponder. The two legitimate functions of social enquiry, Wells argues, are historical sociology and utopian projection; and history and utopia are combined in many of Wells's works, ranging from his novel *Tono-Bungay* to his encyclopedic textbook *The Outline of History*. Further on in his essay, Kumar asks whether present-day sociologists have not begun, hesitantly and unconsciously, to follow in Wells's footsteps. The relevance of utopian thought to sociological study is now at last finding some recognition, and where it is not recognized, as Kumar puts it, "it is modern sociology, not Wells, that is in need of revision."

Cliona Murphy focusses on what is arguably a weakness in Wells's thought. Despite being an ex-teacher and a lifelong champion of educational modernization, Wells had surprising little to say about women's education; indeed Murphy finds it necessary to turn to his novels rather than to his formal treatises to understand what his views may have been. Echoing Bonnie Kime Scott's earlier essay with its consideration of the outcomes of Wells's novels, Murphy observes how often the Wellsian heroine fails to complete her education, since her real destiny lies elsewhere. Wells, it is concluded, was less than wholehearted about education for women; in this he was a "man of his time," "more conservative than he or many of his contemporaries thought."

The purpose of K. V. Bailey's essay, at first sight, is to emphasize the links between Wells and C. S. Lewis, who was not only a science fiction and fantasy writer, but a robustly conservative thinker. If Lewis was once called the "H. G. Wells of Christendom," Wells, so Bailey argues, might plausibly be described as the C. S. Lewis of atheism. Nevertheless, the affinities that concern Bailey are those of mythopoeic imagery and symbolism, rather than of ideology. Tracing the patterns of the apocalyptic imagination in Wells's work, Bailey opens up the possibility of viewing his whole body of writings, fictional and nonfictional, as a single visionary text. Once again this essay offers a remarkably interdisciplinary approach to Wells's writings, connecting biographical research to utopian studies, and science fiction criticism to theology.

Finally, in addition to scaling the visionary heights, Wells succeeded as few other modern writers have done in communicating his vision to ordinary people. Robert Crossley's essay on "Wells's Common Readers" is a study of Wells's fan mail, as it is preserved for posterity in the Rare Book Room at the University of Illinois at Urbana. Showing the responses of readers who range from parsons' wives to rocket engineers and from a Midwestern schoolteacher to a Zulu soldier, this remarkable essay gives unparalleled evidence of the breadth and immediacy of Wells's appeal. We read here of people who found emotional comfort and mental inspiration in Wells's books, of people who felt that their lives had been changed by reading these works, and who found in them an "invigorating, inquiring, activist hope." That he was able to find such readers is the surest vindication of Wells's aims as a visionary, a utopian, and an educationalist.

H. G. Wells: Problems of an Amorous Utopian

John Huntington

H. G. Wells is probably the most significant utopian voice of the twentieth century. From 1901, with *Anticipations,* to almost the very end of his life, he worked to promote education, science, socialism, the world state, the Declaration of Human Rights, and the open conspiracy of rational and well-intentioned people. And it is the utopianism at the heart of his project that has occasioned some of the most severe criticism of Wells. F. R. Leavis speaks to a broad audience when he uses "Wellsian" as an adjective denoting all that is shallow in scientific culture; for Leavis it is sufficient to call C. P. Snow "Wellsian" to show that he is not a novelist.[1] George Orwell, in "Wells, Hitler, and the World State" (1941), while acknowledging the importance of Wells's liberating intellect early in the century, could denounce his "one-sided imagination" that could treat history simply as "a series of victories won by the scientific man over the romantic man." "Wells," Orwell declares, "is too sane to understand the modern world."[2] For such critics, and they are common, the terms "Wellsian" and "utopian" are synonymous with a thin hyper-rationality.

An admirer of Wells has difficulty responding to such criticisms because Wells himself declares that such rationality is the necessary and only salvation of the world. Yet, if Wells is proud of his rationality, we would not be denigrating him or his work if we observed that he is not as purely rational as he believes he is. On the contrary, Wells's work shows signs of a difficult struggle with a deeply selfish and irrational component of himself, and it is for that struggle, rather than for the neat conclusions he champions, that Wells's utopian work may be of greatest interest. To put it somewhat differently, Wells is greater than he himself understands, not because he achieves a pure rationality, but on the contrary, because he describes for us, if we can learn how to read him in this regard, a deep conflict between an ideal rationality and a much less admired, though not therefore comtemptible, emotionality that, however much he will try to smother it, will not be quiet.

Such a reading of Wells, while it clearly opens up dimensions of his understanding that he tried to repress, is not entirely antithetical to Wells's own consciousness. In the meditation on Machiavelli that begins *The New Machiavelli,* for instance, he advocates just such a reading of the author of *The Prince.* Wells appreciates the human, even disreputable qualities revealed in Machiavelli's letters. For Wells, "these flaws complete him."[3]

Let us begin with the ideal that so offends many humanist critics. Toward the end of *A Modern Utopia,* what Wells calls the "Voice" urges clear and bold *will* and *imagination.*

> The new things will be indeed of the substance of the thing that is, but differing just in the measure of the will and imagination that goes to make them. They will be strong and fair as the will is sturdy and organised and the imagination comprehensive and bold; they will be ugly and smeared with wretchedness as the will is fluctuating and the imagination timid and mean.[4]

This is a voice that Wells in 1905 had already practised for a number of years and which he would continue to perfect for many more. It speaks in bold adjectives of a comfortable, efficient, tolerant, and undemanding world with understood rules. And controlling this world would be the Samurai, who would, in the slightly ironic vision of Majorie Trafford in *Marriage,*

> lead lives of hard discipline and high effort, under self-imposed rule and restraint. They were to stand a little apart from the excitements and temptations of everyday life, to eat sparingly, drink water, resort greatly to self-criticism and self-examination, and harden their spirits by severe and dangerous exercises.[5]

A reading of such passages may be affected by the consideration that throughout the period when Wells was publicly developing the idea of his harmonious utopia led by disciplined will and imagination, he was finding the order his wife was so admirably sustaining at Spade House increasingly unsatisfying. The story of Wells's unconventional amatory experiments has been much retold, both by Wells himself and by later writers and biographers.[6] It is not necessary here to enter into this labyrinth in any detail except to keep in mind that according to Wells's own version of his life, within a few years of marrying Amy Catherine Robbins, his second wife, he began to have fantasies about relations with other women, and by the middle of the first decade of the century he had begun a continual series of sexual relationships, some frivolous, some serious, which remained the pattern of his life until well after the death of his wife. Wells was in his life revolting against what his own utopian voice calls its "haunting insistence on sacrifice and discipline" (234).

Wells indeed seems to have been proud of his amorous experiments, and in the late 1930s, in *H. G. Wells in Love,* he explains his persistent womanizing as a search for what he calls the Lover-Shadow. This is not a very clear concept. It resembles a Jungian archetype, a sort of *Ewigweibliche* whose proffered but never-attained satisfactions are a source of desire and aspiration throughout life. Part of the difficulty Wells has talking about the Lover-Shadow is that, while it is social insofar as it draws one out of pure self-centeredness, at the same time it represents a drive that has no regard for social good. An important difference between *H. G. Wells in Love* and the *Experiment in Autobiography* is that the former depicts a Wells relentlessly intent on his private desires.

In *The New Machiavelli,* Wells attempts to focus explicitly on the problems of the disjunction of love and the project to restructure society. Remington's popular phrase, "Love and fine thinking," which he poses as the solution to the political mess, turns out to be a paradox; it points to a union that contains the cause of its own disintegration.[7] The novel is a tale of tragic—toward the end rather operatic—romantic passion. The lovers admit their guilt, and the novel points to the people and causes they betray, but it finally sees them as victims of "the world-wide problem between duty and conscious, passionate love the world has still to solve" (442). Wells acknowledges the conflict, but he poses it as the world's problem, not as a contradiction within his own system of ideals. A better world, so he seems to say, would not have ostracized Remington.

The split between social ideals and personal needs is one that Wells hopes to overcome in his own experience and thought, but even as he tries to reconcile the two, the split remains embedded in his prose. For instance, in the following passage from *H. G. Wells in Love,* the Lover-Shadow appears as something distinct from the social *persona:*

> The sustaining theme of my *Experiment in Autobiography* has been the development and consolidation of my *persona,* as a devotee, albeit consciously weak and insufficient, to the evocation of a Socialist World-State. If I have not traced the development of my Lover-Shadow, and my search for its realization in responsive flesh and blood, with the same particularity and continuity, I have at least given the broad outline of its essential beginnings.[8]

The phrase "consciously weak and insufficient" might seem to anticipate and apologize for the more narrowly personal desire expressed in the phrase "responsive flesh and blood." Wells does not state that the two aspects of personality are in conflict, but his sense of their unavoidable difference can be seen in such an image as "the *persona* and the Lover-Shadow are, as I see it, the hero and heroine of the individual drama most of us make of our lives."[9] The gender antithesis is important here, not because it puts one aspect above the other, but simply because it insists on difference.

In Wells's utopian writings—as opposed to his social novels—the Lover-Shadow is not acknowledged as significant. The usual reading of *A Modern Utopia* finds something like a parody of the Lover-Shadow in the Voice's companion, the botanist, a man apparently determined to make life in Utopia difficult.[10] He can be read as an ironic and finally irrelevant reminder of psychological stances that the utopian future will need to transcend. He comes from and drags with him the world before the Comet, a world of possessive jealousies and amorous fixations. At the end of *A Modern Utopia* a meta-voice opines that the stances represented by the Voice and the botanist are essential and incompatible, one speaking of "a synthetic wider being, the great State, mankind," the other representing "the little lures of the immediate life" (372–73). In this reading, and it seems clearly the one that Wells consciously wanted us to make, the botanist is an embarrassing figure that we have to learn to overcome.

Such a subordination of the desires of the individual to the needs of the whole society or race is one of Wells's favorite themes, and it serves as a rationale for utopian dreams throughout his work. I want to pose a stronger reading of the botanist, however, and hear him as an authentic voice of the Lover-Shadow, a submerged voice that can be heard in one way or another throughout Wells's work, a voice that speaks for aspects of his unconscious that the rational ideals of the utopian world cannot satisfy. If we learn to hear *this* voice as "Wellsian," we shall be in a position to begin to understand some of the central texts of the Wells canon in a new way and to answer the objections of Leavis and Orwell.

2

Behind all the late works in which Wells undertakes to explain as clearly and as forthrightly as he can the amorous dimensions of his life—I am thinking especially of *Experiment in Autobiography,* the recently published *H. G. Wells in Love,* and highly autobiographical fictions such as *Apropos of Dolores* and *Brynhild*—we can point to the long affair with Odette Keun from which Wells had recently disentangled himself. This affair poses an extraordinary puzzle for Wells the rational utopian, one which he can never quite solve: why should a "free" man bind himself voluntarily over a long period of time to a person he finds thoroughly unpleasant? From early in his career as a lover, Wells had complicated his life deeply and, one has to say, compulsively. The relationships with Amber Reeves and Rebecca West are the great instances. Yet these two relationships can be explained because—there is an element of tautology here, but the language is Wells's own—Wells was "in love." But how could the affair with Keun—manifestly a source of considerable discontent, sustained by no social pressures, according to Wells never a "love" affair—continue for eight years? Clearly there is a mystery about the unconscious and about human behavior here that requires psychological explanation and must be taken into account in any rational utopian construction.

In this late period, Wells himself was pointing to the importance of the unconscious as a source of unhappiness. In *The Anatomy of Frustration,* another of his attempts to put together a utopian synthesis, the author's fictional voice, William Burroughs Steele, urges that one of the main sources of "frustration" comes from "that dark undertow of unformulated or disguised impulses" which the modern technique of psychoanalysis has revealed.[11] In a loose way, Steele is here picking up the theme of Freud's almost contemporaneous *Civilization and Its Discontents,* but there is a radical and significant difference between the ways Freud and Wells understand the unconscious. While Freud might agree with Steele's claim that "the psychoanalysts have opened our eyes to the artificiality of our rationalized conceptions of ourselves and our social relations" (52), he would absolutely disagree with the assertion that "our moral confusion and distress" stem from "our inability to impose any systematic direction of conduct upon the impulses from the subconscious that drive us" (60). For Freud, what Wells calls the "release from instinct" (by which he seems to mean *escaping* instinct altogether rather than giving it free rein) and the "restraint upon impulse" are themselves the very sources of "discontent" in civilization. From a very early age, one has emotions towards and thoughts about parents and siblings that the social code says are wrong. One has to repress these forbidden feelings and thoughts, thereby creating the guilt that is intrinsic to civilization. The "systematic direction of conduct" that Wells anticipates will, Freud would argue, increase rather than diminish discontent. Freud would warn us that what is repressed will return to plague us in ways that a Wellsian rationality will be unable to control.

For Wells, the unconscious is not Freud's repressed but active system of values and desires inspired by guilt and in turn generating further guilt, but the instinctual drives that tend to disrupt the rational and ethical organization of civilization. Perhaps it is something like pure *libido* without the complications created by *ego* and *super-ego.* For Wells the unconscious is simply the "primitive" that in his writings of the 1890s he loved to pit against highly evolved "civilization."[12] It is that irradicable trace of the early animal in the evolved human that must be controlled by education and will. Ultimately, Wells's theory of the unconscious is based, not on Freud, but on Darwin and Huxley.

This "evolutionary" conception of the unconscious appears in *Apropos of Dolores,* when Stephen Wilbeck, the novel's narrator and the husband of Dolores, defines Dolores (the Keun figure) as "egotism" and himself (the Wells figure) as "restraint" and argues that the Dolores type must die out in the future. Dolores' egotism, Stephen contends, "is just common humanity unmitigated."[13] He concedes that he and everybody is at the core much the same as Dolores, "but tinted, mercerized . . . , glazed over, trimmed, loaded down," and therefore more advanced, more adapted to the utopian future. For Freud it is the frustration generated by these very overlays that is the source of civilization's discontent. Like Steele's, Wilbeck's analysis, which there is no reason to think of as different from Wells's own, treats the unconscious simply as the evolutionary primitive that must somehow be tamed.

Such an ethical conception of the unconscious may simplify the utopianist's project, but it makes it extremely difficult for Wells to account for his own behavior in the affair with Keun. To allow *Apropos of Dolores* to generate a utopian message rather than a message of despair, Wells must depict Stephen Wilbeck as different from himself in ways that seem minor in the text but are significant given the issues of egotism and restraint. Stephen maintains a strict monogamy. When his first wife has an affair, he promptly divorces her. In his thirteen years of marriage to Dolores, he is never unfaithful. Wells himself—as he makes clear in the *Autobiography, H. G. Wells in Love,* and in his utopian writings—was never committed to monogamy, and in the last years of his affair with Keun he had resumed his passionate relationship with Moura Budberg. The difficult question must arise here: if in the self-justifying fiction of *Apropos of Dolores* he finds it necessary for his moral and social point to make Stephen Wilbeck doggedly and self-sacrificingly "restrained"—and we should note that most of Wells's heroes share these traits of pointed fidelity and rigorous restraint—then what did Wells think of his own comparative unrestraint?

From a utopian perspective, Wells's love life poses a double contradiction. It is, first of all, unrestrained. And yet, and this comes out most clearly in the affair with Keun, it is subject to a mysterious restraint that prevents him from breaking off a relationship he claims he detests. Such a contradiction is common enough in human experience. In Wells's case the experience of his distant and disapproving mother, briefly but movingly depicted in the early scenes of *Tono-Bungay,* may in part account for his clinging to a relationship that seems to offer him very little reward.[14] Nevertheless, my aim here is not to perform an analysis of Wells himself, but to show a point of crisis in Wells's utopian vision. A novel like *Apropos of Dolores* is interesting in this context because in its twistings it reveals some of the strain Wells is undergoing in trying to bring into harmony his own life and his utopian ideals. Wells's anger at Keun and his sense of himself as long-suffering seem to have blinded him to the deeper implications of the affair. But such a work can alert us to issues that we can then find Wells working on, more or less consciously, in his earlier writings. An unstated mystery, which his utopian Voice would like to ignore but which his own life repeatedly brings to his attention, is why, in a world in which happiness should be there for the taking, do people make themselves unhappy. Wells addresses this question quite explicitly even when he is writing about a utopia beyond Sirius or an invasion from Mars.

3

All agree that the botanist in *A Modern Utopia* serves as an increasingly foolish challenge to the main utopian speculations of the book. But the botanist also expresses the "unrestrained" aspect of Wells himself that we have been looking at, which he cannot acknowledge openly, perhaps even to himself, but which he is unable to deny.

This confused and double quality of the botanist, his paradoxical burden of being mocked by the author for speaking matters that are deeply important to the author, is rendered repeatedly in the text. From the beginning, the Voice complains about the botanist in terms that suggest there is more going on here than can be said: "It is strange, but this figure of the botanist will not keep in place. It sprang up between us, dear reader, as a passing illustrative invention. I do not know what put him into my head" (25). This admission of ignorance is casual, but important. It is an acknowledgment that, for the moment at least, the unconscious is dictating. Somewhat later the Voice will again complain that when my whole being should be taken up with speculative wonder, this man should be standing by my side, and lugging my attention persistently towards himself, towards his limited futile self. This thing perpetually happens to me, this intrusion of something small and irrelevant and alive, upon my great impressions. (54)

Such a passage, behind its comedy, speaks to deep issues in Wells's own life and work; if it can be read from the proper angle, the passage warns us that the botanist's presence is not trivial: it is recurrent, important, and, most significantly, "alive." It is essential to Wells's honesty even as he strives to develop his utopia of *will* and *imagination*. The botanist's "paltry egotistical love story" (124; cf. also 69) is, after all, a sketch of the situation Wells will elaborate without comedy in *The Passionate Friends*. "I suppose," the Voice confesses, "I had no power to leave him behind" (179; cf. also 343).

The botanist, then, is an absolutely essential figure for *A Modern Utopia*. Without him, the Voice itself becomes hollow. It might be argued that to attribute so much to such an apparently peripheral figure is to misread the comedy and the repeated trivializations of him in the text. But, as Freud has taught us to see, these very gestures of disregard may be significant; they allow Wells to approach the issues of obsessive and irrational love that the botanist represents and of which Wells himself cannot speak freely and openly.

When the Voice laments, "Is not the suppression of these notes [of amorous sentimentality] my perpetual effort, my undying despair?" (178), he may be acknowledging Wells's own powerful erotic urges in the very act of attempting to exclude them. And the botanist has his own insights into this restrictive aspect of the Voice. At one point, near the end, he complains of the Voice, "You are always talking as though you could kick the past to pieces; as though one could get right out from oneself and begin afresh" (359). This statement is more than just an obstructional balking at utopian energy. In 1904 when he was writing this, Wells may have wished very much that he could "begin afresh" in a number of ways. There are the manifest utopian beginnings, but Wells is also feeling trapped in his marriage. Something here needs to "begin afresh." He is in despair about the power of his amorous impulses, and he dreams of a new, more controlled, utopian self. *A Modern Utopia* can be seen as an attempt to rationalize his frustrations, to keep the botanist in himself, who cannot be entirely denied, at least in his place.

It is a nice irony that a year or two later, when Wells began to meet Amber Reeves at Cambridge, it was the utopian Voice's ideas of group marriage that seem to have, as Wells put it in *H. G. Wells in Love*, "provided all that was necessary for a swift mutual understanding" (75).

4

I am suggesting that part of the power of Wells's work derives from the repressed recognitions in it of desires that he cannot acknowledge and that are incongruent with his rational, utopian ideals but that he is unable to explain away. To put it another way, it is Wells's hypocrisy as a utopian that makes him an honest artist: while he advocates an order of self-controlled Samurai, "advanced" people who will repress and control their egoistic desires, he himself is exploring ways to escape just such repression and control. His writings depict, however covertly, his emotional desires along with his rational ideals.

This complex surface that renders latent and private meanings in terms of a narrative about public events and policies can be seen in fiction that antedates Wells's explicitly utopian formulations of the first part of the century. *The War of the Worlds,* for instance, while on the surface a tale of imperialist guilt and of civilization restored, is also a more private consideration of the emotional drawbacks of the couple. The main symbol of civilization lost and recovered is the narrator's wife, but the attitudes towards the wife are fraught with unexplained negative emotions. It is remarkable that a figure of such profound symbolic import and of such recurrent obligation should be unnamed and undescribed. She is a counter to be moved, an abstract value to be lost.

We get our first clues to the emotional subtext of the novel in the strangely labored quality of the narrator's self-justifications. When he gets his wife to Leatherhead, he gives over the course of two paragraphs three different explanations for why he must leave her again: he has his "promise to the innkeeper," he is "feverishly excited," and he admits "in my heart I was not so very sorry that I had to return to Maybury that night."[15] Any one of these excuses would be adequate; the three of them suggest that the real one is being covered up. Much later he finds himself "praying that the Heat-Ray might have suddenly and painlessly struck her out of being" (428). Of course the manifest meaning here is a humane desire that she be spared suffering, but given the general coolness running through the relationship in the novel, we may well hear a more selfish wish-fantasy in these words.

It is telling that anxiety over the narrator's wife is closely connected with the entrance of the curate. That appearance is a strange narrative moment with an almost hallucinatory quality to it:

> It is a curious thing that I felt angry with my wife; I cannot account for it, but my impotent desire to reach Leatherhead worried me excessively.
>
>   I do not clearly remember the arrival of the curate, so that probably I dozed. I became aware of him as a seated figure. . . . (360–61)

The claim to be anxious about reaching Leatherhead has all the earmarks of a rationalization to prevent further inquiry into the sources of anger that he has just declared to be unaccountable. At this moment of explicit but inexplicable anger at the narrator's wife, the curate appears.

For the middle part of the novel the curate replaces the wife as the narrator's housemate. Now the "anxiety" for the *absent* companion converts to a declared anger at the *present* one, as can be seen in the subtle movement of the following paragraph:

> My mind was occupied by anxiety for my wife. I figured her at Leatherhead, terrified, in danger, mourning me already as a dead man. I paced the rooms and cried aloud when I thought of how I was cut off from her, of all that might happen to her in my absence. My cousin [at whose house she was] I knew was brave enough for any emergency, but he was not the sort of man to realize danger quickly, to rise promptly. What was needed now was not bravery, but circumspection. My only consolation was to believe that the Martians were moving Londonward and away from her. Such vague anxieties keep the mind sensitive and painful. I grew very weary and irritable with the curate's perpetual ejaculations; tired of the sight of his selfish despair. After some ineffectual remonstrance I kept away from him. . . . (399)

The elision of the two figures of the wife and curate that the prose performs here is carried out in the plot. The narrator and the curate live together, squabbling over household economics, until the narrator, in self-defense, to prevent the curate from revealing their hiding place, clubs him and leaves him to be taken by the Martians. It is a moment of ambiguous responsibilities,[16] not unlike that which terminates Dolores' life in the novel written forty years later.

The expressions of irritation at the curate are echoed in the contemptuous descriptions of Mrs. Elphinstone's yearning for her husband "George," which is, of course, Wells's own name. Mrs.

Elphinstone, like the narrator's wife, has become separated from her competent husband, and instead of rising to the occasion (like her sister-in-law), she falls into helpless whinings. She is a completely gratuitous figure as far as the plot of the novel goes, but she is an important presence insofar as she allows the novel to complain about wives without admitting that *the* wife is an object of complaint.

If the curate and Mrs. Elphinstone represent a bitter commentary on the trap of domesticity, the Artilleryman, in his satire on the ordinary man's "little miserable skeddadle through the world" (433) becomes, momentarily, a powerful critic of the domestic ideal: "No proud dreams and no proud lusts; and a man who hasn't one or the other—Lord! what is he but funk and precautions?" "Dreams" here probably mean not utopian ideals, but something like the ambitions of uncle Teddy Ponderevo. Here is a real promise to "begin afresh"! But then the novel takes another twist and renders the vision of amorous liberation as empty boasting. At the same time it treats as impossible the Artilleryman's other dream of an organized underground, a sort of prefiguration of the Open Conspiracy. The amorous and the utopian promises all collapse, and the narrator again leaves home.

The War of the Worlds is an extraordinary work for the way in which it manages to combine creative exuberance and deep pessimism. We can partially account for this combination by observing that the Martians, at one level, offer a fantasy of freedom from the snare of domesticity. Like the Voice in *A Modern Utopia,* they seem to offer an opportunity to "kick the past to pieces" so that the sane man can "begin afresh." The emptiness the narrator feels at the death of the last Martian may be partly caused by his sense that his liberation has been frustrated.[17] And the joy of the final reunion of husband and wife is severely muted. The novel's final words tell, not of promise and renewal, but of the hostile and forbidden thoughts that the novel has lived out: "And strangest of all is it to hold my wife's hand again, and to think that I have counted her, and that she has counted me, among the dead."

5

I do not mean to suggest that Wells was unusual or immoral for having such fantasies. Freud tells us that it is not the fantasies, but the failure to find some outlet for them, that is the cause of "discontent." Wells, of course, went beyond fantasy—not to the point of killing his wife, but certainly to the extent of escaping domesticity. As he became a more active and promiscuous lover, however, he must have had a difficult time reconciling his behavior with his ideals of utopian discipline.

Early in *A Modern Utopia,* the Voice, considering for a moment how energetic and charismatic personalities will fit into Utopia, wonders, "What, for instance, will Utopia do with Mr. Roosevelt?" (28) This is, of course, a serious question in itself, but we may be missing the real implications if we do not see that behind it lies an even more difficult, though private, question: "What will Utopia do with H. G. Wells?" In his fiction, we can see Wells, obliquely to be sure, but relentlessly too, considering the difficulties his powerful emotions create. Wells is half conscious of these difficulties, but he also, for perfectly understandable reasons, is not likely to be the first person to point to them. After all, his utopian ideal of discipline and restraint was not advanced by the complex and disruptive awarenesses his own life and experience generate. If we are to understand the totality of his enterprise, we need to see past the efficient and persuasive rhetorical surface to the more complex dynamics of each individual Wellsian text. This project does not mean denying the surface meaning, but it does involve inspecting it closely, questioning it, and relating it to Wells's own life.

Notes

1. F. R. Leavis, *Two Cultures? The Significance of C. P. Snow. Being the Richmond Lecture, 1962* (New York: Pantheon Books, 1963).

2. George Orwell, "Wells, Hitler, and the World State," *The Collected Essays, Journalism and Letters of George Orwell,* ed. Sonia Orwell and Ian Angus (New York: Harcourt, Brace, and World, 1968). 11:139–45.

3. H. G. Wells, *The New Machiavelli* (New York: Duffield & Co., 1910), 6. Subsequent quotations from this work are cited parenthetically in the text.

4. Wells, *A Modern Utopia* (1905; Lincoln: University of Nebraska Press. 1968), 368. Subsequent quotations from this work are cited parenthetically in the text.

5. Wells, *Marriage* (1912; London: Hogarth Press, 1986), 222.

6. Wells described his mode of life in somewhat abstract terms in his *Experiment in Autobiography* (1934) and in rather more explicit terms in *H. G. Wells in Love* (published posthumously, 1984). For other angles on this matter, *see* Norman and Jeanne MacKenzie, *H. G. Wells* (New York: Simon & Schuster, 1973); Anthony West, *H. G. Wells: Aspects of a Life* (New York: Random House, 1984); and David C. Smith, *H. G. Wells: Desperately Mortal* (New Haven: Yale University Press, 1986).

7. Even as he portrays the lovers in the novel as "bad" people who injure friends and destroy the promise of utopian reform in England, Wells here, as he will do later in *Apropos of Dolores,* finds it necessary to vary from the reality of his own situation. Remington, though he has engaged in some brief sexual escapades before his marriage, is a faithful husband until after his wife locks him out and he falls passionately "in love" with Isabel Rivers.

8. Wells, *H. G. Wells in Love: Postscript to an Experiment in Autobiography,* ed. G. P. Wells (Boston: Little, Brown and Co., 1984), 55.

9. Ibid., 55.

10. The botanist has been discussed by Mark Hillegas in his introduction to the Nebraska reprint of *A Modern Utopia,* by David Hughes in "The Mood of *A Modern Utopia,*" *Extrapolation,* 19 (1977), 56–57, and by myself in *The Logic of Fantasy: H. G. Wells and Science Fiction* (New York: Columbia University Press, 1982), 168.

11. Wells, *The Anatomy of Frustration: A Modern Synthesis* (New York: Macmillan, 1936), 51.

12. Huntington, *The Logic of Fantasy,* 16–17.

13. Wells, *Apropos of Dolores* (New York: Scribners, 1938), 159.

14. *See* Nancy Steffan-Fluhr, "Paper Tiger: Women in H. G. Wells," *Science-Fiction Studies* 37 (1985), 313.

15. Wells, *The War of the Worlds* in *Seven Science Fiction Novels of H. G. Wells* (New York: Dover Publications, 1934), 340. Subsequent quotations from this work are cited parenthetically in the text.

16. *See* Huntington, *The Logic of Fantasy,* 75.

17. Ibid., 63, 81.

Wells and Positivism

Martha S. Vogeler

"Pseudo-scientific interlopers" is what Wells called the English Positivists in 1906 when addressing the fledgling Sociological Society. Yet they were the followers of Auguste Comte, who had coined the term "sociologic" and claimed to have originated the scientific study of society. Wells argued that sociology was neither simply science nor art, but knowledge "rendered imaginatively, and with an element of personality; that is to say, in the highest sense of the term, literature." He was defining sociology to exclude Positivism, as he conceived it, and to include utopias, the literary form in which he excelled.[1] In *Experiment in Autobiography,* published almost three decades later, he acknowledged that he had been unjust to Comte. Though conscious of having "a real personal dislike" for him, as for Marx, and a "genuine reluctance to concede him any sort of leadership," Wells felt obliged to recognize Comte's "sort of priority . . . in sketching the modern outlook." The problem lay in the "deification" of such thinkers. They should "guide as far as they can—and then vanish."[2]

Wells exaggerated the veneration felt for Comte by his English followers. They were, in fact, embarrassed by the personal life of the philosopher, who had died in 1857, a decade before their conversion to his system was completed. They kept their distance from his more orthodox disciples in France, Mexico, and Brazil (even while supporting the Paris organization financially) and, significantly, called themselves Positivists, not Comtists. Highly selective in choosing concepts from Comte's writings for English consumption, they ignored much in the major English versions of his works: Harriet Martineau's free English translation of *The Positive Philosophy,* their own translation of the four-volume *System of Positive Polity,* and Richard Congreve's of *The Catechism of Positive Religion.*[3]

How much Wells knew about these primary sources of Comte's thought is unknown, but the leading London Positivists could hardly have escaped his notice long before their claim to a voice in the Sociological Society. Oxford-educated and well-connected professional men, they had begun contributing to important London journals in the 1860s, and newspapers generously reported their speeches and addresses. They were hence familiar to British intellectuals by 1888, the year Wells at age twenty-one was desperately seeking an escape from underpaid teaching. His strategy was to ask Dr. William Job Collins, a friend of his mother's employer at Uppark, to find him a position as assistant to some busy London writer in the "world of liberal thought." Wells named as prospects Bernard Shaw, "The Huxleys," and Frederic Harrison, the most talented and versatile of Positivist authors.[4] Recalling this episode in his autobiography, Wells depicts Collins as a second-generation Positivist, but I have found no evidence for the label; perhaps it can be explained by the association of Collins and Harrison in London politics. Two years before he was approached by young Wells for help, Collins had enlisted Harrison as the Gladstonian candidate for London University in the General Election (he lost), and after 1889 they were allies in London County Council affairs.[5]

Harrison, who was fifty-six when Wells mentioned him to Collins, had been ubiquitous in London political and religious controversies since the 1860s. He had broken with his former Oxford tutor, Richard Congreve, organizer of the Positivist Society in the late 1860s, and formed a new group with men of his own Oxford generation—John Henry Bridges, a public health physician; and Edward Spencer Beesly, professor of history at University College—along with James Cotter Morison, a man of independent means and something of a dilettante; and Vernon and Godfrey Lushington, twin sons of a noted judge and themselves senior civil servants. In 1881 Harrison's group opened a center for classes, meetings, and socials in a room in the Royal Scottish Corporation building in Fetter Lane, off Fleet Street, and called it Newton Hall.

In naming Harrison as a possible mentor, young Wells chose more wisely than he could have known. A man of considerable independent means and wide cultural interests, Harrison had already proved useful to two aspiring writers, one very poor and the other very rich, and both later friends of Wells: George Gissing, whom Harrison virtually discovered; and Beatrice Potter, whose early studies of labor he encouraged. But Collins declined to intercede for his young friend, and Wells had to make his own way by his pen. Ironically, he later recalled that his first readers included the kind of people who subscribed to the *Positivist Review,* founded by Harrison's associate Beesly in 1893.[6] Wells did not write for it himself; it did not pay contributors, and he needed to augment his teacher's salary. In any case, much in Positivism was at odds with his thinking at the time. In 1895 he gave a harsh reception to a new periodical, *The Evergreen,* one of the many enterprises of the biologist and future town planner Patrick Geddes, who was on the fringe of the Positivist movement, aided by the biologist J. A. Thompson, and Victor Branford, an accountant later active in the early Sociological Society with Geddes.[7] Their laudable attempt to bring science, literature, and art together in their journal was undercut for Wells by their belief that viewing the struggle for existence as nature's "sole method of progress" overlooked the important role of the social virtues in human evolution—reasoning Wells dismissed as a "kind of pulpit science."[8]

Wells probably did not know at the time that Geddes, like himself, had been Huxley's pupil in London. Geddes's student years, a decade before Wells's own, had coincided with Huxley's controversy with Congreve and Harrison over Comte's Religion of Humanity, which Huxley had derided as "Catholicism minus Christianity."[9] Geddes, unconvinced, had sought out the Positivists in their first meeting room, in Chapel Street (now Rugby Street), Bloomsbury, and remained on friendly terms with its leaders and later with the breakaway Positivists at Newton Hall. Though never active in the organized movement—he had too many irons in the fire for that—he became a spokesman for some of its principles.[10] His views about biological evolution, for example, owed something to Comte, who, writing before Darwin or Alfred Russel Wallace, attributed man's ascendancy over other animals to his unique powers of cooperation. Wells in the 1890s conceived of man's emergence in a quite opposite way—as an accident rather than as a product of moral behavior. That Wells thought man closer to his animal ancestors than did Thompson and Geddes is evident in *The Island of Doctor Moreau.* Indeed, Wells was haunted by an even darker notion, man's possible extinction as a species, a theme of *The Time Machine* and *The War of the Worlds.* But before the end of the century, Wells was optimistically turning his attention to "artificial evolution," the process whereby man, the "culminating ape," ameliorates the untoward effects of natural selection through education and applied science.[11]

Once embarked on this new road, Wells planted signposts pointing to variously named destinations: the "New Republic," the "Open Conspiracy," the "World State." But no matter what its windings, Wells's path often seemed headed for a utopia that resembled Comte's because of their common insistence on a planned industrial order, the importance of science and great literature in education, and the notion of a world state that would eliminate nationalism and war. Of course, there were differences between the two social visions. To take only one: Wells anticipated at least some of our ideas of women's expanded role in society, whereas Comte and his followers were even more retrograde on this score than most thinkers of the period. Since Wells's utopian vision changed somewhat from book to book, generalizations are risky. But surely W. Warren Wagar, the scholar who has written most thoroughly on Wells and the world state, is right in saying that Comte would not have felt out of place in some of the societies imagined by Wells.[12]

The development of utopian ideals in Wells's canon can be seen in part at least as a response to Huxley's Romanes Lecture in 1893. Since Wells published one of his earliest essays in the *Fortnightly Review* in 1891, he would surely have known of Huxley's controversy with Harrison in that journal in the intervening year.[13] Harrison, still smarting under Huxley's criticism of Positivism in the 1860s and at meetings of the Metaphysical Society in the 1870s, had demanded that Huxley say whether his agnosticism was merely a state of mind about religion or a substitute for religion. If the latter, Harrison argued, agnosticism should deal with the great moral issues of life, as did Positivism. In his Romanes Lecture, Huxley sought to do just that, declaring in his often-quoted formulation that "social progress means a checking of the cosmic process at every step, and the substitution for it of another, which may be called the ethical process." Harrison purported to regard this assertion as evidence of Huxley's conversion to Positivist theory, and Huxley obligingly declared that they had buried the hatchet.[14] It seems probable that the Romanes Lecture contributed to the shift in Wells's interest about this time from biological issues, such as man's relation to the animals, to social issues, such as man's evolving ethical sense. There is nothing in his 1895 *Fortnightly Review* essay, "Human Evolution: An Artificial Process," to offend a Positivist.

When Wells delivered his paper to the Sociological Society in 1906, Geddes was in the chair. The first commentator he called upon was the Positivist who had succeeded Harrison as head of the Newton Hall group, Hugh Shapland Swinny. He pointed to similarities between Wells's view of sociology and Comte's (their interest in the sequence of social states, and their rejection of experimentation as a method of social study). He also defined a few differences (Comte was more optimistic about objectivity in sociology than Wells, and thought that discovering the laws of social progress was sociology's main goal); and he pressed Wells on his quarrel with Comte. Wells replied that the gist of the matter was whether sociology would make prophecy possible, which he denied.[15] He seems to have harboured the erroneous belief, still common, that Comte's Positivism implied quantification, though Comte had placed sociology at the top of his hierarchy of the sciences to indicate that while it drew some methodologies from them, it differed from them in dealing with issues too complex to allow for prediction or statistical analysis.[16]

However they construed the relevance of science to the study of society, both Wells and the Positivists were unabashed elitists. Moreover, neither he nor they made entirely plain how the enlightened would prevail. Wells's exemplars in the novels often do not. Comte, on the contrary, always exhibited the unreflecting confidence of the zealot. And while Wells frequently depicted his "Open Conspirators" as members of the professional classes, Comte decreed that a combination of male philosophers and working-class leaders would usher in the Positivist era. In his new dispensation, politics and journalism would disappear, their reforming functions no longer needed. Heading the new industrial order would be bankers and engineers; directing the new spiritual realm, which included education as well as religion, would be a priesthood centered in Paris. The Newton Hall Positivists ignored much of the reactionary detail in Comte's blueprint for a new temporal order, practised only attenuated versions of his religious rituals, and stressed the principles most obviously in tune with conventional English assumptions, such as the duty of venerating civilization's great men and women, the moral superiority of women, and the importance of the family. There was no speculation about how different everyday life would be in the Positivist state because of new ideals and technology. Here the contrast with Wells is apparent.

In 1903 Wells's publisher sent *Mankind in the Making* to Harrison, probably hoping for a review. Before finishing the book, Harrison wrote to thank Wells, explaining that guests, who included Henry James (a bit of name-dropping here) had kept taking it from his study. Finally reading the work himself, Harrison said he was "considering many of its problems" (a somewhat ambiguous statement). He added that so complex a subject as the "up-bringing of the race" allowed for differences of opinion. And it was not Wells's opinion but his interpretation of birth and death rates that Harrison faulted, offering his own, for unlike Comte, Harrison used statistics when they served his purposes.[17] The issue, in this case, was minor, however, and Swinny's discussion of Wells's book in the *Positivist Review* was favorable.[18] When Wells wrote to Harrison thanking him for a copy of the issue, Harrison, then retired in rural

Kent, feigned surprise that an author "to whom the future belongs" had consulted an out-of-date post office directory and sent his letter to Harrison's obsolete London address.[19]

Wells took his revenge in his next novel, *The Food of the Gods*, by portraying Harrison, the only actual person named, as a critic of the new "boomfood" that creates giants. Wells has him enlisted by the Society for the Preservation of Ancient Statures (a lovely pun) and writing an essay denouncing the miraculous comestible as "vulgar, and entirely inharmonious with that Revelation of Humanity that is found in the teachings of Comte."[20]

Thus tagged as an old fogey, Harrison could only assure Wells that at seventy-three he still enjoyed the "brilliant fun of those who have the world before them."[21] A similar mixture of irony, admiration, and envy informs his comment to Wells after reading *A Modern Utopia* in 1905: "Dream, young man, dream boldly: and thy Dreams will be prophecies!"[22]

We should remember that in the 1890s, when Wells's literary fame began, the influence of Positivism was declining due to the advanced age or death of its original promoters, their failure to find successors as gifted as themselves, and the waning interest in the Victorian religious controversies in which the Positivists had made their name. After the turn of the century, the Newton Hall group was reduced to meeting in hired rooms until its reunion during World War I with the similarly depleted little band at Chapel Street. Its leader was Philip Thomas, a civil servant whose unimaginative dogmatism not only betrayed the Positivist vision but had already tainted the childhood of his son, the poet Edward Thomas. In the *Positivist Review* in 1909, Philip Thomas embraced the author of *First and Last Things* as "clearly one of those 'instinctive Positivists' mentioned by Auguste Comte in his 'Polity'." Wells's depiction of mankind's history as the slow unfolding of a "sense of community," and his account of the living were rightly seen by Thomas as key Positivist tenets, whether or not Wells was aware of the similarities. But *Ann Veronica* the following year destroyed whatever illusions Thomas may have entertained about Wells as an expounder of Positivism. Reviewing the novel with the same righteous indignation that proved so trying to his son, Thomas warned his Positivist readers that the story was about a woman who "revolts from parental control"; in place of Comte's maxim "*Live for others*" Wells offered Nietzsche's "decadent doctrine": "*Live for yourself alone, and never mind the others.*"[23]

The war that made a poet of Philip Thomas's son made something of a religious mystic of Wells. Despairing over the slaughter in

France and of Europe's future, and no longer confident that scientific rationalism could produce social progress, he surprised and dismayed his admirers with a series of novels presenting religious ideas that were reminiscent of Positivism. Having previously conceived of an emergent collective mind of the species, which recalled Comte's conception of Humanity, in *Mr Britling Sees it Through* in 1917 Wells conjured up a "Finite God, who is king of man's adventure in space and time," the "Captain of the World Republic." Then, by his own account, he turned his New Republic into a "divine monarchy" in *God the Invisible King;* offered a "new personification of human progressiveness" in *The Soul of a Bishop;* and "strongly flavoured" *Joan and Peter* and *The Undying Fire* with "deified humanism." After a final brief appearance of God as a character in *The Secret Places of the Heart* in 1922, he returned, he says, to "the sturdy atheism" of his youth.[24]

Writing of this religious phase in Wells's career, Wagar notes that if it had been Wells's way to work out his ideas in detail, he could have "made something of a splash in twentieth-century religious thought."[25] Perhaps. But he might thereby have met the same fate as the Positivists, whose Religion of Humanity was everywhere ridiculed, though one of its essential ideas, the survival of individuals in the good they have done and in the thoughts of the living, became part of secular humanism. To the Positivists, Wells's "God the Invisible King" seemed both too vague and too close to their own notion of humanity for acceptance. In a dialogue set in an Oxford college, Harrison has a Junior Fellow back from the trenches tell a churchman and an elderly barrister (that is, Harrison) about his conversion to "the invisible God of our premier novelist." The churchman replies that without a bible or system of morals, one couldn't know if such a god inspires truth or falsehood, virtue or vice; and the barrister complains about a mere "sensation" being termed a god. But Harrison, as usual, was having it both ways: his barrister also thinks Wells's god owes much to Comte's idea of humanity—indeed, that Comte was Wells's "Invisible prompter."[26] Philip Thomas said much the same thing in the *Positivist Review,* but without Harrison's wit.[27]

Though Wells thought he had left his religious phase behind him, when his wife was dying in 1927 he began to plan for a quasi-religious service to precede the cremation she had requested. For advice he turned to Dr. Frank Hayward, a Positivist prominent in education circles, who gave him a little book of all-purpose funeral addresses composed by Frederick J. Gould, another Positivist educator. Writing to Gould, Wells explained his intention of "imitating and plagiarizing" the service in the book designed for a person of middle age.[28] According to Mrs. Bernard Shaw's account, the reading of the text Wells devised, the organ music, and Wells's uncontrolled sobs together provided an effect that was "dreadful . . . beyond anything words can describe."[29] We should not be too surprised that Wells proved impervious to quasi-Positivist consolation. He once told an interviewer that his favorite bedside book was *The Service of Man,* by the Positivist Cotter Morison, a work that displeased Morison's own Newton Hall colleagues because it cast doubt on the power of *any* religion to mitigate suffering or insure mortality.[30] Wells, overcome by his loss—and perhaps by guilt, if he thought of the pain his philandering had caused his wife—was in no state to be comforted by mere words.

As a promoter of a world federation of states in the years following the war, Wells seemed to be taking over the Positivist mission. In the shape of things to come according to Comte, large nations would be subdivided to banish the nationalistic fervor that led to war. Nations would be bound in harmony by a common Religion of Humanity rooted in the Positivist reading of social and religious evolution. In Wells's utopian vision also, a common reading of humanity's past unites mankind and provides a vision of the future. It was to provide such a universal history that he produced his most ambitious and ultimately his best selling work, *The Outline of History,* published serially in 1919 and as a book in 1920. Its idealistic purpose, vast scope, and synthetic character inevitably reminded the Positivists of the sketch of human history Comte had provided in his *Positivist Polity* with a purpose not unlike Wells's.

There is indeed evidence that among the many strands of scholarship Wells wove into his rich historical tapestry, several had Positivist origins. In some editions he refers to Gould's "excellent pamphlet" *History, the Supreme Subject in the Instruction of the Young* (1918), which in its title alone states one thesis of Wells's book. Wells also says he found "an admirable summary of human progress" in *The Living Past,* published in 1913 by Francis S. Marvin, another Positivist who promoted history in the schools. Moreover, we know from Wells's correspondence with Marvin that his *Century of Hope: Western Progress from 1815 to the Great War* proved useful when Wells moved into the last part of his long journey from prehistoric to modern man, and that Marvin probably read over part of that section of Wells's text before its publication.[31] In *The Outline,* Wells thanks Marvin, along with Frank Hayward, and, of course, many, many others.

Important among them was Gilbert Murray, the Oxford classicist.

Three decades earlier, at the outset of a long and distinguished career, Murray had been coopted by Marvin to write entries for the Positivists' *New Calendar of Great Men,* a highly ambitious chronological biographical dictionary of the 559 worthies named in the Positivist Calendar. Conceived of by Harrison, the general editor, as a kind of universal history, the work took years to complete, and Harrison's occasional impatience with his collaborators prefigured Wells's complaints as he was producing two sequels to *The Outline of History.* But Wells was richly rewarded for his labors by phenomenal sales of all three works and generally favorable reviews, whereas the Positivist tome proved too scholarly for the ordinary reader and too colored by an alien creed for the educated.[32]

Thus we can imagine what it cost the Positivists to add their voices to the general acclaim that greeted *The Outline of History,* especially since they were just then issuing an enlarged edition of the *New Calendar,* subsidized by the almost defunct London Positivist Society. (The volume had no more appeal than the first edition.) In praising *The Outline of History* in the *Positivist Review,* Marvin remarked on the absence of any reference to Comte.[33] And when Wells published an essay asserting he had been the first to respond to the need for "a general account of man's story in the universe," Harrison fired off a long letter to him claiming priority for the Positivists. They had been popularizing universal history in their lectures and writings for half a century; his own first book, *The Meaning of History,* in 1862, had been just such a synoptic effort. Even more aggressively than Marvin, he taxed Wells for not acknowledging a debt to Comte.[34] Then almost ninety, Harrison had been making such a complaint about other writers since before Wells was born: George Eliot, Ruskin, Mill, Arnold, and Huxley were only some of the Victorians whose works had seemed to him to contain unacknowledged Positivism. In his frustration, he ought to have remembered Comte's teaching that all achievements of mankind enrich collective humanity and benefit all. But such a thought could no more comfort Harrison in his frustration than those quasi-Positivist pieties would comfort the distraught Wells at his wife's funeral.[35]

Notes

1. H. G. Wells, "The So-Called Science of Sociology," *Sociological Papers* (London: Macmillan, 1907), 3:357–69.
2. Wells, *Experiment in Autobiography* (New York: Macmillan, 1934), 562.

3. *See* my *Frederic Harrison: The Vocations of a Positivist* (Oxford: Clarendon Press, 1984) for details on Harrison and the Positivists not otherwise documented in this paper.

4. Wells. *Experiment in Autobiography*, 248, 251–53; Geoffrey West, *H. G. Wells: A Sketch for a Portrait* (London: Gerald Howe, 1930), 74–76.

5. On Collins (who was knighted in 1902), *see* his papers at University of London Library, Senate House, and letters in the Frederic Harrison Collection in the British Library of Political and Economic Science, London School of Economics.

6. Patrick Parrinder, ed. *H. G. Wells: The Critical Heritage* (London and Boston, Routledge and Kegan Paul, 1972), 2, citing Wells to Frederick Macmillan, 26 September 1904 (Macmillan Papers, British Library).

7. Paddy Kitchen, *A Most Unsettling Person: An Introduction to the Ideas and Life of Patrick Geddes* (London: Victor Gollancz, 1975), especially 150–53.

8. Wells, "Bio-Optimism", a review of *The Evergreen: A Northern Seasonal*, in *Nature* 52 (29 August 1895): 410–11, reprinted in *H. G. Wells: Early Writings in Science and Science Fiction*, edited, with critical commentary and notes, by Robert M. Philmus and David Y. Hughes (Berkeley: University of California Press, 1975), 206–10.

9. *See* Sydney Eisen, "Huxley and the Positivists," *Victorian Studies* 7 (June 1964): 337–58.

10. Patrick Geddes, "Introduction," in Susan Liveing, *A Nineteenth-Century Teacher: John Henry Bridges* (London: Kegal Paul, Trench, Trübner, 1926).

11. Philmus and Hughes, *H. G. Wells*, 1–12, 183–86.

12. W. Warren Wagar, *H. G. Wells and the World State* (New Haven: Yale University Press, 1961), 224; many other passages discuss similarities between Wells and Comte.

13. The thesis of "Rediscovery of the Unique," *Fortnightly Review* new series 50 (July 1891): 106–11, reprinted in Philmus and Hughes, H. G. Wells, 22–31, that the mind perceives of relationships among phenomena despite their actual differences, recalls Comte's distinction between objective and subjective reality.

14. *See* my *Frederic Harrison,* 226–27, on a subsequent outburst of Harrison's, and Sydney Eisen, "Huxley and the Positivists," *Victorian Studies* 7 (June 1964): 337–58. On Huxley's influence on Wells, *see* Bernard Bergonzi, *The Early H. G. Wells* (Toronto: University of Toronto Press, 1961), 106.

15. *Sociological Papers* 3:370–71 (Swinny), 3:376–77 (Wells).

16. *See* Christopher Kent's entries on Comte and on Positivism in *The Encyclopaedia of Unbelief,* ed. by Gordon Stein (Buffalo: Prometheus Books, 1985), Vol. I, and the Appendix on Positivism in Sydney Eisen and Bernard V. Lightman, *Victorian Science and Religion: A Bibliography with Emphasis on Evolution, Belief, and Unbelief . . .* (Hamden, Conn.: Archon, 1984).

17. Harrison to Wells, 19 November 1903 (University of Illinois, Urbana-Champaign).

18. H. S. Swinny, "Mankind in the Making," *Positivist Review* 13 (December 1903), 275–78.

19. Harrison to Wells, 15 December 1903 (University of Illinois, Urbana-Champaign).

20. Wells, *The Food of the Gods,* chap. 4, sec. 2, "The Dawn of the Food." (Harrison's first name is given a final k, a common error that annoyed him.)

21. Harrison to Wells, 5 October 1904 (University of Illinois, annotated by Wells, "No answer"). In the months between this and the previous letters, Harrison and Wells had corresponded about Gissing's death and plans for his children.

22. Harrison to Wells, 15 April 1905 (University of Illinois,).

23. "The Positivism of Mr. H. G. Wells," *Positivist Review* 17 (June 1909): 135–41; "The Sins of Ann Veronica," 18 (March 1910): 64–66 (Thomas's italics).

24. Wells, *Experiment in Autobiography,* 574 (quoting from *God the Invisible King*), 8.

25. Wagar, 105.

26. Harrison to Marvin, Easter Monday, 1919 (Bodleian Library, Oxford, MS Eng. lett. c. 266, fols. 68–69); "A Very Invisible God," *Nineteenth-Century and After,* 82 (October 1917), 771–81.

27. P. Thomas, "Mr Wells's Essay in God-Making," *The Positivist Review* 35 (July and December 1917), 153–58, 273. The resemblance to Comte's religion was noted by William Archer, *God and Mr Wells: A Critical Examination of 'God and the Invisible King'* (London: Watts, 1917), 70, 91, 97.

28. Wells, Introduction, *The Book of Catherine Wells* (London: Chatto and Windus, 1928), 31; Wells to Gould, 26 September 1927, photostat in Wells Collection (University of Illinois), quoted; Wells to Hayward (card tipped into a copy of *Experiment in Autobiography* in the Wells Collection, Bromley Public Library). I am indebted to Dr. Ian D. MacKillop for information on Hayward and Gould. On Gould's *Funeral Services without Theology,* published for the Rationalist Press Association (London: Watts & Co., 1906), *see* review by H. S. Swinny in *The Positivist Review* 14 (September 1906), 215, and copy of Gould's text in the British Library.

29. Norman and Jeanne MacKenzie, *The Time Traveller: The Life of H. G. Wells* (London: Weidenfeld and Nicolson, 1973), 353, quoting a letter in Janet Dunbar, *Mrs G. B. S* (New York: Harper and Row, 1963).

30. Georges Connes, *Etude sur la Pensée de Wells* (Paris: Libraire Hachette, 1926), 363; *see also* 362, 377, and Appendix 3.

31. Wells to Marvin, Tues. [23 October 1919], and two undated letters (F. S. Marvin Papers, Bodleian Library, Oxford, MS Eng. lett. c. 266, fols. 212, 216, 222). Wells's lecture, "An Apologia for a World Utopia," at the Unity Schools meetings, August 1920, arranged in conjunction with the League of Nations Union, is in *The Evolution of World Peace,* edited by Marvin, (1921), (Freeport, N.Y.: Books for Libraries Press, 1968), 159–78.

32. *See* my *Frederic Harrison,* 298, 354–56; MacKenzie, *The Time Traveller,* 321; Wells's correspondence with Gilbert Murray in the Bodleian Library.

33. "Mr. Wells's *Outline of History,*" *The Positivist Review* 29 (July 1921): 152–56.

34. Wells, "History for Everybody: A Postscript to *The Outline of History,*" *The Fortnightly Review* 115 (June 1921), 887–910; Harrison to Wells, 25 June 1921 (University of Illinois); *see also* Harrison to Marvin, 11 December 1921, reiterating the complaint (F. S. Marvin Papers, Bodleian Library, Oxford, MS Eng. lett. c. 260, fols. 155–56 [misfiled with 1911 letters]); Harrison to Lord Rosebery, 7 Dec 1920 (National Library of Scotland, Edinburgh), calling *The Outline* "good" and "quite original"; *see* a typed unsigned copy of a letter from Hayward to Wells, 16 December 1939, in a copy of *Experiment in Autobiography,* Wells Collection, Bromley Public Library, asking if he had known Gould, who had tried without success to interest educators in "SYNTHESIS on the basis of HISTORY THE TEACHER" [sic].

35. Letters and a telegram from Harrison to Wells (University of Illinois) show that he questioned but eventually endorsed Wells's unsuccessful Parliamentary candidacy in 1922.

Wells and "the So-Called Science of Sociology"

Krishan Kumar

The Idea of a Scientific Sociology

In a recent discussion on Moscow television, a visiting British minister of state used the term "utopian" disparagingly. A Russian journalist, more knowledgeable about these things perhaps than his counterparts elsewhere, reproved him. He pointed out that it was an Englishman, Thomas More, who invented the term and concept of utopia, and in so doing launched an honorable and fertile tradition of social thought upon the world. It ill became a later Englishman to be so contemptuous of this tradition, and so blind to its constructive possibilities.[1]

The Russians, as is well known, have a fondness not just for More but also for Wells. Despite the official view of him as a "bourgeois" thinker, intellectuals of all kinds have been influenced by Wells's thinking about the future of industrial civilization. They have admired him, that is, as much as a sociologist as an inspired writer of science fantasies. For them, the author of *Anticipations, Mankind in the Making, A Modern Utopia, The Outline of History,* and many other volumes of social criticism and social speculation, is as important as the author of *The Time Machine, The War of the Worlds,* and *The Shape of Things to Come.* Or rather, and rightly, they refuse to put these two kinds of writing into rigidly separate compartments. We may be sceptical of a "sociology of literature"; but Wells's example ought surely to make us look more sympathetically at the practice of "literary sociology," of which he was the supreme exponent in recent English writing.[2]

British sociologists are at one with British politicians in their indifference to, and ignorance of, the native utopian tradition. This may have something to do with British sociology's debt to Fabianism—at least, that orthodox strand of Fabianism that found it impossible to accommodate Wells.[3] When Edward Bellamy's wildly popular *Looking Backward* appeared in 1888, British Fabians were nonplussed by this rendering of socialist ideas in utopian form. George Bernard Shaw's reaction was typical: "We rather turned up our noses at Utopias as cheap stuff until Wells stood up for them." But Wells's championing of utopias was one of the many things that put him explosively at odds with the Fabian leadership. British Fabians were even more anxious than Continental socialists to repudiate the utopian strain in socialism. Socialism was scentific or it was nothing; mere moralizing and metaphysics. Of a piece with Friedrich Engels's canonical rejection of "utopian socialism" was Sidney Webb's stiff-necked response to Bellamy's utopia: "It cannot be too often repeated that Socialism, to Socialists, is not a Utopia which they have invented, but a principle of social organization which they assert to have been discovered by the patient investigators into sociology whose labours have distinguished the present century."[4]

Sociology, like late ninteenth-century socialism, has always striven to be "scientific." It reveres as its founders the Positivist sociologists Auguste Comte and Herbert Spencer, together with their immediate successors such as Emile Durkheim. Karl Marx too it has warmly embraced—but Marx the scientific anatomist of capitalist society, not Marx the prophet and revolutionary. Together with Max Weber, all of these can be pressed into the service of a Positivistic "value-free" sociology. This is a sociology that takes as its paradigm the model and method of the natural sciences. Sociology, like the physical sciences, must observe, compare, classify; it must establish regularities and formulate testable laws, like the laws of physics and chemistry.

It was against this conception of sociology that Wells delivered his counterblast at a meeting of the London Sociological Society in 1906. In a paper entitled "The So-Called Science of Sociology"— one regrettably ignored by Wellsians as much as sociologists— Wells chose "to deny that sociology is a science . . . and to throw doubt upon the value of sociology that follows too closely what is called the scientific method." Sociology was indeed "a new and fruitful system of human inquiry"; but its promise would be stillborn if it were to be developed largely by the disciples of Comte and Spencer. Instead, in a bold reassertion of the continuing relevance of the ancient Greek social philosophers, Wells asks us "to go to Plato for the proper method, the proper way of thinking sociologically."[5]

It is interesting and, in view of the received stereotype of Wells as the archapostle of science, somewhat unexpected that Wells considers and rejects the possibility that sociology might after all be a science, but one of a different kind from physics or chemistry. Why not say, with many apologists for a "scientific sociology," that there are many different kinds of science, suited to different natural and social phenomena? Why should sociology not be considered scientific, differing from physics no less but no more than do astronomy or physiology? But Wells will have none of this. His objection is not simply that such a procedure will cause confusion and imprecision in inquiry and discussion. More fundamentally, he wants to drive a wedge between the inorganic sciences—the sphere of science proper—and all those disciplines concerned with the study of living things. Sociology is not a science because life—and *a fortiori* human social life—cannot be studied scientifically. Wells, despite widespread belief to the contrary, was no Positivist. He did not believe in a single unified scientific method embracing the whole universe. Science *in* society was one thing, and a supremely urgent and important one; a science *of* society was quite another and, in Wells's view, impossible and undesirable.

Let us accept, says Wells, that "science" is that method that we find in the inorganic sciences, expecially those of physics and chemistry. Its peculiar strength here is that it deals in millions of more or less identical units—atoms, ions, and so forth. It is this fundamental homogeneity of material, in bulk quantities, that makes possible the scientific method of counting, comparison, and experimental proof. In both professional and popular understanding, this is unquestionably what is meant by science. And this is as it should be. It does not matter that, philosophically speaking, scientists are in error in supposing that there ever can be any entities, however minute, that are absolutely identical and absolutely commensurable. The point is that, on the basis of this imperfect understanding, great things have been and are being done. This "cocksure science" has proved its practical worth "so far as the movements of comets and electric trams go" (198).

Applied to the sphere of life, however, such an approach will be misconceived in theory and disastrous in practice. This is because its basic postulate—very large numbers of identical units—becomes increasingly untenable the further we depart from the realm of inorganic matter. Life may or may not be "superior" to matter—Wells is too good a Darwinist to pass judgment on such a questionable issue as that of relative "fitness" for long-term survival. But life is undoubtedly different, qualitatively different, from inanimate matter. Where inorganic matter exhibits a fundamental homogeneity and mechanical repetitiveness of form, life is characterized by an equally fundamental heterogeneity and individuality. Where the units of inorganic matter are small and plentiful, those of life are large and relatively few in number. The fewer the forms, the more they exhibit the qualities of individuality and uniqueness. This has to be taken as the essential postulate of all inquiry into living things. "Could you take men by the thousand billion, you could generalise about them as you do about atoms; could you take atoms singly, it may be you would find them as individual as your aunts and cousins" (197).

With the appearance of life, claims Wells, the scientific method strictly so-called loses its validity. It is now in the realm of individuality, not of generality. Its techniques hence become increasingly inappropriate. Biology, he provocatively asserts, is not a science.[6] Darwin would never have reached his epoch-making conclusions had he proceeded according to the logic of the scientific method. Given the object of his inquiry—the evolution of organic forms—his method of work necessarily had more in common with that of the historian or the biographer than of the physicist or chemist.

What is true of biology must be even truer of sociology. Human life is a special case of life in general, and so sociology, the study of human life, must be a special case of biology. But just as life in general progressively departs from the numerical plenitude of dead matter, so human life, as a particular case of organic evolution, carries the concentration and unification of units to the furthest extent yet observable in the living world. With humanity, the number of identifiable units shrinks to just one: human society as a whole. In this sense the Comteans are right to see sociology as standing at the extreme end of the scale from the molecular sciences. "In these latter there is an infinitude of units; in sociology . . . there is only one unit" (199).

Wells considers sympathetically the efforts of those, such as Spencer and Durkheim, who have tried to divide human society into different societies, and to regard them as quasi-independent entities engaged in a competitive struggle for survival, on the analogy of animal species competing within the same environment. But he dismisses this enterprise as ultimately misguided. For not only is it impossible to isolate complete communities of men; it is equally impossible to establish sufficient similarities between different societies to make meaningful comparisons between them. "These alleged units have as much individuality as pieces of cloud; they come, they go, they fuse and separate." Thus not only must we reject, as inappropriate to sociology, the method of observation, experiment, and verification that we find in the "hard" sciences of physics and chemistry; we must also reject "the method of classification under types" that has proved so useful in "the middle group of subjects"—such as comparative embryology or ethology—where the units are finite in number but still relatively numerous. For human society cannot be so split up and subdivided. In the case of humans, there is only one society.

> We cannot put Humanity into a museum, or dry it for examination; our one single still living specimen is all history, all anthropology, and the fluctuating world of men. There is no satisfactory means of dividing it, and nothing else in the real world with which to compare it. We have only the remotest ideas of its "life-cycle" and a few relics of its origin and dreams of its destiny. (200)

Human society being unitary and unique, the only relevant units for study are individual human beings in their relationship to the whole. There has to be a perpetual oscillation of focus, from the individual to the social and back again, as the sociologist attempts both to clarify and to perfect the social nexus. "Sociology, it is evident, is . . . no less than the attempt to bring that vast, complex, unique Being, its subject, into clear, true relations with the individual intelligence." Such an enterprise cannot hope for the certainties and universal regularities of the physical sciences. Individuals are as unique as the human society they inhabit; their relationship to it is bound to be shot through with personal differences and idiosyncrasies. Any account of society, any attempt to present "that great Being . . . in a comprehensible manner," must incorporate the individual point of view as much as the general.

This takes sociology halfway towards the realm of art, in its concern with self-expression. Such a movement is also encouraged by the irreducible fact of subjectivity and consciousness in the relationship of individuals to their world. Unlike other natural entities, human beings are capable of self-reflection, of conceiving purposes, of forming ideal conceptions and setting conscious goals. This makes human society an organism "essentially fluid and moving," possessed of the power of self-creation and self-renewal. It is different in kind from the "given fact" and "dead data" that are the subject of the physical sciences.

Wells however has no intention of giving all the ground to "the subjective element, which is beauty." This must "coalesce with the objective, which is truth." Sociology must be a form of inquiry that lives in the tension between opposing, or apparently opposing, modes: between the subjective and the objective, the individual and the social, the expressive and the rational or technical. This is not,

Wells insists, to drag science in again by the back door, to say that sociology is some amalgam of art and science. Science, as a method, remains excluded. Sociology is not a science. It is rather—curiously enough, as Durkheim also held—a form of inquiry sui generis. The models of other sciences and other disciplines, including artistic ones, are irrelevant. Just as physics and chemistry are appropriate modes for the phenomena they observe, so Wells aims at a sociology that is as precisely suited to its own peculiar subject matter, evolving human society. This involves a distinctive literary mode. "Sociology must be neither art simply, nor science in the narrow meaning of the world at all, but knowledge rendered imaginatively, and with an element of personality; that is to say, in the highest sense of the term, literature" (202).

Sociology as a Literature of Utopias

This is evidently a pretty tall order. What kind of writing is there that has been able to meet the challenge? Surprisingly there was, according to Wells, a considerable amount of it about, although not usually considered sociology by the Positivists and the professional practitioners. Wells here refers to a certain kind of social or sociological history: not history of the ordinary narrative kind, but that "sort of historical literature that seeks to elucidate and impose general interpretations upon the complex of occurrences and institutions, to establish broad historical generalisations, to eliminate the mass of irrelevant incident, to present some great period of history, or all history, in the light of one dramatic sequence, or as one process" (202). He gives as examples T. H. Buckle's *History of Civilisation* and William Lecky's *History of European Morals.* Other examples Wells mentions are Edward Gibbon's *Decline and Fall of the Roman Empire* and Thomas Carlyle's *The French Revolution.*

Wells presumably approved the form, if not altogether the gloomy mood, of Oswald Spengler's *The Decline of the West* (1918–22). He must also have warmly greeted—though I know no evidence that he actually read—Arnold Toynbee's monumental *A Study of History,* the first of whose twelve volumes appeared in the 1930s. Pitirim Sorokin, too, in the 1920s and 1930s, was producing his four-volume *Social and Cultural Dynamics,* a stimulating exercise in comparative sociological history that—like Toynbee's study—has long been dismissed or ignored by European and American sociologists. What, however, might have given Wells even greater pleasure is the belated recognition, especially in British and American sociology, of the essential soundness of his position, and the revival of various forms of historical sociology after more than half a century of neglect. In recent years we have seen works such as Barrington Moore, Jr.'s *The Social Origins of Dictatorship and Democracy* (1966), Perry Anderson's *Passages from Antiquity to Feudalism* (1974) and *Lineages of the Absolutist State* (1974), Immanuel Wallerstein's *The Modern World System* (1974–1980), Theda Skocpol's *States and Social Revolutions* (1979), and Michael Mann's multivolume *The Sources of Social Power* (1986–   ).[7] These works in their different ways represent a veritable renaissance of the historical method in sociology. With their attempt to see history whole, as a single developing entity, or to select particular episodes or particular social phenomena as representing or illuminating general patterns of social stability and change, they move precisely in the direction that Wells would have wished sociology to go.

What links these more recent studies with the examples that Wells himself admired might be termed the assumption of "the philosophical contemporaneity of all history" that Toynbee took as the postulate of his *Study of History*. The past becomes not just a record of origins, or a possible storehouse of moral and social truths—although both of these are important. It becomes relevant to the present in a peculiarly direct and forceful way. In one version, as in Spengler and Toynbee, history is seen not so much to repeat itself as to be the record of various essentially similar attempts to achieve civilizational balance and stability. Present efforts can therefore be seen in the light of, and perhaps under the guidance of, those of the past. It was clear, for instance, to Gibbon's eighteenth-century contemporaries that his account of the decline of Rome was directly aimed, both as a warning and a prophecy, at the prospects of eighteenth-century European civilization. Similarly Carlyle in his sulphurous history of the French Revolution admonished his Victorian contemporaries along the lines of "it could happen here" and—more grimly, perhaps—that it should. Alexis de Tocqueville's view of the same event, in his *The Ancien Régime and the Revolution*, took the alternative line followed by this vein of "philosophical" history. Here, as in the Marx-inspired studies of Anderson and Wallerstein, history is regarded not as cyclical but as unilineal. The past is shown to impinge on the present as a part, necessary both to its understanding and to its future forms, of the still-continuing evolution of human society. Social evolution is a process in which the past persists as an explosive mixture of continuity and contradiction in the present, and so as the key to developments in the future.[8]

The success of these works of philosophical history and their value as sociology depend not just on their intellectual conception but also on their literary execution. Wells is emphatic on this. He praises Gibbon and Carlyle for their endeavor, through their selection of particularly dramatic and important episodes, "to impose upon the vast confusions of the past a scheme of interpretation." But their attempt is "valuable just to the extent of its literary value, of the success with which the discrepant masses have been fused and cast into the shape the insight of the writer has determined." Here the artistic purpose is critical. "The writing of great history is entirely analogous to fine portraiture, in which fact is indeed material, but material entirely subordinate to vision." The vision of these writers imposes artistic form on their work; it is also what enables them to see the significant shapes of history, and to draw the necessary inferences for the present. To restore, as these historians do, "the dead bones of the past to a living participation in our lives," is an achievement at once both literary and sociological (203).

Sociology may have come around to seeing the value of history (though its practitioners are for the most part still woefully lacking in the requisite literary skills). But it is still a very long way from considering, let alone accepting, the need for the second kind of literature championed by Wells in his effort to redirect sociology. It is here that Plato comes in, as Wells had promised at the very outset of his paper. For, argues Wells, sociology can never be purely descriptive; it must, implicitly if not explicitly, evaluate and prescribe. "There is no such thing in sociology as dispassionately considering what *is,* without considering what is *intended to be.* In sociology, beyond any possibility of evasion, ideas are facts" [Wells's emphasis] (203).

Sociologists are certainly prepared now to question the idea of a "value-free" sociology. The inescapable involvement of the sociologist in the life of his or her society; the values and outlook acquired as a member of a particular class, community and culture; the shaping of perceptions by the use of the very medium of description and analysis, language, itself a social tool—all these factors have convinced most sociologists of the absurdity of pursuing the nineteenth-century ideal of a neutral, "objective" sociology.[9]

But while this has induced a certain degree of humility and self-examination—to the point where "the sociology of sociology" threatened to become a growth industry—it has not led sociologists to take the further and more radical step proposed by Wells. For to do so would apparently have meant embracing a certain social philosophy, or philosophy of history, which Wells only briefly adumbrates in his 1906 paper but that underlies practically the whole of his vast literary output. To Wellsians this is familiar in the form of the concept of "the Mind of the Race," and Wells's belief that the whole of human history can be seen as a striving towards the realization of "the world mind" in the context of a world state and civilization. In the 1906 paper, the world mind and the world state have not yet become the central and almost obsessively repeated expressions of this belief; Wells here speaks instead of "the Social Idea."

> The history of civilisation is really the history of the appearance and reappearance, the tentatives and hesitations and alterations, the manifestations and reflections in this mind and that, of a very complex, imperfect, elusive idea, the Social Idea. It is that idea struggling to exist and realise itself in a world of egotisms, animalisms, and brute matter. (203–204)[10]

There is a suggestion of historical determinism and teleological thinking in this passage which is likely to drive sociologists, schooled on Karl Popper's *The Open Society,* even further away from Wells; while the strongly idealist cast of the perspective will upset those Marxists and materialists not necessarily averse to determinism. But it is important to stress that Wells was never a crude determinist, either at the beginning or the end of his long life as a writer. In 1934 he restated in the plainest possible manner his belief that "human life as we know it, is only the dispersed raw material for human life as it might be." Every development in the modern world—in science, in government, in economics—was tending towards the crystallization of the world state, and the "undreamt-of fullness, freedom, and happiness" which that state would make possible. But Wells of all people was keenly aware that there was nothing inevitable about this development. A conscious and deliberate choice, backed by necessary action, had to be made. For "if mankind fails to apprehend its opportunity, then division, cruelties, delusions and ultimate frustration lies before our kind. The decision to perish or escape has to be made within a very limited time."[11]

But even without this disclaimer, it would seem possible and desirable to accept Wells's characterization of sociology's second task. For in drawing attention to the inherently prescriptive nature of sociological inquiry, Wells makes no requirement that we accept some rigidly imposed scheme of social evolution. Indeed he quite explicitly states that the aim should be "to endeavour to disentangle and express one's *personal* version of [the Social] idea, and to measure realities from the standpoint of that idealisation" (204) (my emphasis). This suggests that Wells's prescription for sociology is formal and methodological, rather than substantive. He lays down no one teleological goal, no one conception of the good society, as the necessary guide to sociological investigation. All he insists—and on this he is passionate—is that sociology is a meaningless and trivial activity without reference to some coherent set of values, some standard or ideal, which orders our selection of objects for study and gives us a means of assessing their human worth. It is this—and not submission to some authoritarian or dogmatic statement of creed—that is implied in Wells's carefully-considered declaration:

> I think . . . that the creation of Utopias—and their exhaustive criticism—is the proper and distinctive method of sociology . . . Sociology is the description of the Ideal Society and its relation to existing societies. (204)

Unlike the case of historical sociology, Wells had to admit that there was a paucity of examples of utopian sociology in his own day. It was just for this reason that he felt that it was in this "at present neglected direction" that the "predominant attack" upon the problem of sociology should lie. But at least there was a wealth of past efforts to draw upon. Plato's *Republic* and his *Laws* stood as the supreme examples of sociology as utopia-building. Wells had already paid his homage the year before, in *A Modern Utopia* (1905); later he was to say that "*A Modern Utopia*, quite as much as that of More, derives frankly from the *Republic*."[12] The ancient Greeks also provided Plato's energetic and equally indispensable antithesis in the person of Aristotle, the hard-headed critic of utopias. The utopian current, after a blank period during the "intellectual barbarism" of the Dark Ages, revived in the Renaissance with the rediscovery of the Greeks. More's discussion of pauperism in *Utopia*, and Bacon's model for the organization of scientific research in *New Atlantis*, are commended as exemplary forms of sociological analysis. The utopian impulse remained strong in the eighteenth century: "the yeast of the French Revolution," says Wells, "was Utopias." Wells even finds strong utopian elements in the works of those sociologists, such as Comte, most intent on denying it, in their insistence that they deal only in positive facts.

Even Comte, all the while that he is professing science, fact, precision, is adding detail after detail to the intensely personal Utopia of a Western Republic that constitutes his one meritorious gift to the world. Sociologists cannot help making Utopias; though they avoid the word, though they deny the idea with passion, their very silences shape a Utopia. (204–205)

Wells ends his paper to the London Sociological Society with a characteristic vision. He imagines a "dream book of huge dimensions" containing a picture, in all its varied and interconnected details, of the Ideal Society. "This book . . . would be the backbone of sociology." It would be the reference point, the organizing principle, for all work in sociology, currently disparate and dispersed. "The institutions of existing states would come into comparison with the institutions of the Ideal State, their failures and defects would be criticised most effectually in that relation, and the whole science of collective psychology, the psychology of human association, would be brought to bear upon the question of the practicability of this proposed ideal" (205).

Wells is crisp with the objection that this conception of sociology would leave out that mass of work, currently thought sociological, concerned with immediate social problems: what Wells calls "inquiries concerning the rough expedients to meet the failure of imperfect institutions," "social emergency work."

What to do with the pariah dogs of Constantinople, what to do with the tramps who sleep in the London parks, how to prevent ignorant people, who having nothing else to do, getting drunk in beerhouses, are no doubt serious questions for the practical administrator, questions of primary importance to the politician; but they have no more to do with sociology than the erection of a temporary hospital after the collision of two trains has to do with railway engineering. (206)

This admirably sees off sociology as understood by the Charity Organization Society, and as practised by social investigators such as Charles Booth and Seebohm Rowntree. Sociology, if it is at all to be separated from social administration and social work, must concern itself with society as a system and find its material in the harmonious or discordant functioning of its parts. Here, once more, British sociology has been hampered by its Fabian heritage. Influenced on the one hand by the Continental tradition of Comte and Durkheim, and on the other by the native tradition of Booth, Rowntree, and the Webbs, it occupies an uncomfortable halfway house. It is caught between the haphazard analysis of social structure and the investigation of what is essentially the inheritance of the Victorian Poor Law. The point of view that would offer a perspective on the development of British society as a whole, its strivings, accomplishments, and failures, is signally lacking. There is available some splendid sociological history—though written largely by historians such as Eric Hobsbawm and Edward Thompson rather than by sociologists themselves. But it rarely connects with any vision of British society in its whole movement, a vision that would link past, present, and possible future. It lacks, that is, what Wells would have called a properly utopian dimension.[13]

It is clear in this example, as it must already have been to the attentive listener of Wells's paper, that the two types of sociological literature that he advocates are really two aspects of the same thing. More precisely, the utopian function subsumes the historical. It supplies the necessary reference point for historical inquiry. It is this that leads Wells to call the construction of utopias "the most central and essential portion of sociological work." For the first part, the historical part, "will in effect amount to a history of the suggestions in circumstance and experience of that Idea of Society of which the second will consist, and of the instructive failures in attempting its incomplete realisation" (206). Here, at that time in his life when the world of thought and letters still lay gloriously spread out before him, when every new work by him was received by an attentive public, Wells set himself what amounted to an agenda for his life's work.

Wells the Sociologist

It is one thing to prescribe a method, quite another to apply it, to provide the material by which the method may reasonably be judged. How far did Wells himself carry out the precepts of his 1906 paper? What is there of Wellsian sociology?

The historical task was triumphantly executed, to vast popular and even professional acclaim. In *The Outline of History* (1920) and *The Science of Life* (1930), Wells linked the Darwinian perspective on nature and the Progressivist philosophy of Winwood Reade and others to produce just that account of the emergence of the Social Idea that he had held to be one of sociology's prime needs. The guiding thread was "the growth of association since the dawn of animal communities," "the gathering coordination of lives." The *Outline of History* traced, as one continuous story of "expanding relationship," the development of the social idea from its earliest appearance among premammalian creatures to its full-blooded expression in the "aeroplane-radio-linked human world of today."[14]

No more than in any of his other writings did Wells see the growth of the social idea—now clearly identified with the idea of the world state—as a tale of continuous and uninterrupted triumph. "History has never gone simply forward."[15] For Wells, history was a record of oscillating advances and setbacks in the slow and painful progress of the idea of a world order. At the time that he was writing, Wells saw the promise of the most recent advance—the industrial and scientific revolution of the nineteenth century—threatened by narrowness of vision and short-sighted egotistical strivings. The Great War of 1914, the culmination of an epoch of nationalist rivalries and imperialist wars, had shown that there had been "a real *de-civilization* of men's minds."[16] History remained, as always, open. The choice between disaster and the gathering up of the fruits of humanity's long endeavour was there to be made. Either national antagonisms and racial passions would lead mankind to world-wide destruction; or the enlightened elites of all nations would come together in pursuit of the goal of a world civilization based on science.

Wells had taken over from T. H. Huxley the concept that human life was inherently dualistic.[17] There was a permanent conflict between the ethical process—the creative, constructive, civilizing process that contained the best of human history—and the evolutionary process, that system of brutal competition and mutual annihilation in which man was implicated along with all other species. It was a dialectical conception of history in which ideas and instincts interact to produce an ultimately forward movement, but one marked by many lapses and reverses.

> From Plato with his Utopianism, confident in the power of man to change his state, and Aristotle with his insistence upon the supremacy of reason and proven fact, right down to the constructive effort and science of today we have seen the human mind feeling its way to creative freedom. And always the forces of instinctive conservatism, of privilege and dogmatic authority have resisted or prevented that advance. True there is a great development of world-wide political, social and moral ideas, but will they bear fruit?[18]

In the end, though, Wells had a characteristic faith in "the power of reason and in the increasing good-will in men." "Clumsily or smoothly, the world, it seems, progresses and will progress." The forces making for world unification were so urgent and palpable that men must soon acknowledge their "necessity and logic." Ultimately, too, as always, the struggle would be won or lost on the field of ideas. "All human history is fundamentally a history of ideas." It was consequently above all to education, education for world citizenship, that Wells looked for the realization of the world idea. He was convinced that "for a new order in the world there must be a new education and that for a real world civilization there must be a common basis of general ideas. . . ."[19] Human history had become "more and more a race between education and catastrophe." *The Outline of History, The Science of Life,* and *The Work, Wealth, and Happiness of Mankind* (1932), were all intended by him to be contributions to this educative enterprise. They were elements in the construction of "a world citizen's ideology." The understanding of mankind's history and its contemporary predicament would, Wells hoped, "push the mind irresistibly, in spite of the clashes of race and tradition and the huge difficulties created by differences in language, towards the belief that a conscious struggle to establish or prevent a political world community will be the next stage in human history."[20]

The Outline of History ends with a utopia. Wells sketches, in some detail, a scientific world civilization, free from drudgery and dedicated to adventures of the mind and body. The very last lines strongly echo the remarkable closing pages of Reade's *The Martyrdom of Man*. Wells, like Reade, pictures an all-powerful and triumphant humanity reaching out to the stars.

> Men will unify, only to intensify, the search for knowledge and power, and live as ever for new occasions. Animal and vegetable life, the obscure processes of psychology, the intimate structure of matter and the interior of our earth, will yield their secrets and endow their conqueror. Life begins perpetually. Gathered together at last under the leadership of man, the student-teacher of the universe, unified, disciplined, armed with the secret powers of the atom, and with knowledge as yet beyond dreaming, Life, for ever dying to be born afresh, for ever young and eager, will presently stand upon the earth as upon a footstool, and stretch out its realm amidst the stars.[21]

Nothing could more clearly indicate the link, in Wells's mind, between the historical and the utopian tasks of sociology. History takes one to the brink of utopia. It is the intimations of what could be, imperfectly grasped, fitfully attempted, always instructive in its failures as much as its achievements. The future does not grow out of the brain of the utopist, a Plato or a Bacon, however inspired the vision. Although Wells had little respect for Hegel and Marx, he concurs essentially in their view that the past is not a meaningless and useless record of obsolete practices but contains the building-blocks of the future. The elements of the future world state are at least partly to be found in the intellectual and expressive prefigurations of the great world religions, and the political prefigurations of the "world empires" of such men as Alexander and Caesar. It is necessary, of course, in getting a clearer conception of the world state, to expose the weaknesses of these past attempts. But without their existence as tried, human practices, as models of a sort, no amount of utopian exhortation is likely to carry conviction. Wells can scarcely be accused by anyone as a worshipper of the past. But he would surely have agreed as much with George Santayana's well-known saying, that "those who know no history are condemned to repeat it," as with C. Wright Mills's less well-known dictum, that "we study the past in order to be rid of it."

Still, an awareness of historical intimations and limitations can only take us so far. There remains the work of utopia construction, the central task, as Wells had seen it, of a reconstituted sociology. Wells may be said to have discharged that task with almost excessive zeal. From *Anticipations* (1901) onwards, in a stream of books that included *A Modern Utopia* (1905), *The World Set Free* (1914), *Men Like Gods* (1923), and *The Shape of Things to Come* (1933), Wells instructed mankind tirelessly on the need to build a new world and provided striking portraits of what that world could be like. Wells is the greatest—one might almost say the only—utopist of the twentieth century. Practically everything subsequently that has been written in a utopian vein has borrowed from him, while for the anti-utopists he has always been the supreme target.

This is not the place to elaborate on Wells's utopia of a world order based on scientific understanding and scientific organization. It is well enough known in its main outlines, even though the stereotypical portrayal of it as a mechanical and soulless civilization can sadly at times mislead even Wellsians.[22] What perhaps we rather need to remind ourselves is that most of Wells's utopias are in the form of novels. Now it is true that, at least since Thomas More invented the modern utopia in 1516, the literary forms of utopia and of the novel have heavily overlapped one another. Utopias are by definition fictions; more recently too they have generally avoided the dialog form favored by Plato (and partly imitated by Wells in *A Modern Utopia*) in preference for the narrative form of the modern novel.

But, in the modern utopia, the balance between imaginative

fiction and more or less straight sociological analysis and prescription has varied enormously. Some utopias, such as Bellamy's *Looking Backward* and B. F. Skinner's *Walden Two,* are closer to formal political disquisitions such as Locke's *Two Treatises of Goverment* and Rousseau's *The Social Contract* than they are to the mainstream modern novel. This is very rarely true of Wells. Even in *A Modern Utopia,* which comes closest to the presentation of a utopia in the classic mold, the complex literary devices employed produce an ambiguous portrait of the good society that frequently leaves us unsure of the author's intent and even of his fundamental faith in his utopian vision. Similarly with *The World Set Free* and *The Shape of Things to Come:* Wells's concern to warn mankind to act before it is too late leads him to project images of apocalyptic disaster that have more in common with his early antiutopian science fiction, such as *The War of the Worlds,* than his more formally sociological works such as *Anticipations.* Wells never forgot, even at his most prophetic and utopian, that he was writing imaginative fiction. This was not just the pride of a writer who considered himself first and foremost a novelist. It also spoke precisely to the sociological purpose of the utopian writing. Wells had commended Gibbon and Carlyle for the visionary quality of their historical writing. Their literary strength was not some aesthetic bonus but a direct measure of their worth as historians and sociologists. In his own case too Wells was aware of the need to present his utopian vision in as compelling a form as possible. This meant avoiding the rigidity and aridity of the conventional treatise in politics or sociology. The novel form allowed an exploration of possibilities, together with the indication of complexities and contradictions, quite beyond the scope of the political tract. Wells admired Bellamy, and paid him the compliment of borrowing certain ideas from him; but in his utopian writing he is closer to More's *Utopia,* with its subtlety, its allusiveness, its satirical edge and its frequent shifts of mood.

In his utopian works, Wells takes the cosmic vision. "No less than a planet," he says, "will serve the purpose of a modern utopia."[23] His unit is mankind as a whole. This is in line with his conviction that sociology has only one subject, "that vast complex, unique Being," world society. Earlier utopias, such as More's and Bacon's, were to be found on isolated islands or in mountain valleys. Such isolation was a practical possibility in earlier times. It was not therefore implausible for utopias to be conceived as pockets of perfection in a generally imperfect world. This conception is no longer possible, says Wells. The technology of war and modern communications has forced the world to see itself as it has always really been, one entity, one interdependent system. Utopia must match this reality. "World-state, therefore, it must be."[24]

But there is also, elsewhere in Wells's writings and less often noted, another version of utopia, or at least of one of the most important features of utopia. While the *Outline of History* and the utopian works take as their subject the history and prospects of the whole of mankind, there is in Wells another linking of history and utopia that points towards a more concrete and more historically specific sociology. It is drawn from the history of England, and it is to be found in a number of Wells's works. But it is most clearly developed in his novel *Tono-Bungay* (1909), where Wells states his "Bladesover theory" of English society.

In *Tono-Bungay,* the hero George Ponderevo reflects on the importance in English history and culture of gentry households such as Bladesover House where—like Wells himself at Up Park—George has spent much of his childhood as the housekeeper's son. England, George decides, is still to a good extent Bladesover writ large. The whole social system still reverberates with the impact of the gentry culture consolidated after the "Glorious Revolution" of 1688. The gentry class has been manifestly in decline in recent times, but no new class has arisen to displace its authority. The obvious contenders—the merchants, financiers, and industrialists—have proved lacking in the requisite creative and constructive qualities. In the absence of viable alternatives, gentry culture—enfeebled but still seductive—continues to dominate English society. "Everybody who is not actually in the shadow of a Bladesover is as it were perpetually seeking after lost orientations."[25]

The importance of the gentry was that it was not simply a self-interested and self-serving ruling class of the old kind, but a directing intelligence for society as a whole. Gentry rule was a civilizing agency of immense conseqence, perhaps the most creative force the world has seen hitherto. Gentry power cannot be revived, but it is just this kind of constructive rule that is needed in twentieth-century industrial society. In his *Autobiography,* Wells, in a striking passage, returned to this theme. Gentry culture, now thought of as a generally European phenomenon, was seen not simply as the impetus to but as the very model of the coming world state.

Now it is one of my firmest convictions that modern civilization was begotten and nursed in the households of the prosperous, relatively independent people, the minor nobility, the gentry, and the larger bourgeoisie, which became visibly important in the landscape of the six-teenth century, introducing a new architectural element in the towns, and spreading as country houses and chateaux and villas over the continually more orderly countryside. Within these households, behind their screen of deer park and park wall and sheltered service, men could talk, think and write at their leisure. They were free from inspection and immediate imperatives. They, at least, could go on after thirteen thinking and doing as they pleased. They created the public schools, revived the waning universities, went on the Grand Tour to see and learn. They could be interested in public affairs without being consumed by them. The management of their estates kept them in touch with reality with-out making exhaustive demands on their time. Many, no doubt, degen-erated into a life of easy dignity or gentlemanly vice, but quite a sufficient number remained curious and interested to make, foster and protect the accumulating science and literature of the seventeenth and eighteenth centuries. Their large rooms, their libraries, their collections of pictures and "curios" retained into the nineteenth century an at-mosphere of unhurried liberal enquiry, of serene and determined in-subordination and personal dignity, of established aesthetic and intellectual standards. Out of such houses came the Royal Society, the *Century of Inventions,* the first museums and laboratories and picture galleries, gentle manners, good writing, and nearly all that is worth while in our civilization to-day. Their culture, like the culture of the ancient world, rested on a toiling class. Nobody bothered very much about that, but it has been far more through the curiosity and enterprise and free deliberate thinking of these independent gentlemen than through any other influences, that modern machinery and economic organization have developed so as to abolish at last the harsh necessity for any toiling class whatever. It is the country house that has opened the way to human equality, not in the form of a democracy of insurgent proletarians, but as a world of universal gentlefolk no longer in need of a servile substratum. It was the experimental cellule of the coming Mod-ern State.[26]

What Wells has done here, as in *Tono-Bungay* and a number of the other novels of English life, is to show how a fundamentally utopian conception can inform our use and understanding of his-tory. But the level now is not the most abstract and general, the history of mankind, as in the *Outline*. It is the most concrete and specific, the most immediate and homely, the history of one's own country. Wells seems to be saying that it does not matter very much from which level one starts. The world or the nation, mankind or English society, the bird's-eye or the worm's-eye view, both can be equally illuminating routes to the understanding of present dilem-mas and future possibilities. Wells, as the supreme practitioner at both levels, moved easily from one to the other—sometimes even in the same work, as in *In the Days of the Comet* (1906). The guiding thread at all times was utopia. It was the vision of the future world state that cast its broad beam backward on history, lighting up here particular details of a nation's history, there, in a wide arc, the strivings of mankind as a whole in the rise and fall of civilizations. The two levels could moreover be shown to be intimately linked. Starting with the analysis of the disintegration of nineteenth-century English society, Wells is led, by a natural progression, to the diagnosis of the predicament of contemporary world civilization, and from there to the prescription and prediction of a coming world order governed by the creative force of science. Past and future run into each other, history and utopia become one. The English gentry of the eighteenth century are transformed into the Samurai of *A Modern Utopia.*[27]

There is a tendency, especially for those who know only Wells's science fiction and perhaps some of the utopian writing, to see Wells as obsessed with the cosmic vision of humanity. Wells is thought, rather like the Martians of *The War of the Worlds,* to regard the world in a detached Olympian manner, with an intelligence "vast and cool and unsympathetic." So concerned was he to save humanity, it is felt, that he neglected individual human beings and their daily concerns. It is perhaps this that Joseph Conrad had in mind when he made his famous comparison in a letter to Wells: "The difference between us is fundamental. You don't care for humanity but think they are to be improved. I love humanity but know they are not."[28]

This has some truth perhaps, certainly as far as Conrad is concerned; but no one who has read Wells's "social" novels of the early 1900s, or who knows anything of the tempestuous nature of his personal life, can doubt that Wells was intensely alive to the claims of the individual life. His utopian vision always took in the need for individual fulfillment and personal happiness as well as for the realization of social goals of abundance and equity. Or perhaps one might better say that Wells was always conscious that the social goals were not ends in themselves but the instruments of individual fulfillment.

In *A Modern Utopia,* he makes the point comically. A lovelorn botanist, distracted by his "poor little love affair" on earth and indifferent to the grand schemes of Utopia, is given as companion to the rationalist narrator, enthusing over Utopian marvels of social engineering. Wells has fun with the querulous botanist, but he makes it plain that he takes his claims—the claims of the personal life—seriously. In a more extended treatment of the same theme, in his novel *The New Machiavelli* (1911), Wells goes further. Here a politician, Richard Remington, sacrifices a promising career for an adulterous love affair that drives him into exile abroad. Remington, like an earlier exiled politician, Machiavelli, sets about writing a political treatise. But unlike Machiavelli, he finds he cannot leave the individual life of sex and the passions outside the study door. He decides that any vision of the good life that cannot find a central place for the life of the emotions is worthless.

> It is this gradual discovery of sex as a thing collectively portentous that I have to mingle with my statecraft if my picture is to be true. . . . I began life ignoring women, they came to me at first perplexing and dishonouring; only very slowly and very late in my life and after misadventure, did I gauge the power and beauty of the love of man and woman and learnt how it must needs frame a justifiable vision of the ordered world. Love has brought me to disaster, because my career has been planned regardless of its possibility and value. But Machiavelli, it seems to me, when he went into his study, left not only the earth of life outside but its unsuspected soul. . . .[29]

Wells never gave up his conviction that there had to be a harmonious match between the microcosmic life of personal relations and the macrocosmic order of society. We might say, stretching the point a little, that his "Bladesover theory" of English society interposed a middle level between the individual and the cosmic. The gentry class were as preoccupied with the cultivation of the individual mind and body—with following something like the disciplined "Rule" of the Samurai of *A Modern Utopia*—as they were with the affairs of state. This was a necessary condition of their fitness to rule in society. The individual and the social, the personal and the public, are linked through the development of a particular social class, with a particular ethos. The Bladesover theory requires that a class similar in character to the gentry should arise to give the lead to modern industrial society. This is a matter partly of sociological analysis, partly of political organization and action. The development of society over time has to be studied to see what new forces are emerging and what can be encouraged to grow in strength. Wells, in a number of sociological works starting with the conception of the "Efficients" in *Anticipations,* singled out the new middle class of scientists, technicians, and managers as most fitted to direct the scientific civilization of the modern world. The utopias reworked the sociology of modern society by picturing a time when practically everyone would be absorbed into the "expanded middle class" in "a scientifically organized classless society."[30] It is something of a surprise, given the conventional view of Wells as a technocratic elitist, to find that like Marx he constructed a sociology whose axial principle was the utopia of a future classless society. Unlike Marx though, and consistent with his belief in the indispensability of utopias for sociology, Wells was prepared to spell out in detail what this future society could and should look like. This exposed him to the contempt not just of Marxists but of the professional self-styled "scientific" sociologists. Having seen something of the results of the refusal of the Marxists to think through the requirements of the future society,[31] having also for well-nigh half a century been surfeited with the fruitless products of scientific sociology, we may well feel that there is infinitely better reason to follow Wells's example than theirs.

Wells and Modern Sociology

Modern western sociology has persistently turned away from utopian thought, as incompatible with its status as a social science. At the same time it has reared structures of theory—Marxism, Positivism, functionalism—which to most outside observers and even some sociologists are manifestly steeped in utopianism.[32] That this utopianism is for the most part concealed makes, if anything, for a worse situation. Sociologists, as Wells said, cannot help making utopias; "their very silences shape a Utopia." Why not accept this fact and build on it rather than attempt to bury or sidestep it?

Wells's own precepts and practice suggest two promising directions for modern sociology. It might, following Wells, think of these as the Platonic and the Aristotelian modes. The Platonic mode encourages us frankly to construct utopias, or at least to attempt a form of futurology with a strong constructive and utopian element. This need not mean, any more than it does in Wells's own practice, exercises in mere fancy or fantasy. All important utopias, from More to Marx, and from Bellamy to Wells, build on existing forces and tendencies. Utopists have seen the need to engage in a wide-ranging historical sociology, to analyze the past for the significant components that make the present and prepare the future. Only on the basis of the understanding of what has been and what is do they seek to construct their utopian accounts of what might be. We may even say that without this understanding there is no utopia—none at any rate within the tradition of western utopianism. We need not fear, as Thoreau said, to build castles in the air: "that is where they should be." The important thing, he continued, is to "put the foundations under them"[33]—a matter, to some extent, of indicating the historical building-blocks.

The second direction for sociology, the Aristotelian, is precisely to examine and assess those foundations and the utopias reared on them. This is for sociology its task as critic, its role as sceptic and gadfly. It is a role in which sociology is notoriously well-experienced, but more often in the spirit of scornful dismissal than of constructive criticism. The most important aspect of this activity might well turn out to be—again, as Wells suggests—not just the theoretical criticism of utopian schemes, but even more the critical study of practical utopian experiments, past and present. This would allow sociologists to test the limits of social experimentation, to explore, as David Martin has said, "the impossible possibility without which very little is possible." "Sociology does not encourage us to give up hope but it does show us . . . what the genuine limits of hope are."[34]

And there are other aspects of hope that sociology might consider. Wells not only wrote utopias, he wrote the sociology of particular moments and periods of creativity and progress in the history of mankind. His "Bladesover theory" of creative elites is one of his contributions to such a sociology. Sociology might therefore attempt to establish the social and political conditions of cultural and intellectual "renaissances," somewhat as Jacob Burckhardt attempted to do with the Italian Renaissance.[35] It might also, if Marx is right in regarding political revolutions as "the locomotives of history," not leave the study of revolutions to the historian but see it as an indispensable part of political sociology.

Utopia and history: the more one considers it, the more convincing does Wells's advocacy of their centrality to sociology appear. History, as we have seen, is already beginning to attract the attention of a good number of sociologists. They remain on the whole still suspicious of utopia; but there are signs too here that the tide may be beginning to turn. As late industrial civilization wakes up to the reality of technological unemployment on a mass scale, scarce natural resources, the dangers of nuclear power in peace as much as in war, the global environmental impact of machine technology, and the spread of practically instant worldwide communications, utopian intimations and aspirations are not hard to find. The Green parties of Europe and North America are perhaps the clearest expression of the new utopianism; but there are now as well several interesting examples of attempts at a utopian sociology that would have been very much to Wells's taste.[36] Utopia does not necessarily spell optimism (although it does spell hope); but in a time of radical and often threatening changes, it keeps alive, as Raymond Williams has said, "the belief that human beings can live in radically different ways, by radically different values, in radically different kinds of social order."[37] In an age when, as Wells so clearly saw, mankind needs to realize that the choice is world society or no society, utopia and the utopian tradition can stand as a powerful challenge to the complacent parochialisms of time and place.

It is surely clear that it is modern sociology, not Wells, that is in need of revision.

Notes

1. The British minister of state was Timothy Renton; the discussion was broadcast on BBC 2's *Newsnight,* 5 February 1987.

2. For a discussion of one of his books in these terms, *see* Krishan Kumar, "A Book Remembered: *A Modern Utopia,*" *New Universities Quarterly* 36, no. 1 (Winter 1981/82): 3–12. *A Modern Utopia* is of course an extreme case, where the fiction is severely subordinated to the sociological purpose. But Wells never loses sight of the fictional character of the work; and conversely most of his fiction have strong sociological themes—*Tono-Bungay* is perhaps the most ambitious enterprise of this kind.

3. For the Fabian influence in British sociology, *see* Philip Abrams, *The Origins of British Sociology 1834–1914* (Chicago and London: University of Chicago Press, 1968); Raymond A. Kent, *A History of British Empirical Sociology* (Aldershot: Gower, 1981). For Wells's meteoric passage through the Fabian Society, *see* Norman and Jeanne MacKenzie, *The First Fabians* (London: Quartet, 1979), 328–52. Wells's own brief and dismissive account of "that storm in a Fabian tea-cup" can be found in his *Experiment in Autobiography* (1934; London: Jonathan Cape, 1969), 2:660–63.; and, thinly fictionalized and at greater length, in *The New Machiavelli* (1911).

4. Sidney Webb, *The Difficulties of Individualism,* Fabian Tract no. 69 (London: The Fabian Society, 1894), 1. For the frequently ambivalent Marxist attitude to utopianism, *see* Krishan Kumar, *Utopia and Anti-Utopia in Modern Times* (Oxford and New York: Basil Blackwell, 1987), 49–65; Vincent Geoghegan, *Utopianism and Marxism* (London and New York: Methuen, 1987). For the Fabians' reaction to Bellamy, *see* Sylvia E. Bowman, et al., *Edward Bellamy Abroad: An American Prophet's Influence* (New York: Twayne, 1962), 86–118.

5. H. G. Wells, "The So-Called Science of Sociology," in *An Englishman Looks at the World* (London: Cassell, 1914), 192–93. Subsequent quotations from this work are cited parenthetically in the text. The paper was first published in 1906 in the *Sociological Papers* of the London Sociological Society. Wells recalls of the delivery of his paper that "the subsequent discussion was entirely inconclusive. Mr Wilfred Trotter thought it was an 'Attack on Science' and Mr Swinny defended Comte from my ingratitude." (*Experiment in Autobiography,* 2:658).

6. This statement may surprise those readers who are aware of Wells's book, *The Science of Life,* and the frequent references to biology as a science in Wells's other writings. No doubt Wells was deliberately out to shock his positivistically minded audience at the London Sociological Society. For them the scientific status of biology was the bedrock of their view of the scientific status of sociology. Wells's contrary assertion in this lecture therefore has a polemic intent. At other times he was quite happy to call biology a science. But the substance of his point is entirely seriously meant. There can be a "science of life," but only if science is understood in a quite different sense from that derived from the model of the inorganic sciences. In fact, at bottom Wells is questioning the whole conventional notion of science as exemplified in the method of physics or chemistry. Even at the most fundamental level of

matter, where units such as atoms or ions appear identical, there is an irreducible individuality and uniqueness of elements that is glossed over by the conventionally scientific method of comparison and statistical generalization. For most practical purposes, this does not matter; the danger lies in elevating a false concept, built on this practice, as the only acceptable scientific method. In his 1906 lecture, Wells for the purposes of argument is prepared to accept the conventional characterization of science. On *this* basis, biology is not a science. In fact, though, even in this lecture Wells briefly throws out the suggestion that, owing to the immense practical success of the inorganic sciences, "it was scarcely suspected that the biological sciences might perhaps, after all, be *truer* than the experimental . . ." ("The So-Called Science of Sociology," 197). This is because biology—and sociology—are forced to recognize the individuality that inheres in all things. Wells does not, in this lecture, attempt the reconceptualization of science that is implied in this perception. But such a radical rethinking is to be found in many of his other works, from the earliest—the article "The Rediscovery of the Unique" (1891)—to the latest, his London doctor of science dissertation "On the Quality of Illusion in the Continuity of the Individual Life in the Higher Metazoa. . . ." (1943).

7. Evidence of the revival of interest in historical sociology appears in the form of long-delayed recognition of Norbert Elias's great work of historical sociology, *The Civilizing Process*, (1939) 2 vols (Oxford: Basil Blackwell, 1978–82). Other outstanding examples of the kind of history advocated by Wells are Alexis de Tocqueville, *The Ancien Régime and the Revolution* (1856; English translation, London: Fontana, 1966); and Leon Trotsky, *History of the Russian Revolution* (1932; English translation, London: Gollancz, 1965). Further back, and as the source of much of this kind of history, is the *histoire raisonné* or "conjectural" or "natural" history of the eighteenth-century Enlightenment, such as Adam Ferguson's *Essay on the History of Civil Society* (1767).

8. A masterly critical discussion of various approaches in the philosophy of history is Karl Löwith, *Meaning in History* (Chicago: University of Chicago Press, 1949); see also Frank E. Manuel, *Shapes of Philosophical History* (Stanford, Cal.: Stanford University Press, 1965) and, for a useful recent survey, David Bebbington, *Patterns in History* (Leicester: Inter-Varsity Press, 1979).

9. The best statement of this position is Peter Winch, *The Idea of a Social Science and its Relation to Philosophy* (London: Routledge and Kegan Paul, 1958). *See also* Alfred Schutz, *The Phenomenology of the Social World*, trans. G. Walsh and F. Lehnhert (London: Heinemann, 1972).

10. This conception is strongly present in Winwood Reade's popular Victorian classic, *The Martyrdom of Man* (1872), which, according to the MacKenzies, "had a profound and enduring effect upon Wells" and that he drew upon freely in the writing of *The Outline of History*. *See* Norman and Jeanne MacKenzie, *The Time Traveller: The Life of H. G. Wells* (London: Weidenfeld and Nicolson, 1973), 55, 321.

11. Wells, *Experiment in Autobiography*, 1:27. On the very next page, however, Wells frustratingly withdraws some of this voluntarism with his affirmation that "the coming great world of order is real and sure," and that "the great tomorrow is certain"; ibid., 28.

12. Wells, *Experiment in Autobiography*, 2:658. Elsewhere in *Autobiography*, Wells recalls the impact that the discovery of Plato's *Republic* had had on him as a schoolboy. It was, he says, "a very releasing book indeed for my mind. . . . Here was the amazing and heartening suggestion that the whole fabric of law, custom and worship, which seemed so invincibly established, might be cast into the melting pot and made anew," 1:138.

13. In the absence of sociological efforts in this direction, it has been left to a literary critic and cultural historian, Raymond Williams, to attempt such a necessary task. *See* especially his *Culture and Society 1780–1950* (Harmondsworth: Penguin Books, 1963), *The Long Revolution* (Harmondsworth: Penguin Books, 1965), and *The Year 2000* (New York: Pantheon Books, 1983), published in Britain as *Towards 2000*. It is interesting that in the latter work Williams expressly calls for a renewal of utopian writing as an essential part of a proper sociology of the modern world. And for a sympathetic discussion of Williams's own utopianism, *see* Patrick Parrinder, "Utopia and Negativity in Raymond Williams," in his *The Failure of Theory: Essays on Criticism and Contemporary Fiction* (Brighton: Harvester Press, 1987), 72–84. Wells would have liked Parrinder's characterization of Williams's stance:

". . . he found present culture unsatisfactory, not by comparison with an idealised past, but from the perspective of a possible future," ibid., 74.

14. These remarks on intent are in Wells, *Experiment in Autobiography*, 2:718.

15. Wells, *The Outline of History*, Eighth Revision (London: Cassell, 1932), 1150.

16. Ibid., 1147 (Wells's emphasis).

17. See T. H. Huxley's 1893 Romanes Lecture, "Evolution and Ethics," reprinted in T. H. Huxley and J. S. Huxley, *Evolution and Ethics, 1893–1943* (London: Pilot Press, 1947).

18. Wells, *Outline of History*, 1143–44.

19. Wells, *Experiment in Autobiography*, 2:721.

20. Wells, *Outline of History*, 1151. For the other quotations in this paragraph, see ibid., 1146, 1158.

21. Ibid., 1159.

22. For an account of Wells's utopianism, focussing particularly on *A Modern Utopia*, see Kumar, *Utopia and Anti-Utopia*, 168–223.

23. Wells, *A Modern Utopia* (1905; original reprint, Lincoln: University of Nebraska Press, 1967), 11.

24. Ibid., 12.

25. Wells, *Tono-Bungay* (1909; reprint London: Pan Books, 1964), 18. And *see*, for what George Ponderevo calls "my Bladesover theory of the British social scheme," 12–19, 85–89, 156. Gentry domination of English society would have been an obvious feature of Edwardian times when Wells wrote his novel. For a recent study that runs close to Wells's view of the gentry's role in English history and culture, *see* Martin J. Wiener, *English Culture and the Decline of the Industrial Spirit 1850–1980* (Cambridge: Cambridge University Press, 1981).

26. Wells, *Experiment in Autobiography*, 1:135–36.

27. For a development of this conception of the character of the Samurai, *see* Kumar, *Utopia and Anti-Utopia*, 214–19.

28. Letter of Joseph Conrad to H. G. Wells, 25 September 1908, quoted in Lovat Dickson, *H. G. Wells: His Turbulent Life and Times* (Harmondsworth: Penguin, 1972), 289.

29. *The New Machiavelli* (1911; Harmondsworth: Penguin, 1966), 14.

30. Wells, *Experiment in Autobiography*, 1:94. C. Wright Mills's phrase about James Burnham, "a Marx for the managers," applies equally to Wells. For Wells's concept of a classless society, *see* Kumar, *Utopia and Anti-Utopia*, 218–19.

31. On the disastrous consequences of the Marxist antipathy to utopian thinking, especially as seen in the development of the Soviet Union, *see* Martin Buber, *Paths in Utopia* (1949; Boston: Beacon Press, 1958). *See also*, for a similar view, Steven Lukes, "Marxism and Utopia," in P. Alexander and R. Gill, eds., *Utopias* (London: Duckworth, 1984), 153–67.

32. On the utopian element in Marxism, *see* note 4, above. On utopia and functionalism, *see* R. Dahrendorf, "Out of Utopia: Toward a Reorientation of Sociological Analysis," *American Journal of Sociology*, 64, no. 2 (1958): 115–27. The utopian aspects of nineteenth-century sociology are well brought out in Barbara Goodwin, *Social Science and Utopia* (Hassocks, Sussex: Harvester Press, 1978). *See also* R. Levitas, "Sociology and Utopia," *Sociology* 13, no. 1 (1979): 19–33.

33. Henry David Thoreau, *Walden* (1854; New York: New American Library, 1960), 215.

34. David Martin, "Foreword" to John Whitworth, *God's Blueprints: A Sociological Study of Three Utopian Sects* (London: Routledge and Kegal Paul, 1975), xi. And compare to Leszek Kolakowski: "It may well be that the impossible at a given moment can become possible only by being stated at a time when it is impossible. . . . The existence of a utopia is the necessary prerequisite for its eventually ceasing to be a utopia"; "The Concept of the Left," in his *Toward a Marxist Humanism: Essays on the Left Today* (New York: Grove Press, 1969), 70–71. Whitworth's book is, as Martin says, a very good example of the kind of sociological study of utopian experiments that is required. Another excellent example is Rosabeth Moss Kanter's study of nineteenth- and twentieth-century American utopia communities: *Commitment and Community: Communes and Utopias in Sociological Perspective* (Cambridge: Harvard University Press, 1972).

35. Jacob Burckhardt, *The Civilization of the Renaissance in Italy* (1860; London: Phaidon Press, 1955). Arnold Toynbee made a brave attempt at such a sociology of renaissances in vol. 9 of his *A Study of History* (London: Oxford University Press, 1963).

36. *See* especially André Gorz, *Farewell to the Working Class: An Essay on Post-Industrial Socialism* (London: Pluto Press, 1982); Gorz, *Paths to Paradise: On the Liberation from Work* (London: Pluto Press, 1985); Rudolf Bahro, *The Alternative in Eastern Europe* (London: New Left Books, 1978); Bahro, *From Red to Green* (London: Verso, 1984); Alvin Toffler, *The Third Wave* (London: Pan Books, 1981). These and related thinkers are studied in Boris Frankel, *The Post-Industrial Utopians* (Oxford: Polity Press, 1987). Somewhat different in conception, but of equal interest as utopian speculation are Norman Macrae, *The 2024 Report: A Concise History of the Future 1974–2024* (London: Sidgwick and Jackson, 1984); Charles Handy, *The Future of Work* (Oxford: Basil Blackwell, 1984); James Robertson, *Future Work: Jobs, Self-Employment and Leisure After the Industrial Age* (Aldershot: Gower, 1985). An interesting mixture of utopia and dystopia is Brian Stableford and David Langford, *The Third Millennium: A History of the World AD 2000–3000* (London: Paladin, 1988).

37. Williams, *The Year 2000*, 13.

H. G. Wells: Educationalist, Utopian, and Feminist?

Cliona Murphy

Among Wells's many interests, education took a prominent place. In *Mankind in the Making* (1903) and later in *World Brain* (1938), he gave exhaustive plans of various curricula and educational schemes, and in true Wellsian style a novel was written to discuss the subject. *Joan and Peter* (1918) was published just after the First World War and was greeted by Virginia Woolf as another of Wells's "hybrid books," indicating her irritation at his mixture of fiction and sociological essay.[1] Appropriately enough, it had the subtitle "The Story of an Education."

Wells felt well-qualified to write about education and at one stage called himself "an old and seasoned educationist."[2] He obtained his bachelor of science degree from London University and one of the first books he published was a biology textbook.[3] He taught for a few years in various capacities but, he said, "I realized that if I did not get out of the profession it would fling me out."[4] Thus, like many others who did not enjoy practising education, he decided to write about it.

Not surprisingly, he found much wrong with the education of Edwardian Britain. He and many others had serious doubts about Britain's status in the world in the decade or so before the First World War. With the humiliation of the Boer War and the ever-growing German threat, the question of education had become a central issue to national confidence. For Wells, too much time was devoted to the classics and ancient history, while not enough emphasis was put on educating the pupil to be a citizen. The trappings of the educational establishment certainly did not impress him. One of his spokesmen on education, William Clissold, argued that there can be no presumption that "a man who has a diploma, or whatever they call it, of M.A., is even a moderately educated man."[5]

Another preoccupation of Wells's in the early twentieth century was the so-called "woman question." Many of his contemporaries, with perhaps the exception of Rebecca West and one or two others, considered him to have feminist sympathies.[6] He certainly saw himself as a spokesman for women's rights. One observer, Ward Clark, commented that Wells "has stated his problem, the problem of the young woman of today, in the most masterly fashion." Clark was of the opinion that when one of Wells's heroines "voices her inmost beliefs one hears not the observations of a man on the woman question, but the authentic note of the modern woman who, striking out in blind protest against she knows not what, has given a new meaning of the word feminism."[7] Others went further and saw Wells as an outrageous radical. John O'London accused him of inviting the British daughter "to run amuck through life in the name of fulfilment."[8]

Wells labeled a group of his Edwardian novels his "writings about sex." In *Experiment in Autobiography* (1934), he wrote that they were "essentially negative enquiries, statements of unsolved difficulties, protests against rigid restraints and suppressions; variations of 'why not?'" With the hindsight of 1934, he believed that they played a major part in making a generation question its traditional sexual mores, and certainly, judging from contemporary comment, they caused quite a few ripples.[9] In one of the novels concerned he grandly declared: "I want this coddling and browbeating of women to cease. I want to see women come in, free and fearless, to a full participation in the collective purpose of mankind."[10] Almost every aspect of what was known as the woman question was discussed in these novels. In *Ann Veronica* (1909), the growing independence of young women and the reaction of their parents and society was examined. The suffragette violence that appears most notably in *Ann Veronica* appears in almost all of Wells's novels of the period—particularly *The Wife of Sir Isaac Harman* (1914), and *The Soul of a Bishop* (1917). *Marriage* (1912), *The New Machiavelli* (1911), and *The Wife of Sir Isaac Harman* dealt with social attitudes to marriage and traditional motherhood. In other areas, too, Wells let his interest in the position of women be known. Free love was seen by him as essentially a very liberating concept for women, though others then and since have seen it as an excuse for his own self-indulgence. While not doubting the sincerity of his declarations, their ambiguity and lack of consistency and their embodiment into the world state ideal would hardly make them pleasing to feminists today.

The lack of material on women's education in Wells's writings is perplexing. When it is appreciated how much he was involved in discussing both education and the woman question, this silence becomes more mystifying. In the two studies of Wells the educationalist by Doughty and Hammond,[11] no room is given to Wells's view on women's education. Whether this reflects the authors' own biases or is merely a reflection of Wells's bias is a subject for debate. What does this omission in Wells's writings tell us about Wells the utopian, the educationalist and feminist?

In his sociological and utopian writings, the male young were ultimately the subject of his planning. In all these writings, female education is scarcely mentioned. This perhaps could be cited as evidence of his feminism, his nonsexism, if one could argue that Wells was referring to both sexes. This defense does not, however, hold ground. It must be conceded that it is peculiar that one who was so interested in both the educational question and the woman question did not see fit to devote an article or two, out of hundreds, to this topic; particularly in a period when women's education was a controversial issue. If he was a feminist, he should surely have realized that he could not have spoken collectively of reform for both sexes, since so many anomalies existed between them in terms of educational standards and aims. Though he sometimes implied that he was referring to both, when it came to specifics, the question of male education was given predominance. For example, in *Joan and Peter,* after having digressed into a rather lengthy monologue, Wells reminds himself that he had better "get on with the education of Joan and Peter—and more particularly of Peter."[12] This is the subsequent emphasis of the book.

One possible explanation for Wells's lack of interest in the subject of women's education could be found in the circumstances that led him to be overly concerned about the state of male education. This is related to his interest in Social Darwinism. The proponents of this philosophy were concerned with the decline in Britain's imperial position. They felt that Britain needed more mothers if she was to maintain her position as a world power. It followed that women who wished to pursue their careers were being selfish and neglecting the needs of their country. It was assumed that women who went to university were either less likely to marry or less inclined to marry, and in some extreme cases that they might possibly damage their reproductive systems. Thus the nation would eventually suffer. We can see this especially in the writings of Lucas Malet.[13] It should be pointed out that these views were not peculiar to Britain but were quite evident in Germany[14] and the United States[15] as well. Wells's essay "The Endowment of Motherhood" reflected some of these concerns of the period, and its main argument was that the state should make it worthwhile for women to have babies.

Wells saw women playing a major role as breeders of his new race. He advocated independence for women so that they would not have to depend on inferior men for survival. They could perform a better service to the state if supported by the state. This independence (or perhaps we could say new type of dependence?) was to become possible as a result of state endowment.[16] In *A Modern Utopia* (1905) Wells wrote that things would be equalized between the "sexes in the only possible way, by insisting that motherhood is a service to the State and a legitimate claim to a living." He wrote that his state would make "thoroughly efficient motherhood a profession worth following."[17] It is reasonable to suppose that one who felt that motherhood should be enshrined into the state to this extent would not be overly concerned with the cultivation of women's minds.

However, in spite of this neglect in his educational and sociological writings, the state of middle-class women's education before the advent of World War I can, to some extent, be examined by a closer reading of the above-mentioned novels and one or two others. Many of these have women as their central characters. All of these women went to secondary school and most went to university. Though Wells may not have given it as much serious thought as he had given to other women's issues, he did, in these novels, leave his readers with an interesting impression of women's education of the period. Through his power as a novelist over his characters' fates, he also left indications of his views on the subject. By looking at the women involved in education in these novels and how they were portrayed, some conclusions as to Wells's position may be possible.

Starting first with the schools; in these novels Wells provides a varied picture of the secondary education middle-class girls received. Two very different schools are portrayed in *The Wife of Sir Isaac Harman* and *Joan and Peter*. In the former a Wimbledon girls' school was portrayed thus:

> There was no hockey played within the precincts, science was taught without the clumsy apparatus or objectionable diagrams that are now so common, and stress was laid upon the carriage of the young ladies and the iniquity of speaking in raised voices.[18]

Joan's school was at the opposite extreme and, significantly in the context of assessing Wells's feminism, was portrayed satirically as a more advanced type of girls' school:

> The school resounded always with the achievements of the one important sex, . . . The staff at Highmorton had all a common hardness of

demeanour; they were without exception suffragettes. . . . They played hockey with great violence, and let the older girls hear them say "damn!". The ones who had beauty aspired to subvirile effects.[19]

Although on the surface these seem like two very different schools, both are shown with a mixture of mockery and gentle toleration, and neither would appear to have been very successful in the long run. Certainly the reader does not detect any of that constructive criticism which was so much a feature of Wells's social novels.

Wells's portrayal of women schoolteachers supports the traditional view that they were mainly incompetent, badly trained, and lacking in qualifications. They were all unmarried: Miss Murgatroyd, Miss Mills, and Miss Jevons in *Joan and Peter;* Miss Moffat in *Ann Veronica;* Miss Mergle in *The Wheels of Chance;* Miss Maltby Neverson in *Christina Alberta's Father* and Miss Beeton Claver in *The Wife of Sir Isaac Harman*. Miss Murgatroyd was the headmistress of the School of St. George and the Venerable Bede, the elementary school in *Joan and Peter.* She turned to teaching because of "a love disappointment." This had aroused in her "a passion for the plastic affections of children." She "was so overpoweringly moved to teach that what she taught was a secondary consideration."[20] Neither she nor her assistant Miss Mills had any qualifications.

The avoidance of examinations in these schools by both the teachers and the pupils was a feature of the separatist movement in women's education—which is investigated at length in Carol Dyhouse's book on girls growing up at this period.[21] Give women an education, certainly, but of a less competitive kind than their brothers received. This would make them interesting companions for men but ones who would not pose a threat. Did Wells support this view?

Though progress had certainly been made in the last quarter of the nineteenth century in the sphere of women's higher education, there was still a lot to be done. Girton College, Cambridge, and Somerville College, Oxford, strove to match the academic ambitions and achievements of the male colleges. Newnham College, Cambridge, and Lady Margaret Hall, Oxford, pursued less strenuous courses and made concessions to womanhood. It is significant that the majority of Wells's females who attended university attended the latter colleges. Joan *(Joan and Peter),* Margaret *(The New Machiavelli),* and Clementina and Eleanor *(The Soul of a Bishop)* all attended Newnham. Ann Veronica was unsuccessful in her attempts to persuade her father to allow her to attend either Somerville or Newnham. To a staunch antifeminist, one was as bad as the other.

Whatever type of school or college Wells's women attended, they usually encountered opposition if they took it very seriously, especially at tertiary level. The belief that education desexed a woman was very prevalent and Wells showed his women coming up against it on a few occasions. When Ann Veronica's sister went to visit her after she had run away from home, "she exhorted Ann Veronica not to become one of 'those unsexed intellectuals, neither men nor women.'"[22] Her father, having met a Somerville girl, "believed that sort of thing unsexed a woman."[23]

Besides sexuality, health was also shown unable to survive the rigors of education. In *The New Machiavelli,* Margaret, who attended Newnham, eventually succumbed to the fate of her sex: "There in her third year she made herself thoroughly ill through overwork, so ill that she had to give up Newnham altogether and go abroad with her mother." To be fair to Wells, it must be stated that he did not see this illness as springing totally from her gender. "She made herself ill, as so many girls do in those university colleges, through the badness of her home and school training. She thought study must needs be a hard straining of the mind."[24]

There was also the belief that if they got through education unscarred, it was more than likely they could put it to practical use. "It was very much at the back of Marjorie's mind that after Oxbridge, unless she was to face a very serious row indeed . . . she would probably have to return [home]."[25] Even Ann Veronica who left home to pursue her education soon abandoned her ambitions when she became involved with Capes. If a girl was permitted to go to college it was seen as a great social sacrifice on the part of her parents. This "gift" would be withdrawn should their daughter give them any reason to believe that her education was affecting her in a perilous manner. Christina Alberta, on hearing that she had won a scholarship to the London School of Economics, "went, without consulting her mother or anyone, to a hairdresser's and had her hair bobbed. To Mrs. Preemby this was almost a worse blow than the scholarship."[26] By the time she started the second year of her scholarship, she was obliged to leave because she had stayed out late and "had gone to a discussion of the Population Question" and had come back "smelling so strongly of tobacco."[27] Similarly, when Marjorie went against her father's wishes and became involved with Trafford, her father decided to stop paying for her education at once.

In assessing Wells's views on women's education in the context of his overall feminism, one has to be wary of inferring certain attitudes because of lack of material. Wells discussed marriage, divorce, women's suffrage at length—both within and without the confines of his fiction. Already certain explanations have been suggested as to why he did not devote the same energy to discussing the education question. There are obvious dangers in the temptation to infer that the lack of successful, educated women in his novels is an indicator of his antifeminism or at least of his indifference. Graham Hough's *An Essay on Criticism* argues that for a novel to be a novel it must have a basis in a reality with which the readers can identify.[28] Thus a novel full of female professors in 1910 would not be a novel but, in Hough's terminology, a fantasy. Despite this, certain questions occur and recur to the reader of these novels that have implications for an assessment of Wells's views. Why did most of his females go to separatist colleges if he was hailed as a supporter of women's rights? Why did so many of his females abandon their education and return to the hearth? One can perhaps understand Marjorie giving up her education for Trafford since she seemed a rather weak character in the first place. But why did Ann Veronica give up her studies for Capes? Why did Margaret become ill after three years of university? Why were female teachers and earnest female students portrayed satirically? Why was Girton College mocked when it symbolized the supreme assertion on the part of women of their ability to compete on equal terms with men?

Since Wells did not deem the topic serious enough for discussion in his sociological writings, and it was dealt with in the above manner in his novels, it is reasonable to suggest the following. Wells was a man of his time, however much he attempted to break from it. He was more conservative than he or many of his contemporaries thought. It seems fair to state that he was interested in *women's* education and sympathized with the difficulties women encountered trying to pursue it. Going by Hough's definition, it would still have been reasonable and credible, in this period, for Wells's women not to have gone to university—yet most of them did. The colleges they attended on the whole were separatist and from this it can be deduced that Wells too was a separatist. Wells was not ready in the Edwardian period to present women being educated along the same lines as men. His idea of equality between the sexes did not extend this far. It was fine for women to be educated and go to university, but his idea of equality seemed to stop there. It is impossible not to refer to his private life where he always liked to be in control of situations regarding women. Apart from the fact that his idea of women's ultimate role was as breeders for the world state, he generally seems to have disliked the idea of a nation of independent educated women as entities in themselves. Educated women would have control over their own destiny. In the end Wells's females always have to return to the fact that they are women, reminded either by their emotions or their health—these in his view control them. One cannot help concluding that the concept of a woman educated to the extent that, in intellectual terms, she is finally independent of man was one which Wells, despite his desires to be avant-garde, could not entertain.

Notes

1. Virginia Woolf, "Joan and Peter," *The Times Literary Supplement,* 19 September 1918, 439.

2. F. H. Doughty, *H. G. Wells: Educationist* (London: Jonathan Cape, 1926), 16.

3. H. G. Wells, *Text-Book of Biology* (London: W. B. Clive, 1893).

4. Doughty, *H. G. Wells,* 18–19.

5. Wells, *The World of William Clissold* (London: Ernest Benn, 1926), 98.

6. Rebecca West, review of *Marriage, Freewoman,* 19 September 1912, 346–48.

7. Ward Clark, review of *The Passionate Friends, Bookman* 38 (January 1914): 554–57.

8. John O'London, review of *Ann Veronica, T. P.'s Weekly,* 22 October 1909, 537–38.

9. Wells, *Experiment in Autobiography* (London: Victor Gollancz and Cressett Press, 1934), 2:467.

10. Wells, *The New Machiavelli* (London: John Lane, 1911), 411–12.

11. Doughty, *H. G. Wells;* J. R. Hammond, "H. G. Wells as Educationist," *The Wellsian* 4 (Summer 1981): 1–6.

12. Wells, *Joan and Peter* (London: Cassell, 1918), p. 163.

13. Lucas Malet, "The Threatened Re-Subjection of Women," *Fortnightly Review,* January–June 1905, 806–19.

14. George Bernstein and Lottelore Bernstein, "Attitudes toward Women's Education in Germany 1870–1914," *International Journal of Women's Studies* 2, no. 5 (September/October 1979).

15. Maxine Seller, "G. Stanley Hall and Edward Thorndike on the Education of Women: Theory and Policy in the Progressive Era," *Educational Studies,* 2, no. 1 (Spring 1981): 365–74.

16. Wells, "The Endowment of Motherhood," *An Englishman Looks at the World* (London: Cassell, 1914), 229–34.

17. Wells, *A Modern Utopia* (London: Chapman & Hall, 1905), 187–8.

18. Wells, *The Wife of Sir Isaac Harman* (London: Macmillan, 1914), 75–6.

19. Wells, *Joan and Peter* 369–70.

20. Ibid., 138.

21. Carol Dyhouse, *Girls Growing Up in late Victorian and Edwardian England* (London: Routledge & Kegan Paul, 1981).

22. Wells, *Ann Veronica* (London: T. Fisher Unwin, 1909), 99.

23. Ibid., 5.

24. Wells, *The New Machiavelli,* 186.

25. Wells, *Marriage* (London: Macmillan, 1912), 52.

26. Wells, *Christina Alberta's Father* (London: Jonathan Cape, 1925), 35–6.

27. Ibid., 36.

28. Graham Hough, "The Novel and History," *An Essay on Criticism* (London: Gerald Duckworth, 1966), 111–20.

H. G. Wells and C. S. Lewis: Two Sides of a Visionary Coin

K. V. Bailey

The surmised lampooning of H. G. Wells in C. S. Lewis's novel *That Hideous Strength* (in America *The Tortured Planet*) gains special irony when we read in David Wingrove's *Science Fiction Source Book* that Lewis is considered by many to be the H. G. Wells of Christendom.[1] There is a paradox perhaps worth examining.

My intention is to look at a number of parallels taken from their writings and to offer the conclusion that, while the two authors are in opposition as to overt worldviews and philosophies, there are certain underlying imaginative patterns, certain apperceptions, modes of symbolism consciously or subconsciously exercised, which make the aphorism I quoted less superficial than it might first appear, and may even justify a half-serious reciprocal estimate of Wells as the C. S. Lewis of atheism.

Before presenting these brief case studies, however, I will open up the theme in reviewing a number of biographical and experiential elements of common significance or overlap. The two authors belonged to different though successive generations, and in the 1930s were contemporaneously writing science fictions, allegories, and fantasies. Thus *The Pilgrim's Regress* and *The Shape of Things to Come* were both published in 1933; *Star Begotten* and *Out of the Silent Planet* in 1937–38.

Their young lives were lived in socially dissimilar circumstances but were subject to comparable influences and traumas. In *Surprised by Joy,* Lewis names his first school "Belsen" and says that if in his books he speaks too much of Hell, the explanation lies less in his Ulster Protestant childhood than in the Anglo-Catholicism of the church at "Belsen," where he feared for his soul.[2] Lewis's mother died when he was ten, and he writes: "With that all settled happiness, all that was tranquil and reliable disappeared from my life. . . . It was sea and islands now, the great continent had sunk like Atlantis."[3] This specific trope, "sea and islands," assumes large symbolic significance in many of his writings—for example,

Perelandra, The Voyage of the Dawn Treader, and particularly *The Last Battle* (to which I will return).

Wells's experience of childhood was stamped by his mother's piety—again with Ulster Protestant roots. He dreamt of Hell traumatically and vividly. "I feared Hell dreadfully for some time," he writes in *Experiment in Autobiography.*[4] His reaction against what he calls "a bleak Protestant God"[5] was early and violent, but the impress of the Bible, particularly in matters of guilt, apocalypse, damnation, salvation, however much metamorphosed, never faded from his writings; in fact it often structured them, all the way from a virtual Last Judgement before the Grand Lunar of Cavor, and his subsequent plunge as human surrogate into everlasting darkness, through to the salvaging of the Elect in *All Aboard for Ararat.* Wells did not suffer maternal bereavement as a child, but he did feel that in his mother's eyes he was valued less for himself than as a substitute for the sister who had died before he was born; that with the loss of her "Possy," Sarah Wells was in the grip of "a dark undertow of doubt" and consequently "never touched his heart."[6] She retreated, Wells believed, into a life of reverie that might embrace visions "of meeting her lost little Possy in some celestial garden, an unchanged and eternal child"[7]—an image that emerges as persistently in Wells as does the "sea and islands" in Lewis: in Weena of the paradisal Thames Valley in *The Time Machine;* in the fair welcoming girl of the enchanted garden in "The Door in the Wall"; in Sunray in *The Dream,* kneeling beside Sarnac as he wakes from death and hellish memories to those bright mountain meadows of asphodel.

Both authors have left autobiographical records of their reading and other aesthetic experiences, as these affected their young imaginations. Of Wells's childhood reading, Wood's *Natural History* stays in his memory and, during a convalescence, fascinated porings over bound volumes of *Punch* which brought delight in ideas of nations personified as the British lion, Bengal tiger, Uncle Sam, and so on; and vague erotic stirrings evoked by *Punch*'s curvaceous Brittanias, Erins, and Mariannes—stirrings further aroused by the Greek statuary casts at the Crystal Palace, in the gardens of which huge reconstructed dinosaurs led his thoughts to the past.[8] At the same age of about eight, Lewis records, E. Nesbit's *The Amulet* opened his eyes to "the dark backward and abysm of time," while he pored endlessly over bound volumes of *Punch,* where Tenniel's Russian bear, Egyptian crocodile, and British lion gratified a passion for "dressed animals."[9] It was from this time that revelations of imaginative ecstasy seized him—the cherished miniature garden which gave him what he described in retrospect as Milton's "enormous bliss" of Eden; Beatrix Potter's *Squirrel Nutkin,* which gave him experience of what he calls the Idea of Autumn—an extra-dimensional, out-of-this-common-world experience; and the lasting haunting of "Northernness," which came on him with his first reading of Longfellow's "Tegner's Drapa."[10] After an adolescence of classical education, but one also romantically orientated to Wagnerian myth and what he calls the cosmos of the Eddas,[11] he came by way of stinking trenches and a wounding, a "young atheist" as he describes himself,[12] to Oxford. Using a kind of "Hound of Heaven" metaphor, he describes how there he was chased out of the Hegelian Wood by a pack, which included not only his own intuitions of ecstasy, but Dante, Plato and George Herbert. He thus reached a theistic idealism out of which the Christian apologist was eventually to emerge. This stance involved for him the certainty that "in passing from the scientific view to the theological, I have passed from dream to waking . . . I believe in Christianity as I believe that the sun has risen not only because I see it but because by it I see everything else."[13]

Wells's adolescence knew no war, though he fought in reverie bloody strategic battles over the London fringe of the North Downs.[14] As a teenager with access to the Uppark library, he discovered Voltaire, Swift, and Plato[15]—*The Republic* eventually proving seminal to *A Modern Utopia*—and indeed much else. Then as a scholarship student at the Normal School of Science (now Imperial College), he found further reading of high significance—an influence that in those years was only surpassed by the intellectual impact and spell of T. H. Huxley. He confesses to having found his geology professor, Judd, no spellbinder and to having worked *less* strenuously in his laboratory than in the Dyce and Foster Reading Room and Art Library where he read discursively but intensively, aiming both at an understanding of socialism and of comparative religion and at an acquaintanceship with, among others, Milton, Dryden, Carlyle, Goethe, and Shelley. He found, in folios of drawings and the Prophetic Books, that Blake seemed to have everything to say, while Judd had nothing. "Almost subconsciously," he recalls, "the notebooks and text books drew themselves apart into a shocked little heap and the riddles of Blake opened of their own accord before me."[16]

These various grists to the imaginative and intellectual mills were utilized creatively in various ways; but together they went to provide content in an authorly phenomenon common to the two men. In his preface to "The Country of the Blind," Wells describes how eidetic images, forming the nucleus of his stories—sunlit oceans, gardens, battles, monsters—in a manner quite inexplicable floated into his mind out of darkness and nothingness. "I would discover that I was peering into remote and mysterious worlds ruled by an order logical indeed but other than our common sanity."[17] C. S. Lewis in a taped discussion with Brian Aldiss and Kingsley Amis denied having constructed *Perelandra* for preconceived didactic purposes. "It started," he said, "with the mental picture of floating islands. The whole of the rest of my labours consisted of building up a world in which floating islands could exist. And then of course the story about an averted fall developed."[18] Elsewhere he wrote that all of his Narnia books began with pictures in the head. The first of them began with a picture of a faun with an umbrella in a snowy wood that had haunted his mind for a quarter of a century. Presaged by actual dreams, the lion Aslan came bounding in one day and then took over the story.[19]

What we are here concerned with are the creative poetic processes, and the poetic mind as spontaneously a vehicle of myth. Bernard Bergonzi and Patrick Parrinder have both given consideration to Wells's romances as "ironic myths."[20] *The Time Machine* is one such: it takes shape around images of a paradisal garden, a demonic pit, a fire battle, and a final solar eclipse. It is a multivalent myth, ultimately, says Bergonzi, of the opposition of ugliness and beauty, darkness and light.[21] In a paper given to the Oxford Socratic Club, Lewis said: "In a certain sense we spoil a mythology for imaginative purposes by believing in it."[22] His lectures, *Prolegomena to Mediaeval Studies,* in book form became *The Discarded Image* of which the epigraph to the Epilogue consists of the words of Theseus in *A Midsummer Night's Dream:* "The best of this kind are but shadows"—this kind being the rustic actors playing their "tedious brief scene" as Lion and Moonshine. Theseus's metaphor is Platonic, and Lewis intends it to be applied to "models" which might variously include the Great Chain of Being, the Teilhardian Omega Point, a universe of bent space-time, and the pneumatology of Plato who, Lewis says, "was modifying, in the interests of ethics and monotheism, the mythology he had received from his ancestors."[23]

Wells and Lewis both created and used myths of similar patterns, their seminal images deriving, as all poetic creations must, from particular historical contexts; from both the associative cultural bondings, the "hooked atoms," and the subliminal "sleeping images" of *The Road to Xanadu;*[24] and from the shaping of all of these by those modes of psychic functioning that Coleridge called "the powers and privileges of the imagination."[25] I would like now to offer a few paired examples.

The first is the myth of the long-sleeper, waking apocalyptically to transform a decayed world: a myth appearing in many forms, but at its deepest level one of the soul asleep in matter. Lewis in *That Hideous Strength* has such a figure in Merlin; Wells's is Graham in *The Sleeper Awakes*. This latter book obviously owes something to Bellamy and to Morris; but perhaps also something to subliminally recollected Blake. Albion of Blake's *Jerusalem* and Graham-as-Atlas are both sleeping-giant metaphors; both wake to fight with and defeat tyrant opponents (Gog-Magog and Ostrog respectively) who, while the sleepers slept, have channeled England's pastoral heritage into mechanistic bondage. Blake's epic has both spiritual and political dimensions. Wells's themes—technological mastery and its utopian/dystopian implications—are deployed within a mythic frame. Graham, resurrected, is striven for by rival powers. To the enslaved he is "the King Arthur, the Barbarossa, long awaited";[26] he is confused with the legendary Merlin. He dies wrecking in flames Ostrog's repressive horde; and his valedictory speech, with its references to Christ's crucifixion and to humanity's immortality, is that of a sacrificial hero-god.[27]

Lewis's awakened sleeper, Merlinus Ambrosius, is also contended for by opposed powers—the one Positivist and exploitive, the other theistic and hierarchical. The former's manifesto is what Lewis over-facilely dubbed "Wellsianity,"[28] implying, in part, Ostrog's (and the Artilleryman's) creed that "some day the Overman may come (and) the inferior, the weak, and the bestial may be subdued or eliminated."[29] The opposing camp of Ransom, the Pendragon, is a bridgehead on quarantined earth for the shaping and redeeming planetary gods. Merlin, as their instrument, is made, in confounding the enemy, to reintroduce the curse of Babel, and in their destruction to yield up his energies in light and flame. Here, on the coin's reverse, is the imprint of the same myth. Paradoxically, it is an "Ostrog" that is the enemy in each case.

There are even closer imaginal and ideational correspondences in my second paired examples. The first, from Lewis's *The Great Divorce,* is a vision in a dream. An assembly of giant soul-forms stands motionless and silent looking into a silver table. On it, chesswise, move puppets, idola of the immortal spectators, delineating in pantomime the spectators' inmost natures.[30] The companion piece from *The First Men in the Moon* is Bedford's journey earthwards in the sphere. It seems to him that he sits through eternities on a lotus leaf, growing ever bigger among the stars. He looks down on Bedford as from outside space and time, as through a peephole, observing detachedly the antics of his earthly life, yet bound to the stress of that small figure's emotions until its life should end. "And what then?" he asks.[31]

This enlarges to the question "What after Man?" which is implicit in my third pairing—Wells's path to entropic finality in *The Time Machine* and Lewis's in *The Last Battle.* Both writers in their imagery are indebted to the *Revelation of St. John,* and Lewis also, surely, to Wells. Lewis's myth-populated Narnia, his surrogate earth, sinks (security gone) beneath the waters, blood-red under a dying sun which, with octopus-like tentacles of flame, draws in the moon, before being itself reduced by a giant hand to icy darkness. But, we are told, all of the old Narnia that matters has passed through the Door, where all is as different as is the real thing from a shadow. We enter beyond time and space by visual metaphor into a Platonic heaven.[32] Wells's traveler moves differently, machine-magicked backwards through space-time away from the "terrible dread" of "that remote and awful twilight" until "the sun got golden again and the sky blue."[33] In the Epilogue, however, the narrator asks if civilization is but a foolish heaping awaiting inevitable destruction—what then? The answer is to live as though it were not so. Weena's gift of flowers (reminiscent of Coleridge's flowers brought back from a dream of paradise),[34] though faded, symbolizes the persistence of human values.

Neither at that time nor later does Wells wish to align his thought and beliefs with what through the mouth of Keppel in *Star Begotten* he describes as Ghostland[35]—the human mind slithering off into dreams, irrationalities, and moral irresponsibility. Yet within his entropic universe, labeled Shadowlands by Lewis,[36] Wells creates in fictional metaphor doors which sometimes recall, or shadow, the Platonic Narnian Door. For early Wells, in "The Door in the Wall," the protagonist, deluded or not, had a sense of something "that in the guise of wall and door offered him an outlet . . . into another and altogether more beautiful world."[37] For late Wells, in *Star Begotten,* Keppel envisages a Samurai-like "starry race" with power over space and time, and a future "like a great door opening" on to life such as would make previous history seem like a "nightmare before the dawn."[38] In that control of space and time, Wells both consciously incorporates a Stapledonian influence and evokes from way back his own Martian *War of the Worlds* in which, unless we humans preempt the responsibility, it may be the evolved Martian brains with whom the future lies, who may be the carriers of dominating life "spreading slowly from this little seedbed of the solar system throughout the inanimate vastness of sidereal space."[39] Yet in *Mind at the End of Its Tether,* seeing "no way out or round or through," he writes that "the door closes on us for ever more," and that "*Our* universe . . . is going clean out of existence, leaving not a wrack behind."[40]

There were certain qualities and experiential phenomena—beauty, mutual tenderness, remembrance of things past—that Wells only reluctantly yielded to any ultimate dissolution, "leaving not a wrack behind," as symbolized in *The Time Machine* (or in Narnia). In *First and Last Things,* he wrote of beauty as "the unveiling of things seen but dully and darkly"[41]—a figure both Pauline and Platonic. In *The Dream,* following Sarnac's "death" and return to the flowering upland meadow, Starlight asks: "What do we know of the stuff of memory that lies on the other side of matter . . . of the relations of consciousness to matter and energy?"[42] Plato probed the question, she says, and millennia later it remains. It is there for Wells to take up again in *The Brothers* when, after Bolaris has concluded that our minds are prisms and mirrors whose wonderful reflected worlds disappear for ever when they are shattered, he rejects this, and speaks of the relationship of unseen, unknown planetary beauty to the human mind, and of a day when "the monstrous discrepancy between our lives and the starry intervals will cease to be a disharmony."[43] But as to mind and the "starry intervals," theory in the 1930s already surmised that biological organisms will only exist between the time of the formation of the stars and that of their death in an aging universe.

Lewis in the last chapter of *Perelandra* makes Ransom ask the young King a Wellsian question: ". . . we doubt if any shape or plan or pattern was ever more than a trick of our own eyes, cheated with hope, or tired with too much looking. To what is it all driving? What is this morning you speak of?"[44] He is answered by voices emanating from the Great Dance, the participatory visualization of the intertwinings of light, matter, consciousness, and transcendent spirit. These planetary voices speak of all entities, from dust grains to the angel-like *eldila,* as mirrors accepting and reflecting to its source the deific ray; and of the Dance as a pattern of interlocking plans, wherein each movement becomes in its season the breaking into flower of the whole design.[45]

Lewis, like Wells, uses metafictional and referential frames, and in the one that concludes *Out of the Silent Planet,* Ransom urges the publication of his experiences in fictional guise, hoping to effect, if only in a few readers, "a change-over from the conception of Space to the conception of Heaven."[46] This concept of "heaven" is further symbolized and fictionalized in *Perelandra*. Space there is matrix of worlds: the Spirit's "broad fields of the sky" of Milton's *Comus*.[47] "Heaven" is made sensible through Ransom's experience of the Great Dance, first "woven out of the intertwining of many chords and bands of light," embodying corpuscles, phenomena, individuals, qualities; then those circlings are revealed as the "mere superficies" of a vaster multidimensional pattern that, at the zenith of its complexity, dissolves into the pellucidness of an empyrean of pure and Dantesque intellectual light.[48]

Although, in Wells, it is to the conquest of no more than, as it were, "mundane" space that the young giants (of *The Food of the Gods*) launch out from footstool-earth, intimations of an interface between space and a paradoxically timeless but momentary "heaven" do occur. In "The Story of the Last Trump," for example, the cracked mausoleum, the earthquake, and the dust cloths are spatial incidents, but the "something" that happened before the world once more became opaque "was a light, it was a beauty, it was high and solemn, it made the world seem a flimsy transparency."[49] In that other momentary angel-over-the-Haymarket apocalypse of *A Modern Utopia*, Parrinder has seen a possible pointing to the Platonic city of *The Republic* "laid up as a pattern in heaven, which he who desires may behold."[50] Job Huss in *The Undying Fire* is in anaesthetic dream caught up in a version of the Great Dance, but suffers alienation within it. His feet on the crystalline pavement whose translucent depths contain the stars, he tries to thrust "through bars and nets and interlacing curves of many-coloured blinding light" towards a clarity beyond; but "the iridescent net that had seemed to grow thin grew dense again" and black doubts that had momentarily lifted swept down upon his soul.[51]

A dictum of Lewis's was: "If you have a religion it must be cosmic." For him "religion" would imply the addition of "and transcendental"; and his religion would not allow that "the supreme moral end is the perpetuation of our species," particularly if this involved "Overman" and individual-disregarding ethics, or implied the hubristic species presumption of "taking over" the universe.[52] Parrinder writes: "For Wells . . . man is a cosmic animal, whose purpose is to maintain and extend its biological empire in the face of hostile forces that can never be wholly subjugated." Faced with the impossibility of such biological species self-perpetuation, it is understandable that, as Parrinder has observed "the *samurai* are preoccupied by the Second Law of Thermodynamics."[53] There seems across all the anti-utopian and uto-

pian years, across the years of *Mr Britling* and those of a return to
"a sturdy atheism," to have been one who was like the Cabinet
Minister of "The Door in the Wall," "the responsible head of the
most vital of all departments, wandering alone—grieving—sometimes near audibly lamenting—for a door, for a garden!"[54]

In *The Brothers*, Bolaris looks towards a future in which men
may think and work for a common end without being identical
twins. Wells and Lewis, far from being identical twins, are oddly
assorted. Their ideological ends were divergent—so divergent that
there sometimes seems to be a circularly arrived at rendezvous in
some Eden of innocence or at some world's ending; and the intuitions, the myths, and the methods involved, suggesting a comple-
mentarity in their polarity, perhaps make my bracketing of them as
presenting two sides of a visionary coin not entirely misconceived—though what the current currency of such a coin may be is
surely a matter for further thought and question.

Notes

1. David Wingrove, ed., *The Science Fiction Source Book*, (London: Longman, 1984),
188.
2. C. S. Lewis, *Surprised by Joy* (London: Geoffrey Bles, 1955), 31.
3. Ibid., 27.
4. H. G. Wells, *Experiment in Autobiography*, (London: Victor Gollancz and The Cresset
Press, 1934), 1:67.
5. Ibid., 1:82.
6. Ibid., 1:66.
7. Ibid., 1:76.
8. Ibid., 1:76–82.
9. Lewis, *Surprised by Joy*, 19–22.
10. Ibid., 23. The first two stanzas of "Tegner's Drapa" evoke the nostalgia that, as he puts
it, "enslaved" him:

> I heard a voice that cried,
> "Balder the Beautiful
> Is dead, is dead!"
> And through the misty air
> Passed like a mournful cry
> Of sunward sailing cranes.
> I saw the pallid corpse
> Of the dead sun
> Borne through the Northern sky.
> Blasts from Niffelheim
> Lifted the sheeted mists
> Around him as he passed.

Longfellow used a version of *Frithiof's Saga* by the Swedish poet, Esaias Tegner.
11. Ibid., 79, 157.
12. Ibid., 213. Lewis's spiritual experiences at Oxford in the course of the 1920s are
chronicled in the last three chapters of his *Surprised by Joy*, 187–224.
13. C. S. Lewis, "Is Theology Poetry?" *They Asked for a Paper* (London: Geoffrey Bles,
1962) 165.

14. Wells, *Experiment in Autobiography,* 1:100–101.
15. Ibid., 138, 177.
16. Ibid., 241.
17. Wells, *The Country of the Blind and Other Stories* (London: Nelson, 1911), Preface.
18. C. S. Lewis, ed. Walter Hooper, *Of Other Worlds: Essays and Stories* (London: Geoffrey Bles, 1966), 87.
19. Ibid., 42.
20. Bernard Bergonzi, *The Early H. G. Wells* (Manchester: Manchester University Press, 1961), 61; Patrick Parrinder, "Utopia and Meta-Utopia in H. G. Wells," *Science-Fiction Studies* 12, pt. 2 (1985): 122–24.
21. Bergonzi, *Early H. G. Wells.*
22. Lewis, "Is Theology Poetry?" 152.
23. C. S. Lewis, *The Discarded Image* (Cambridge: Cambridge University Press, 1964), 2.
24. John Livingston Lowes, *The Road to Xanadu* (1927; London: Picador, 1978), 312ff, 324ff. Lowes's "sleeping images" there refer to Coleridge's "Kubla Khan" dream. Norman Fruman, discounting the dream origin, writes that the poem embodies "themes and images not logically related by the waking consciousness but offered by the mind of the poet in a state of reverie brought on by opium, or representing the familiar half-sleep, half-waking state. . . ." (*Coleridge, The Damaged Archangel* [London: George Allen and Unwin, 1972], 349). Such hypnogogic images were experienced by both Wells and Lewis, and were related to the "hooked atoms" of subliminal memories. Wells, in his preface to *The Country of the Blind, and Other Stories* (see note 13) writes of his hypnogogic images as having "an uncommon logic of their own."
25. S. T. Coleridge, *Biographia Literaria,* (1817; Oxford: Oxford University Press, 1907), 1:202.
26. Wells, *The Sleeper Awakes,* in *The Atlantic Edition of the Works of H. G. Wells* (London: T. Fisher Unwin, 1924), 2:380.
27. Ibid., 456. For discussion of Graham's role as hero-savior, *see* K. V. Bailey. "The Sundering Sea: A Mid-distant View of British SF," *Foundation* 30 (March 1984): 24–25.
28. Lewis, "Is Theology Poetry?" 154(f). In embracing it, Lewis attributes the term "Wellsianity" to another member of the Oxford Socratic Club, and uses it to describe a limited aspect of what, he says, "we may loosely call the Scientific Outlook."
29. Wells, *The Sleeper Awakes,* in *Atlantic Edn.,* 2:395.
30. C. S. Lewis, *The Great Divorce* (London: Geoffrey Bles, 1945), 116.
31. Wells, *The First Men in the Moon,* in *Atlantic Edn.,* 6:192.
32. C. S. Lewis, *The Last Battle* (1956; London: Penguin/Bodley Head, 1964), 136–38, 153–55.
33. Wells, *The Time Machine,* in *Atlantic Edn.,* 1:110.
34. Ibid., 113. Coleridge's Notebook entry *(Anima Poetae)* was: "If a man could pass through Paradise in a dream, and have a flower presented to him as a pledge that his soul had really been there, and if he found that flower in his hand when he awoke—Aye! and what then?" (Coleridge: *Select Poetry and Prose,* ed. Stephen Potter [London: The Nonesuch Press, 1933], 189).
35. Wells, *Star-begotten* (1937; London: Sphere, 1975), 102.
36. *See* note 32 above.
37. Wells, "The Door in the Wall," in *Atlantic Edn.,* 10:396.
38. Wells, *Star-begotten,* 117.
39. H. G. Wells, *The War of the Worlds,* in *Atlantic Edn.,* 3:450. The impact on the later Wells of Olaf Stapledon's cosmic and speculative imaginings is explicitly voiced in Wells's *Star-begotten,* 56.
40. Wells, *Mind at the End of its Tether* (1945) in *The Last Books of H. G. Wells,* ed. G. P. Wells (London: H. G. Wells Society, 1968), 75, 77.
41. Wells, *First and Last Things,* in *Atlantic Edn.,* 11:258. Many references to the Epistles occur in Wells's writings. Here there is an echoing of I Corinthians 13:12. The context in that chapter of the Epistle is of the transience of knowledge and prophesy and of the endurance of love—a quality signified surely by the lasting "gratitude and mutual

tenderness" recorded in the Epilogue to *The Time Machine* and symbolized by Weena's "two strange white flowers."

42. Wells, *The Dream,* in *Atlantic Edn.,* 18:649.

43. Wells, *The Brothers* (London: Chatto and Windus, 1938), 136–37.

44. C. S. Lewis, *Perelandra* (1943; alternative title *Voyage to Venus;* London: Pan, 1953), 181.

45. Ibid., pp. 181–86. This is one of the most sustained passages of Lewis's "visionary" writing. Without suggesting direct correspondences, one can see its relationship to representations of the Dance of Shiva, to Dante's paradisal vision, to Turner's "Light and Colour," to Blake's visionary engravings, and to the cosmic revelation which concludes Olaf Stapledon's *Star Maker.* These are expressions of and variations on shared spiritual insights. As noted below in the present paper, it is an insight reflected though imperfectly realized in Huss's anaesthetized experience in *The Undying Fire.*

46. C. S. Lewis, *Out of the Silent Planet* (1938; London: Pan, 1955), 179–80.

47. At the conclusion of Milton's *Comus,* the Attending Spirit speaks of:

> happy climes that lie
> Where day never shuts his eye
> Up in the broad fields of the sky.

When in *Out of the Silent Planet,* 35–36, Ransom first saw space (Lewis's "Deep Heaven") while traveling through the solar system (Lewis's "Fields of Arbol"), he "quoted Milton's words to himself lovingly, at this time and often."

48. Lewis, *Perelandra,* 186.

49. Wells, "The Story of the Last Trump," *The Complete Short Stories of H. G. Wells* (London: Benn, 1927), 595.

50. Parrinder, "Utopia and Meta-Utopia," 124. The quotation is from Jowett's translation of the *Republic,* book 9.

51. Wells, *The Undying Fire,* in *Atlantic Edn.,* 11:159. *See* note 45 above.

52. C. S. Lewis, "Unreal Estates," *Of Other Worlds,* 90.

53. Parrinder, "Utopia and Meta-Utopia," 126.

54. Wells, "The Door in the Wall," in *Atlantic Edn.,* 10:395.

Wells's Common Readers

Robert Crossley

In the summer of 1918, H. G. Wells received a letter from a soldier in France, Eric Williams, who told how he had "built up from your writings a sort of unseen parent stirring me to a better & finer way of living, & teaching me an altogether new & splendid conception of life." Many such letters came to Wells during the Great War and, as he often did, he invited the soldier to visit him at Easton Glebe. The opportunity never arose, but 21 years later Wells came home from his 1939 lecture tour to Australia to discover a letter from the same Eric Williams. He had heard Wells speak in Sydney but, unable to meet him, he wrote enclosing a snapshot of himself along with the letter Wells had sent to him in the trenches in 1918. This is what Eric Williams said:

> For every one of your followers who could be classified as "distinguished" there are many thousands of ordinary people who look to you as the World Leader in clarified thinking. . . . When I was a youth—the discovery of your writings marked a complete revolution in my thinking. The continued reading of your books made me, in actual fact, "a new man." The confused ideas lodged in my mind were swept away, permanently, by the logic of your reasoning & your lucid presentation of facts. For this I owe you a personal debt of gratitude which is quite beyond the range of adequate expression.[1]

Unlike some correspondents, Eric Williams was not asking for something (a gift of money, influence in getting a manuscript published, or assistance in being freed from a mental asylum—to name the three most common requests made of Wells in his fan mail). But Williams's two letters typify the responses of the ordinary, undistinguished readers who wrote letters of thanks to Wells throughout his career. The private and public observations of celebrities have become part of the gospel about Wells: how Conrad exclaimed over *The Invisible Man,* what Bennett made of Wells as a doctrinaire reformist, Zamyatin's enthusiasm for the romances, and James's disappointments with the discussion novels. But the finely turned phrases of reviewers and fellow writers may not offer the most useful insights into Wells the populist utopian—a writer who wanted to be an educational force in the world, who wanted to stimulate the moral imagination and critical awareness of the widest possible range of readers, who wanted especially to improve the quality of ordinary people's lives. Studying some of the letters from unknown readers in the Wells Archive at Illinois deepens one's appreciation for the *difference* Wells made in the lives of a great variety of people. Let me itemize a few of them: the Anglican priest for whom *Kipps* had been "an event in my life" and who found in Wells's wartime writing about religion a mirror of his own doubts and faith; the sailor from Glasgow who borrowed a copy of *The Work, Wealth and Happiness of Mankind* from the library of the Seafarer's Education Service and finished it exclaiming, "Now I have read a real history"; the New York bricklayer who told Wells that his "dayly [sic] efforts to keep the misery of Boots at a minimum" were relieved by the two authors he most cherished, "Victor Hugo and Yourself, dear Sir"; a French boy for whom *Mr Polly* "was the first thing I read that showed me that many things in our life were stupid and irrational and should be changed"; a self-described "obscure American schoolmaster" from Missouri whose reading of *Experiment in Autobiography* made him "estimate what the development of your brain has meant to the development of mine"; an Irish apprentice in a shipyard inspired by *The New Machiavelli* to work for a bachelor of science degree in his spare time; a British civil servant in Calcutta, recalling *The Passionate Friends* as the "bright star" in his reading and thanking Wells "for the effect of your literary work on my existence."[2] Such a roll call could be extended, and even an indiscriminate miscellany of Wellsian common readers would be instructive, but the chief themes of Wells's correspondents can be seen to best advantage in a selection of responses grouped according to three overlapping phases of Wells's authorship: those of the scientific romancer, the sociological novelist, and the utopian propagandist.

Wells the scientific romancer can be treated most briefly. The Wells archive contains relatively few letters prompted by the early romances, the most delightful of which came from the proprietor of a gentleman's bootshop offering Wells a "quantity of *Bones,* apparently of the Neolithic period" in gratitude for "A Story of the Stone Age."[3] But, remarkably, most readers say little about the art or adventure of Wells's scientific romances and instead lavishly admire them as vehicles for social and scientific ideas. Unaffected by the consensus of literary critics of the past sixty years, these readers see no falling-off in Wells's desertion of romances for sociological fiction and polemical essays. Wells's eagerness to apply his ingenuity as a fabulator to a commitment to educate the citizens of a new world met with a corresponding eagerness on the part of his readers. They liked Wells because he stretched their minds, and they therefore felt no strain between art and ideas or between the earlier and later work. An American student started reading *The Food of the Gods,* moved on to others of what he called Wells's "fabulous yarns," and, as a result, he told Wells that: "I have really started a new life. I know now what I'm doing and I am leaving my stuffy Arts course where you learn about life for a Science course where you handle life and become part of it. . . . You have taught me a hundred times more than all the prosy little professors and now that I am launched on a great quest I know that I get more out of their poetry (or rather the poetry they handle) than they and all their classes put together."[4] A young French reader asked Wells in 1910 for a new romance that would make socialism attractive to the masses: "People want to be shown realities in the light of dreams, & it is your special capacity to do it. *People are thirsty for idealism and imagination.*"[5] One correspondent, who would have to be classified as an *uncommon* reader when he wrote to Wells in 1932, called up a memory of himself as an ordinary adolescent reader 34 years earlier: "In 1898 I read your 'War of the Worlds.' I was sixteen years old, and the new viewpoints of scientific applications, as well as the compelling realism of the thing, made a deep impression. The spell was complete about a year afterward, and I decided that what might conservatively be called 'high altitude research' was the most fascinating problem in existence." That teenager, R. H. Goddard, became a pioneer of twentieth-century rocketry, but in 1932 recalled the scientific romances only to emphasize his "greatest admiration" for Wells's later work, whose optimism he found "inspiring" and which he considered, as he believed Wells must, "much more important than your writings of the nineties."[6] Readers who communicated with Wells about his scientific romances were likely not to value them exclusively but to see them as a prologue to his life's work of educating world citizens.

As a novelist about society in transition, Wells received some of his most impressive letters. Most literary critics assume that Henry James "won" the dispute with Wells over the nature and purpose of fiction.[7] But a jury of common readers might reach a different verdict. Mabel Dearmer, the wife of a parson, wrote Wells after *Ann Veronica* was denounced in the *Spectator* to insist that such attacks were merely the product of male discomfort: " 'Ann Veronica' puts the truth about women absolutely clearly. Of course women are not free (I don't mean a mere vote)—they are always at the mercy of some man or another. Ann Veronica was never free—there was always some man waiting to devour her." Women readers, Mrs. Dearmer told Wells, did not condemn the book as immoral or as artless because they understood the immorality of women's social condition and because they knew the book offered a portrait of things as they were.[8]

Mrs. Dearmer may have been wrong to assume that gender, rather than social station or aesthetic temperament, was the decisive factor in judgments of Wells's discussion novels. Virginia Woolf, for example, scorned *Joan and Peter* because it lacked the cool detachment of the modernist aesthetic, because it sinned by telling too much and moralizing too earnestly, because it was allegorical rather than symbolic, because its ideas had priority over its form, because, as the final sentence of Woolf's review transparently reveals, Wells was and aimed to be a *popular* writer.[9] But place Woolf's debunking next to this analysis by an utterly unknown reader from Surrey:

> I don't see how you can write a book like "Joan and Peter" and escape pestering letters. This is one of them. I have just closed it with a bang & an indrawn breath. . . . You have turned our minds up towards the sun & made things grow. You have made us infinitely indebted to you. But, in the heat of reading, you seem to me to have done more than that. It seems to me a mental history of these days—a picture of our unrest, confusion, outreaching & aspiration. I found it wholesome, stirring & inspiring. It set me tingling with desire to be a worker in the new order. This is no bit of photography. It's deep sea sounding. . . . It's the public who read & they have opinions. Mine is that everyone who feels as I do ought to write & tell you how tremendously big it seems, how vastly important & how grateful to you it makes him feel. And having written he should not expect you to spend your time replying to his outburst. That's how I feel.[10]

While talk of wholesome and inspiring novels might have occasioned amusement in Bloomsbury, some themes in this letter from F. J. Paradise recur in many other letters written about Wells's sociological fiction: the acknowledgment of a permanent debt for a way of thinking and for the prospect of a more satisfying life; a conviction that Wells speaks for ordinary citizens on contemporary issues and that he teaches them the words and forms for naming their own aspirations;[11] the energizing effect of wanting to work to implement Wells's social ideas; Wells's canonization as a chronicler of the modern era rather than a high priest of modernism; and finally, the touching wish simultaneously to tell Wells the practical and immediate good he has done and to protect him from any sense of obligation to those he has helped.

Of all Wells's novels, the one that produced the greatest outpouring of mail was *Mr Britling Sees It Through*. In recent years patronized as an unwieldy literary souvenir of the Great War, *Mr Britling* remains a fascinating hybrid of the kind of self-referential sociological novel Wells favored before the war and the utopian propaganda that is the outstanding achievement of his final decades. It may also be one of the most perfect expressions of Wells the populist educator; Mr. Britling himself prefigures the "sample brain" that narrates the *Experiment in Autobiography,* an impersonation designed to represent the group mind of an age, making articulate the doubts, frustrations, and longings of the ordinary citizen.[12] In the draft of his open letter to Germany that concludes the novel, Mr. Britling writes that "the common man here is in a state of political perplexity from the cradle to the grave."[13] As Mr. Britling becomes the spokesman for those perplexities, shaping them into a political and ethical agenda for the future, so too Wells wanted to name and thereby to tame the anxieties of an age in order to release his readers to think and act more productively. Through the medium of an ambiguously patriotic fiction, he disclosed a larger vision for the future, finding in the catastrophic mistakes and horrors of the Great War the signposts for a great utopian reconstruction.

That *Mr Britling Sees It Through* did not—and could not—fully satisfy such ambitions is less important than the obvious impact it had on how people thought about the war. A German woman from a Junker family wrote to Wells from New York:

> I wonder whether a thousand victories on either side could accomplish what Mr. Britling will accomplish—and I know that they cannot destroy the good it will do. While I was reading I caught myself wishing that the author were one of my countrymen . . . , but that only showed that I had not yet learnt the book's lesson. I will understand better as time goes on, and help others to understand here and in my own country. We are all so hypnotized into certain beliefs that even as I write I have moments of doubt as to whether in doing so I am not disloyal. But if loyalty means denying the truth or leaving it unspoken, I will chose to be disloyal. I am holding out my hand to you across the ocean. Will you shake?[14]

Civilian readers told Wells that *Mr Britling* appeared at the crucial psychological moment when uncertainty about the aims of the war—and more importantly about what would come after the war—was growing in intensity among ordinary citizens. The question preoccupying Mr. Britling—"What is all this for?"—was increasingly in the minds if not on the lips of a great many people on the home front.[15]

The book altered the lives of people who did not think of themselves as intellectuals or even as readers. Many soldiers received *Mr Britling* as a Christmas gift in 1916,[16] and a Red Cross nurse described to Wells the reactions of one wounded infantryman she was caring for: "He asked me where he was, & I told him *Essex,* at which he sat up & said in a muted voice, to my intense astonishment—'Oh! I'm fine & glad I'm in Essex. That's H. G. Wells Country.' I thought he must have been some servant of yours, but he told me, no—only, *the only book he'd ever read was 'Mr. Britling'*—he knew it almost by heart—& launched at once into Letty's View of the War."[17] In addition to soldiers, Wells also heard from bereaved parents. Two letters are particularly striking. William Farren wrote in 1917 thanking Wells for "the one book written during this war that brings comfort to the stricken—most surely you have touched all our hearts and given consolation and hope and what more can any great writer hope for?"[18] Like many letter writers, he took Hugh Britling as the exemplar for many young soldiers and he guessed incorrectly that Wells might have lost his own son in the war. The other letter worth special attention is from Florence Collins who had written many years earlier about *Love and Mr Lewisham* and had received a kind reply. In early 1917 she read *Mr Britling* with an anxious sense that the fictional parent's struggle to deal with the loss of his son in the war might be prophetic. Shortly afterwards, she heard that her son's ship had struck a mine and that he had died at sea. In her grief she wrote to Wells: "I find it quite impossible to take any comfort from the usual sources. . . . One craves for the human touch and grasp of his big hand; and a remote heaven leaves me cold. I want my son as he *was,* the splendid big funny boy. . . . I am like poor Mr. Britling, incessantly tormented by 'if only'—and the thousand little memories of trivial lovely things, which made my boy so adorable. Now there is nothing but the pride in his sacrifice, and a black wall in front of me which shuts out all my happiness. Can you help me?"[19]

To resurrect after 70 years Florence Collins's *cri de coeur* from a letter marked "Private and Confidential" is, I hope, not a ghoulish act but a demonstration of the extraordinary empathy Wells had with readers who were, in effect, anonymous to him. He was their voice, their intellectual leader, their champion, their substitute parent, their comrade-in-arms, their vocational counselor, their psychotherapist, their neighbor across counties and oceans. Wells the busy world traveler hobnobbing with the political, scientific, and literary figures of his day is so familiar an image that it is worth emphasizing the bond he also felt with the ordinary citizen, the common reader. There is no doubt that Wells had very mixed feelings about that mythological being named "the common man." W. Warren Wagar has demonstrated how paternalistic Wells's view of the common person was, and Patrick Parrinder has made a careful analysis of the slipperiness of Wells's concept of the "common man" as both an idealized vision of possibility and a rhetorical figment invented to accommodate Wellsianism to a mass audience.[20] From the devastating caricature of newspaper readers at their breakfast table in *The War of the Worlds* to the gloomy assessment forty years later in *The Fate of Homo Sapiens* of the difficulty of increasing the ordinary man or woman's level of critical reading, there is a measure of impatience and dismay in Wells's account of the common reader. He knew from his own painful self-education some of the limitations of the unprivileged, and unlike Samuel Johnson he did not "rejoice to concur" with the common reader's judgments. Wells wanted to exhort, surprise, intrigue, admonish, and push readers; he wanted to show the way, not trust them to follow their instincts. At the same time, he could identify himself powerfully with the interests of ordinary readers, as in his famous letter scolding James Joyce over *Finnegans Wake* and *Ulysses:* "You have turned your back on common men—on their elementary needs and their restricted time and intelligence, and you have elaborated. What is the result? Vast riddles. Your last two works have been more amusing and exciting to write than they will ever be to read. Take me as a typical common reader. Do I get much pleasure from this work? No. . . . So I ask! Who the hell is this Joyce who demands so many waking hours of the few thousands I have still to live for a proper appreciation of his quirks and fancies and flashes of rendering?"[21]

Was Wells disingenuous to ask Joyce to take him as a "typical common reader"? As with his persona of a "sample brain" in the *Autobiography,* there may be as much truth as calculation in Wells's pose as a typical reader. His correspondents repeatedly testify that his books remained alive to the issues that mattered to people. An American woman, watching the last of her children grow up, recited a list of the formative books of her own youth from *Tono-Bungay* to

Joan and Peter and recalled how she "first began to find some answers in your books to questions which parents and school did not or could not answer." Wells taught her generation, she said, that no one "could remain indifferent to the meaning of world events and their relationship to our personal lives, nor fail to make an attempt to find light and hope in the muddled darkness of men's stupidity."[22] An Englishwoman also wrote retrospectively of a lifetime's reading of Wells: "When you were young you interpreted us to ourselves. . . . We grow old but you seem perennially young, with a mind open to fresh ideas."[23]

As befits a writer whose utopian perspective was global, Wells had readers responding to him from every part of the earth. He must have been pleased when he heard from J. B. S. Haldane that Charlotte Haldane, visiting China in 1938, found many women soldiers in Mao's army reading *The Shape of Things to Come*.[24] But one extravagant letter from a foreign reader may reveal more about Wells's power to reach all the potential citizens of a new world. The letter came late in Wells's life and proposed that his works on human rights were "much greater than any other book that this world has," including the Bible. As a moral force who "all the time wrote & told the truth about the *treatment* of a common man by this world," Wells had, according to his correspondent, only one rival, and that was Jesus Christ.[25] When Wells replied to Lance-corporal Aaron Hlope, he began with a gruff dismissal of the most hyperbolic of the letter's comparisons: "What you write about Jesus Christ and me is the most utter nonsense." Instead, he insisted that he was a representative voice, a sample brain rather than a lone prophet: "I happen to be a speculative writer who has made one or two good guesses at the problem of tomorrow, but what I think, a lot of other English and American people are coming to think, and you mustn't compare one single man with the whole movement of liberal thought in the world."[26] Wells, who could be devastating when he suspected shamming or stupidity, nevertheless wrote affectionately to Aaron Hlope; indeed Hlope's letter inspired both a speech and a newspaper article from Wells in the following months.[27] The reason for Wells's thoughtful response is not hard to find. In his concluding page, Hlope apologizes for his shaky command of English, reveals his race and nationality, and connects Wells's "world of ideas & ideals" to his own most recent experience as a Zulu in the Middle East Forces in Cairo in the summer of 1942:

What has shocked every black man from South Africa is the behaviour of your British Tommies. Their character is wonderful & to explain it, can need many pages. They shake hands with us, they talk to us, they sit next to us in cinemas, they drink beer with us, they smoke cigarettes with us. Even when one goes to the British hospital, he gets the same food with them, he lines into one line with them, he is given a bed in the ward same to other beds & blankets, he is sent to the ward according to the nature of his sickness. They have offered us more kindness than God has done. It is the first time in life that we have seen people of that kind.

In Aaron Hlope's mind, Wells stood as both teacher and proto-type of those British soldiers, and what the Christian Bible had not accomplished among white South Africans he hoped the utopian vision of H. G. Wells might yet supply. Half a century has elapsed since Hlope and Wells exchanged letters, and the official Anglo-American response to the oppression of black South Africans might seem reason enough to be depressed by the world's re-calcitrance to Wells's utopian vision. Nevertheless—and that is the word that reading the letters sent to Wells by people like Aaron Hlope, Mabel Dearmer, Florence Collins, and F. J. Paradise seems always to demand—just as the British Tommies in Egypt exem-plified a higher standard of common humanity than the world figures who had brought them to war, so our hope for a future may be strengthened in the conviction that Wells's words remain potent enough to continue to educate readers to a more generous global vision than that provided by the current political leaders of the West. It was just such an invigorating, inquiring, activist hope that seems to have been the essential appeal of Wells to the ordinary reader.

Notes

1. The two letters of Eric Williams to H. G. Wells are dated 18 July 1918 and 17 March 1939. Like all other unpublished letters cited, they are deposited in the Wells Archive at the University of Illinois Library. I gratefully acknowledge the energetic assistance of the curator, Gene Rinkel, and the Rare Book Room staff, particularly Louise Fitton.

2. Letter from John A. Leng to Wells, 10 May 1917; letter signed "SGD" to the Seafarer's Education Service, 20 April 1936, enclosed in a letter from the organizing secretary of the service to Wells, 23 April 1936; letter of Emil Eriksen to Wells, 10 December 1922; letter of Henri Jullien to Wells, 16 February, year not given; Letter of Blandford Jennings to Wells, 22 September 1936; letter of Richard Lee to Wells, 6 August 1926; letter of Godfrey T. B. Harvey to Wells, 30 January 1917.

3. Letter of Sydney Hook to Wells, 7 December 1903.

4. Letter of Harry C. Elliott to Wells, 13 June 1926.

5. Letter of E. J. Coulomb to Wells, 31 December 1910.

6. Letter of R. H. Goddard to Wells, 20 April 1932.

7. Although some doubts have been registered in recent years, by far most Anglo-American literary historians have championed the Jamesian virtues of formal delicacy and theoretical rigor and have gleefully declared Wells the loser for his unseemly didacticism, his preference for saturation over selection, and his disdain for modernist canons of art. But see Kirpal Singh's "Genius Misunderstood: Towards on Asian Understanding of H. G. Wells"

(above), which argues that Asian readers are never embarrassed by the notion of the writer as sage and teacher and that they assume that Wells properly repudiated James's stingy and inhumane aesthetic.

8. Letter of Mabel Dearmer to Wells, 11 December 1909. She told Wells that during a supper party at the vicarage, a man launched into a diatribe on the "infamy" of *Ann Veronica* and every woman at the table, "decent conventional women, turned on him."

9. Virginia Woolf's unsigned review appeared in *The Times Literary Supplement*, 19 September 1918, 439, and is reprinted in Patrick Parrinder, ed., *H. G. Wells: The Critical Heritage* (London and Boston: Routledge & Kegan Paul, 1972), 244–47. Woolf concludes her review with a dismissal of what she takes to be Wells's indifference to anything but the needs of the present moment: "But if he is one of those writers who snap their fingers in the face of the future, the roar of genuine applause which salutes every new work of his more than makes up, we are sure, for the dubious silence, and possibly the unconcealed boredom, of posterity."

10. Letter of F. J. Paradise to Wells, 31 October 1918.

11. Compare two similar observations: Rosalind Scott Dunkin's acknowledgement in a letter of 24 July 1925: "Two big things I get from reading your writings—I am stimulated to think and I find you crystalize for me thoughts that have been groping around in my mind unable to find adequate expression"; and Sir William Rothenstein's metaphors sprung from the Great War, in a letter to Wells of 16 June 1918: "It is your particular privilege to be able to express in strong & trenchant form the beliefs most people hold in a shadowy & timid one. You give them courage & body & coax their halting minds to peep over the top. Barbed wire keeps men's imagination in as well as the enemy out & the world is too much sandbagged, there are too many & too deep saps in which men's instincts & generosity take shelter: you bring back open warfare."

12. Note, for instance, Wells's reference to Mr. Britling's brain as a "specimen" of the "multitude of other brains" in Europe in 1914; his description of Britling as "a sample Englishman"; and Mr. Britling's inclination to see his own son Hugh as "a fair sample of his generation." Wells, *Mr. Britling Sees It Through* (1916; London: Hogarth Press, 1985), 132–33; 205; 317.

13. Wells, *Mr. Britling*, 425.

14. Letter of Irmgart Hutcheson to Wells, 24 June 1917.

15. Besides Irmgart Hutcheson's letter, the other most revealing civilian letter is from J. Melbourne Shortliffe, 1 January 1917 [misdated 1916], which claims that *Mr Britling* embodies his own evolving reactions to the war: "Moreover the thoughts I had already had about the war and about war in general and about the underlying causes of all wars prepared the way for my appreciation of Mr. Britling's repeated query—what is it all about?" On the impact of the novel on the civilian population at large, *see also* Robert Crossley, ed., *Talking Across the World: The Love Letters of Olaf Stapledon and Agnes Miller* (Hanover and London: University Press of New England, 1987), 90–92, 202–4.

16. R. L. Henderson wrote Wells on 15 January 1917 while on sick leave at a Swiss Red Cross hospital with 14 other officers, nearly all of whom, he said, had just received a copy of *Mr Britling*.

17. Letter of Mrs. M. Calverley to Wells, 25 August [1918?].

18. Letter of William Farren to Wells, 23 January 1917.

19. Letter of Florence Collins to Wells, 3 August 1917.

20. See W. Warren Wagar, *H. G. Wells and the World State* (New Haven: Yale University Press, 1961), 172, and Patrick Parrinder, *H. G. Wells* (New York: Putnam's, 1970), 100–102. A dramatic instance of Wells's dismay at the sentimentality and recidivist patriotism of the average Briton is his reaction to the street celebrations at the end of the Great War: " 'And this,' thought I, 'is the reality of democracy; this is the proletariat of dear old Marx in being. This is the real people. This seething multitude of vague kindly uncritical brains is the stuff that old dogmatist counted upon for his dictatorship of the proletariat, to direct the novel and complex organization of a better world!' " Wells, *Experiment in Autobiography: Discoveries and Conclusions of a Very Ordinary Brain (Since 1866)* (New York: Macmillan, 1934), 590.

21. Letter of Wells to James Joyce, 23 November 1928, as printed in Patrick Parrinder and Robert Philmus, eds., *H. G. Wells's Literary Criticism*, (Sussex: Harvester Press; New Jersey: Barnes & Noble, 1980), 177.

22. Letter of Virginia E. Bray to Wells, 7 May 1941.

23. Letter of Esther Grierson to Wells, 31 March 1932.

24. Letter from J. B. S. Haldane to Wells, 26 October 1938.

25. Letter of Aaron J. Hlope to Wells, 6 August 1942. Startling as these comparisons must seem, they were not quite unique in Wells's fan mail. The Chicago clubwoman Rosalind Scott Dunkin used to tell her associates that the foundation of any good library was "The Bible, Shakespeare and H. G. Wells" (24 July 1925), and the Anglican priest John Leng, while insisting that "I could not for a moment look to you as I look to Jesus of Nazareth," came close to idolatry in saying about Wells's performance in *God the Invisible King:* "I have come to regard you as one who is really bearing the sins of the world."

26. Letter of H. G. Wells to Aaron Hlope, 24 November 1942.

27. The article prompted by Hlope's letter, "What a Zulu Thinks of the English," was a prophecy of "the inevitable adjustment" and "convulsion" that must lie in the future if "the petty white tyranny" in South Africa continued to resist "the breath of freedom" blowing through Africa as through the rest of the world. It appeared in the *Evening Standard,* 16 March 1943, 6, and was expanded in Wells's *'42 to '44: A Contemporary Memoir* (London: Secker & Warburg, 1944), 68–74. Aaron Hlope appeared again in a speech called "On Putting the Common Man Back Where He Belongs," delivered to the Roadfarer's Club early in 1944. An excerpt from the speech, focussing on the letter from Hlope, was printed in the *New Leader* as "Back to the Old Round?—No Fear," 11 March 1944. The typescript of the complete speech is in the Wells Archive at the University of Illinois Library.

PART FIVE
Epilogue

Introduction

Julius Kagarlitsky, the leading Soviet H. G. Wells scholar, was unable to attend the 1986 symposium (see General Introduction). The following short paper, written for delivery at the symposium, was read by Professor Kagarlitsky to a meeting of the H. G. Wells Society in London on 11 April 1987.

Wells the "Culturologist"

Julius Kagarlitsky

Our conference is called H. G. Wells under Revision, and it seems to me that the forty years that have passed since his death enable us to take a fresh look at his work. H. G. Wells foretold all the most significant historical events of the first half of this century and all of them occurred during his lifetime. He foresaw two World Wars and he lived through two World Wars. In the First World War, he visited the front as a war correspondent, and he refused to leave London during the German air raids in the Second World War. He anticipated the Russian Revolution; it took place and he saw postrevolutionary Russia with his own eyes. He anticipated the collapse of old Europe, and the Europe that we live in today is, indeed, very different to old Europe. He was the first major English writer to take a stand against Fascism and he did this at a time when no one could have imagined that the hooliganism of Mussolini's black shirts would develop into Hitler's extermination camps. He predicted the atomic bomb and the first two atomic bombs exploded while he was still alive. In a word, everything that Wells foretold he saw for himself.

Let us ask ourselves why it is that we still find Wells so interesting when all the events that he foretold have already taken place. I believe that to answer this question we need to adopt a much broader approach to H. G. Wells, and to regard him not only as a kind of prophet but also as a one-man think tank. Wells's shortcomings and achievements as a writer are due to his tendency to see each person from the point of view of his mentality, and the most interesting thing for us today is the mentality of H. G. Wells himself. For a long time scholars argued who in reality was H. G. Wells: was he a writer or a journalist? Wells was in the habit of calling himself a journalist, though he did this at moments of irritation when he was being accused of being a poor artist. He was a good journalist only when he was a writer. Of course, he wasn't an artist in the meaning of the term used by Henry James. When it comes down to it, he was a writer and nothing but a writer, only he was a writer of a very special kind. Wells's mentality and personality—and, therefore, his work—contained a multitude of heterogeneous elements, or I should say elements that were considered to be heterogeneous before Wells fused them together. The word writer when applied to Wells fails to convey his originality. In some way we can apply to him another word—culturologist. But this word also has its limitations when applied to H. G. Wells. He doesn't belong to *Kulturwissenschaft* in the old meaning of the word, because culture for him integrates science, the humanities, manners, beliefs, prejudices, modes of living, religions, and the historical heritage imprinted in the human mind. I should say that without such a broadened, Wellsian kind of *Kulturwissenschaft,* we would have understood nothing about the Iranian Revolution and many paradoxical events of our history that seemed unpredictable. I come from a country that has traveled a long and complex road in those forty years since Wells's death. I believe that the history of other countries during those forty years has not been a simple one. In the course of the historical process, it is not only economics and politics that play a role but also the state of the human mind that depends, in its turn, on many other factors. I think you know how popular Wells is in our country. All Wells's major works have been published many times in our country in editions running into many millions of copies. In the Soviet Union, H. G. Wells's collected works in many volumes have been published. And the number of editions of his works in the Russian language issued by central and provincial publishing houses approaches the thousand mark. The last anthology of H. G. Wells's work, for which I had the pleasure of writing a preface, was published in an edition of four hundred thousand copies. His popularity doesn't fade. Something of what we received from Wells has already become part of our consciousness. It is not surprising that Wells is so needed in a country with such strong social dynamics. And I believe the renewed interest in Wells is to be explained not only by whims in literary taste, but also certain social reasons. I believe that our conference will have a wider impact than an academic one. It was of great use to me, and I believe to all others present.

Notes on Contributors

PATRICK PARRINDER is professor of English at the University of Reading, England, and chairman of the H. G. Wells Society. He is author of *H. G. Wells* (1970) and editor of *H. G. Wells: The Critical Heritage* (1972) and *H. G. Wells's Literary Criticism* (1980) (with Robert M. Philmus). His other books include *Science Fiction: Its Criticism and Teaching* (1980) and *James Joyce* (1984).

CHRISTOPHER ROLFE is a senior lecturer in English at the Polytechnic of North London and has also taught at the State University of New York at Cortland. He is the honorary general secretary of the H. G. Wells Society and editor of the *H. G. Wells Newsletter*. He has written widely on modern literature and criticism.

BRIAN W. ALDISS is a vice-president of the H. G. Wells Society and a leading British novelist. He has written numerous science fiction novels and stories, including the highly Wellsian *Moreau's Other Island* (1980). He has also written much criticism, including a standard history of science fiction, *Trillion Year Spree* (1986) (with David Wingrove).

KENNETH V. BAILEY is the author of books on the history of radio and television, on education and the environment, and of a number of children's books. He has been senior lecturer in history at Daneshill College and chief education officer at the British Broadcasting Corporation. He has written a number of critical studies and reviews of science fiction.

MARIA TERESA CHIALANT is associate professor of English literature at the University of Naples (Istituto Universitario Orientale). She has published articles on Victorian novelists and on Orwell, Forster, and Rex Warner. She is coeditor of a collection of critical essays, *La città e il teatro: Dickens e l'immaginario vittoriano* (1988).

ROBERT CROSSLEY is professor of English at the University of Massachusetts at Boston. He is author of the *H. G. Wells* volume in the Starmont series of readers' guides and has edited the Wells-Olaf Stapledon correspondence. He has recently published *Talking Across the World,* an edition of the love letters of Stapledon and Agnes Miller.

CHRISTIE DAVIES is professor of sociology at the University of Reading. A graduate of Cambridge University and former BBC radio producer, he has published widely on the sociology of humor and comedy. His books include *Jokes are about Peoples* (forthcoming). His father, also named Christie Davies, did research on H. G. Wells at the University of Wales.

J. R. HAMMOND is the founder and former secretary of the H. G. Wells Society. His books include *H. G. Wells: An Annotated Bibliography of his Works* (1977) and *An H. G. Wells Companion* (1979). He has also edited a collection of Wells's unreprinted short stories, *The Man with a Nose* (1984). His latest book is *H. G. Wells and the Modern Novel* (1988).

JOHN HUNTINGTON is the author of *The Logic of Fantasy: H. G. Wells and Science Fiction* (1982). He teaches at the University of Illinois at Chicago.

JULIUS KAGARLITSKY is a member of the Union of Soviet Writers and was formerly a professor at the Lunacharsky Theatrical Institute in Moscow. He has edited Wells's collected works in Russian, and his book *The Life and Thought of H. G. Wells* was translated into English by Moura Budberg (1966). He is a vice-president of the H. G. Wells Society.

KRISHAN KUMAR is professor of social thought at the University of Kent at Canterbury, England. He has been a BBC radio producer, a visiting fellow at Harvard University, and a visiting professor at the University of Colorado at Boulder. His books include *Utopia and Anti-Utopia in Modern Times* (1987) and *The Rise of Modern Society* (1988).

CLIONA MURPHY studied at the National University of Ireland and at the State University of New York at Binghamton, where she took her Ph.D. She is author of *The Women's Suffrage Movement and Irish Society in the Early Twentieth Century* (forthcoming), and is an assistant professor at California State University, Bakersfield.

JOHN R. REED is professor of English at Wayne State University, Detroit. He has written widely on nineteenth- and twentieth-century British literature, and his books include *Victorian Conventions* (1975), *The Natural History of H. G. Wells* (1982), and *Decadent Style* (1985). He has just completed a book-length study entitled *Victorian Will*.

ROMOLO RUNCINI is associate professor in the sociology of literature at the University of Naples, Italy. He has published numerous books and articles on literary history and sociology, including studies of Gothic fantasy and romance such as *Il Romanzo fantastico* (1983).

W. M. S. RUSSELL is professor of sociology at the University of Reading, vice-chairman of the British Social Biology Council, and vice-president and past president of the Folklore Society. His publications include six books, more than a hundred articles, and a prize-winning, science fiction story.

BONNIE KIME SCOTT is professor of English at the University of Delaware. She is author of *Joyce and Feminism* (1984) and *James Joyce* (Feminist Readings series, 1987) as well as of numerous articles on Irish literature, women writers, and feminist theory. She is currently working with a team of twenty scholars on a revisionary feminist anthology, *The Gender of Modernism*.

KIRPAL SINGH is senior lecturer in English at the National University of Singapore. He has published extensively on modern fiction and is writing a book-length comparative study of Wells and Tagore. His books include *Palm Readings* (1986), *Critical Engagements* (1986), and *The Writer's Sense of the Past* (1987). He is also a poet and short story writer.

LEON STOVER is professor of anthropology at Illinois Institute of Technology, Chicago, where he teaches two courses on Wells. He is author of *The Shaving of Karl Marx* (1982), a work of novelized literary criticism, and *The Prophetic Soul: A Reading of H. G. Wells's "Things to Come"* (1987). A further study, *The Science Fiction Novels of H. G. Wells and Their Films*, is in preparation.

MARTHA S. VOGELER is professor of English and comparative literature at California State University, Fullerton. She has published *Frederic Harrison: The Vocations of a Positivist* (1984), and has edited Harrison's *Order and Progress* (1975). She has also written on Victorians such as George Eliot, George Gissing, and Matthew Arnold.

W. WARREN WAGAR is distinguished teaching professor of history at the State University of New York at Binghamton and is a vice-president of the H. G. Wells Society. He is author of *H. G. Wells and the World State* (1961) and editor of *H. G. Wells: Journalism and Prophecy* (1966). He has also written about Wells in several books on modern thought, including *The City of Man* (1963), *Good Tidings* (1972) and *Terminal Visions* (1982).

Index